Can We Play You Every Week?

Can We Play You Every Week?

A journey to the heart of all
92 football league clubs

MAX VELODY

First published in 2008
by Short Books
3A Exmouth House
Pine Street
EC1R 0JH

10 9 8 7 6 5 4 3 2 1

A CIP catalogue record for this book is available from the British Library.`

ISBN 978-1-906021-47-4

Printed in Great Britain by Clays

Cover design: Two Associates

Foreword

"You have to respect what football is. It came out from the roots of the country through local communities who identified themselves with their team, and we have to be careful not to destroy that."
Arsene Wenger, 2008

Factory workers, railwaymen, church groups and teenagers founded England's football league clubs. They formed the teams while their earliest supporters played a pivotal role in building up the clubs, donating kit, rattling collection tins, clearing sites, building grounds.

More than a century later and not much has changed. Which seems mad on the face of it – since the Premier League was formed in 1992 English football has become big business on an unimaginable scale. It boasts the best footballers on the planet, attracts billions of viewers worldwide, numbers multi-billionaires among its owners and rakes in billions of pounds from global TV rights, merchandising, and the highest ticket prices in Europe.

And yet English football has never been poorer and the role of the fan has never been more important. Most of the money has been trousered by players, agents, and astute businessmen. The so-called Big Four clubs have massive annual incomes but even they carry two billion pounds of long-term debt. Further down, it's grim. In the last 15 years an astonishing 46 league clubs – that's half of them – have slumped into administration, unable to pay their bills, many of them surviving only through the unswerving support of fans who have organised raffles, rattled collection tins, cleared derelict sites and even formed political parties to keep their club alive. They are the true heirs of the founders of the game, and the stars of this book.

There are lots of statistics in the pages that follow but it isn't aimed at anoraks – it's about the stories and the people that have made each club what it is. The quotes are there for comedy value but many of them reveal more in one line about the condition of a club than any number of words.

Now, for the important bit. When the Premier League broke away from the Football League, the Football League didn't want to sound second-rate. So the Second Division ws renamed the First Division, the Third Division became the Second Division, and the The Fourth Division was the Third Division.

Confusing? It got more confusing in 2004 when the First Division was rebranded The Championship, the Second Division became League One, the Third Divison – League Two. At a stroke, the common language that football fans used to discuss the game was destroyed. The championship isn't the same as the Championship. There are 92 clubs in the English football league, but only 72 in the Football League. Writers trying to compare and contrast different footballing eras have two choices. They can include copious and tedious footnotes explaining which league meant what when. Or they can bang on tortuously and endlessly about top flight clubs, second-tier teams, and basement leagues. I tried that myself but it quickly got very repetitive. So in this book...

– The top tier of English football is called the first division up until 1992. Since then, the Premier League.
– The second, third, and fourth tiers of English football are called the second division, third division, and fourth division, throughout.
– The fifth tier of the English football is called the conference, throughout.
– The knock-out cup open to all 92 league clubs is called the League Cup.
– The knock-out trophy competed for by teams in the third and fourth divisions is called the Football League Trophy.

Clubs

Accrington Stanley

Aldershot Town

Arsenal

Aston Villa

Barnet

Barnsley

Birmingham City

Blackburn Rovers

Blackpool

Bolton Wanderers

AFC Bournemouth

Bradford City

Brentford

Brighton & Hove Albion

Bristol City

Bristol Rovers

Burnley

Bury

Cardiff City

Carlisle United

Charlton Athletic

Chelsea

Cheltenham Town

Chester City

Chesterfield

Colchester United

Coventry City

Crewe Alexandra

Crystal Palace

Dagenham & Redbridge

Darlington

Derby County

Doncaster Rovers

Everton

Exeter City

Fulham

Gillingham

Grimsby Town

Hartlepool United

Hereford United

Huddersfield Town

Hull City

Ipswich Town

Leeds United

Leicester City

Leyton Orient

Lincoln City	Rochdale
Liverpool	Rotherham United
Luton Town	Scunthorpe United
Macclesfield Town	Sheffield United
Manchester City	Sheffield Wednesday
Manchester United	Shrewsbury Town
Middlesbrough	Southampton
Millwall	Southend United
Milton Keynes Dons	Stockport County
Morecambe	Stoke City
Newcastle United	Sunderland AFC
Northampton Town	Swansea City
Norwich City	Swindon Town
Nottingham Forest	Tottenham Hotspur
Notts County	Tranmere Rovers
Oldham Athletic	Walsall
Peterborough United	Watford
Plymouth Argyle	West Bromwich Albion
Portsmouth	West Ham United
Port Vale	Wigan Athletic
Preston North End	Wolverhampton Wanderers
Queens Park Rangers	Wycombe Wanderers
Reading	Yeovil Town

Accrington Stanley

"It is like a fairytale. March 6th, 1962, was a black day for Accrington. We went down in history as the first club to not fulfil their fixtures. Hopefully now we will be known for the right reasons."

Owner Eric Whalley rejoices that 44 years and 40 days later,
the Minnows are back with the big fish.

Mystic Meg may be an Accrington lass but even she wouldn't have had the balls to predict the miracle that has transfigured her home town. For generations of footie fans Accrington Stanley only ever meant one thing – it was the club that went kaput.

Whenever the imagination strayed to Accrington – obviously not often – it conjured up a dank and dreary mill town at the arse-end of Lancashire, a black and white world where players in baggy shorts won bugger-all with relentless consistency at a club that spent little but earned less so went bust and was forced to resign from the fourth division mid-season.

Accrington Stanley's only legacy was as a dusty footnote in football folklore, its demise a dire warning of what goes wrong when clubs spend more than they earn. Synonymous with failure. We thought. The Football League Review certainly thought so. Its 1962 edition included a photo of the ground, crumbling, derelict and overgrown, beneath a headline that read: "Remember what happened to Accrington – don't let the grass grow under your feet." There was even a patronising ad from the Milk Marketing Board in the 1980s featuring Liverpool idol Ian Rush with a punchline ridiculing Stanley's demise.

Fast-forward to Woking 2007 where a 1-0 win ensured the Minnows were back in the Football League 44 years and 40 days after they folded. Watching that day was 80-something Jack Barrett. It was Barrett who took it upon himself to reform the club back in 1968. By 1970 the club was admitted to the second division of the Lancashire Combination, and the long climb back was under way.

Key man in the revival was Eric Whalley, a local businessman who played for the reserves in 1958 and was later manager. He bought it for £80,000 in 1995 and quickly realised its potential – all over the world people knew about Accrington Stanley. Americans made pilgrimages to see them, while the Norwegian branch alone had 200 members at a time when a typical crowd numbered 500. Whalley worked energetically exploiting the brand – Accrington Stanley do their own Merlot in the club shop – and ploughing the money back into the club.

Nickname Stanley, the Minnows or the Reds

Kit Red shirt, red shorts, red socks

Ground Fraser Eagle Stadium – 5,050 (1,200 seated)

Address Livingstone Road, Accrington, Lancs BB5 5BX 01254 356950

Website www.accringtonstanley.co.uk

But none of it would have been possible without striker Brett Ormerod. Once a textile worker in the town, Stanley picked him up after he had been discarded by Blackburn and had the guile to negotiate a sell-on fee when they let him go. Which meant that when Ormerod was transferred from Blackpool to Southampton,

11

Stanley netted a whopping £250,000, enough to build a new stand, without which they would never have been allowed back into the Football League.

As it is, the ground is fit for Minnows – with a capacity of just over 5,000 it's the smallest in the league. But it is not the grim wasteland of the imagination, surrounded as it is by mature trees with green fields rolling upwards towards the foothills of the Pennines.

It was there in 2001 that Stanley, still in non-league football, performed an act of generosity that was applauded by everyone that cares about football. With neighbours Bury in very real danger of going to the wall, Stanley staged a fundraising benefit for the Shakers, with every penny going to their emergency fund. Whalley remembered there was no one to turn to when Stanley went under in 1962 and was determined that wouldn't happen to another Lancashire club.

Believe it or not... when Stanley ran out of money in 1962, owing £60,000, the club sent a letter to Football League secretary Alan

Hardacre tendering its resignation. But within a week, new backers came forward and the club asked Hardacre to rip it up. Although Hardacre hadn't yet presented the letter to the Football League committee, he refused. Why would he do that? If you believe the conspiracy theorists, he was allegedly in cahoots with Burnley owner Bob Lord who hoped to snaffle up Stanley fans if the club folded.

Back from the dead

Aldershot Town

"When the club died, people cried, some went to sit in the stands with flasks of tea and just looked at the grass."

Save Our Shots stalwart Terry Owens remembers the day Aldershot FC went to the wall.

The phoenix has risen. When Aldershot FC went bust back in 1992, the supporters formed a new club and added that mythical bird to the club crest. Sixteen years and five promotions later, the garrison town in Hampshire can once again boast a Football League team.

Aldershot FC is the only club in the last 40 years to have gone bust mid-season, mired in debt and owing the taxman more than a million. When the plug was finally pulled, all its fixtures for that season were declared null and void, its assets and club memorabilia flogged off, the Recreation Ground stripped of all fixtures and fittings, and the keys returned to Rushmoor Council.

How had it come to this? The club had never been that successful – two appearances in the FA Cup fifth round and success against Wolves in the very first play-off final back in 1987 was about as good as it ever got in 70 unbroken years of league football.

But the writing had been on the wall for a while. In 1990 the club had come within minutes of being wound up. The players had gone three months without pay, some had their phones cut off and it was all over barring a miracle.

Enter Spencer Trethewy, a teenage property tycoon who turned up out of the blue professing a love for the club and, more importantly, waving a signed affidavit for £200,000 to clear the Shots' debts.

He seemed too good to be true, and he was. Trethewy was kicked off the board after three months when directors discovered he had borrowed the money to save the club and couldn't pay it back. The 19-year-old continued to make headlines – at one stage he boasted of plans to start an airline to rival Richard Branson's Virgin, while singer Whitney Houston served him with a writ banning him from saying he was acting on her behalf. He went bankrupt. And in 1994, in an unrelated case, was jailed for 27 months for fraud.

He left the club in turmoil but the town struck lucky twice. A covenant on the Recreation Ground meant it couldn't be sold off for flats but had to remain in sporting use. And one man had seen the future and was ready for it. Less than a month after Aldershot FC had folded, Aldershot Town was born. Terry Owens had been behind the Save Our Shots campaign that battled to save the old club – and when 700 fans turned up to a public meeting to find out what might happen next, they found Owens had already been busy planning a new company, board, chairman, manager, and with enquiries already in about league membership for the following season.

Nickname The Shots

Kit Red and navy blue shirt, red shorts, red socks

Ground Recreation Ground – 7,100 (2,000 seated)

Contact High St, Aldershot, Hants, GU11 1TW 01252 320211

Website www.theshots.co.uk

That league turned out to be the Isthmian, division three, a full five divisions below the Football League. But the rest, as they say, is history. In their first season Aldershot Town won ten games on the spin and promotion by 18 points. After another three promotions and two unsuccessful conference play-offs, they turned professional in 2004, and last season they ran away with the conference, clocking up a record 101 points.

Heroes? On management and playing side, too many to mention. Left-back Jason Chewins made nearly 500 appearances starting in the mid-nineties, while Gary Abbott thumped home 120 goals in just three years.

Whatever happened to… Spencer Trethewy? Believe it or not, he's back in football. Now calling himself Spencer Day, he has resurfaced as the owner/manager of Chertsey Town in the Combined Counties League.

Arsenal

**"When I heard Jonathan repeat the figure of £ 55k,
I nearly swerved off the road 'He is taking the p***, Jonathan!'
I yelled down the phone. I was trembling with anger."**

When Ashley "Cashley" Cole's agent told him he was being offered an insulting pay rise, the Arsenal defender was very cross. His autobiography "My Defence" turned out to be the funniest book written in 2006. Want to know how Cole was treated like a slave, shown no respect, and had his loyalty flung back in his face? The hardback edition is available from online retailer Amazon at the very reasonable price of one penny.

Just like watching Brazil? There was a South American swagger about Arsenal's League Cup side when they crashed six goals past Liverpool and Sheffield United in 2007 and 2008. And that was just the kids, the average age of the team against the Blades just 19.

The first team? At their best, breathtaking artistry played at an explosive pace. But… no trophies since the FA Cup win in 2005 because of a tendency to over elaborate, and sometimes a failure to cope with physical teams who won't let them play.

Founded in 1886 by munitions factory workers in Woolwich, the club moved to North London in 1913. From 1930, they bagged seven first division titles and three FA Cups in 22 years under Herbert Chapman, George Allison and Tom Whittaker. Decline in the fifties and sixties was followed by success in the seventies after club physio Bertie Mee turned manager and led Arsenal to the Double in 1971.

Nickname The Gunners

Kit Red and white shirt, white shorts, white socks

Ground Emirates Stadium – 60,432

Contact Highbury House, 75, Drayton Park, London N5 1BU

Tickets 0207 619 5000

Website www.arsenal.com

"Boring Boring Arsenal"? A legacy from George Graham's side, title winners in 1989 and 1991, frustrating opponents and their fans nationwide with a ruthlessly perfected offside trap.

Arsene Wenger? Arrived in 1996 and led Arsenal to a Champions League Final, three titles and four FA Cups, his team unbeaten throughout the 2003-04 season. While his rivals in Manchester, Merseyside and West London snapped up world superstars, Wenger confounded Arsenal fans by bringing in young unknowns and developing them into world-class players. His greatest success? Spotting the goalscoring potential of Thierry Henry who managed just 31 goals for club and country in his five years prior to Arsenal. But 262 in seven years with Wenger.

A selling club? The Gunners failed to retain Henry and Cole, and in 2008 had the heart ripped out of their midfield when Alex Hleb went to Barcelona and Mathieu Flamini to Milan. Although its annual wage bill is still £100m, the club has insisted on financial prudence, especially while it's still paying for its £300m new ground which opened in 2006.

UEFA calls it "The Arsenal Stadium", some fans call it The Grove. A magnificent well-lit four-tiered bowl with plush padded seating and generous legroom for 60,000? Or, as fanatical Gooner and Sex Pistol John Lydon told me, a horrible soulless corporate monstrosity with no atmosphere and lots of accountants. It's certainly quieter than their notoriously silent former home at Highbury, known affectionately as "The Library". During quiet spells at the Emirates fans continue the age-old tradition of putting fingers to lips and hissing "shush".

Heroes? Thierry Henry broke the club scoring record during his seven years, an astonishing combination of poise, grace, balance and electrifying speed. Dennis

> **Bizarre injury…** Arsenal defender Steve Morrow's arm snapped in two when skipper Tony Adams hoisted him aloft at the end of the 1993 League Cup final. And dropped him.

Bergkamp, less prolific and infinitely slower but possessed with touches of genius that opened up the tightest defence and conjured up fantasy goals. While Tony Adams confronted the alcoholism which put him in jail and could have scuppered his career to become the only player to captain a side to three titles in three different decades.

Greatest moment? Lifting the first division title at Anfield in 1989. In an emotional game played just weeks after 96 Liverpool fans were killed at Hillsborough, Arsenal needed to win by two goals and pulled it off when Michael Thomas lifted the ball over Bruce Grobbelaar in the second minute of stoppage time. The Kop? Applauded Arsenal when they paraded the trophy before them.

> **Disastrous signing…** Frannie Jeffers. Arsene Wenger paid £9m to sign the so-called "fox in the box" from Everton in 2001. Scored four goals in three years at Highbury.

Aston Villa

"Referees should be wired up to a couple of electrodes and they should be allowed to make three mistakes before you run 50,000 volts through their genitals."

Former Villa manager John Gregory talks bollocks.

There was a huge sigh of relief at Villa Park when American Anglophile Randy Lerner took control back in 2006. He came with an excellent track record after doing a fine job running NFL outfit the Cleveland Cowboys. At a time when the Premier League had three billionaire owners who kept their own counsel, he was refreshingly open and direct. And he'd bought the club with his own money, a welcome change.

Change was what was needed at Villa, which had stagnated for decades under the control of previous incumbent, the legendarily tight Doug Ellis. Lerner quickly won a reputation as a man who listened - and delivered. He ploughed money into youth development and facilities at training ground Bodymoor Heath, undertook a massive if controversial facelift for the legendary Holte End, and involved fans with redesigning the club crest. He organised a weekend of festivities celebrating the 25th anniversary of Villa's European Cup triumph of 1982, thus satisfying the huge numbers of fans who felt the club had never adequately recognised the achievement.

Hell – he even has a bona fide purple–heart winning former Marine

Corps Commandant as his right hand man!

General Charles C. Krulak has a wide-ranging brief, or should that be briefs? As a surprising but regular contributor to fan club websites, he'd called for the club shop to stock a more comfy range of women's knickers, revealed he'd acquired a Villa kit for his 94-year-old dad, and had a well-publicised spat with Birmingham owner David Gold.

Villa has a special place in football folklore. Not only were they one of the original 12 clubs that founded the Football League, it was their idea. The hard work was done by then chairman William McGregor in 1888, and for a long time Villa were indisputably England's top club – by 1920 they'd won an unrivalled six League championships and six FA Cups. Since then, they've won the cup and the first division just once, although the title-winning team of 1981 went on to beat Bayern Munich and win the European Cup the following year. The heroes of that team – goalscorer Peter Withe, captain Dennis Mortimer and midfield wizard Gordon Cowans – come up regularly whenever there's talk of erecting a statue to a Villa hero.

Nickname The Villans

Kit Claret and light blue shirt, white shorts, light blue socks

Ground Villa Park – 42,640

Contact Trinity Rd, Birmingham B6 6HE 0121 327 2299

Tickets 0800 6120970

Website www.avfc.co.uk

One man who won't be getting a statue erected is deeply unpopular former manager David "Dreary" O'Leary, sacked by the 82-year-old Ellis as a final act before selling up to Lerner. There's been a newfound confidence in the club since Martin O'Neill was installed, after the loonies at the FA overlooked his overpowering credentials for the

England managership and plumped for loser Steve McClaren.

Could have been a contender? Ashley Young may be the most fleet-footed and best dribbler in the 2008 Villa team but he was second-best at school. Who says so? Formula 1 race ace and former schoolmate Lewis Hamilton, who claims he was "faster and had more skill" in the footie team.

Tom Hanks, a Villan? The double Oscar-winning film star paraded down the red carpet at the premiere of his political movie *Charlie Wilson's War* flaunting a claret and blue Villa scarf. Why? "I don't follow football, I just love the name Aston Villa. Here in England you have other footballing entities like Manchester and Arsenal and Chelsea… and here's Aston Villa! What suburb of Rome is Aston Villa from?"

Bizarre injury… Aston Villa defender Shaun Teale was ruled out of a UEFA Cup tie against Turkish side Trabzonspor in 1994 after gashing his arm on the family fish tank.

Disastrous signing… Bosko Balaban. The Croatian international striker cost Aston Villa £5.8m and was on £20,000 a week when signed from Dinamo Zagreb. Stayed three years, started two matches, never scored.

Club hero?… Has to be Paul McGrath. An alcoholic with deeply dodgy knees that required no fewer than eight operations over his career, his former club Manchester United took pity in 1989 and offered early retirement and a £100,000 pay-off. McGrath turned it down and moved to Villa. Unable to train and occasionally unavailable, he confessed to taking to the field under the influence more than once. It didn't appear to affect his performance. An exceptionally skilful giant at the back, he was the dominant figure during his seven years at Villa, guiding them to two second places and winning the League Cup in 1985 against Manchester United. He won the Professional Footballers' Association Player of the Year award when at Villa Park. When the Football League celebrated its centenary in 1998, McGrath featured in the all-time list of 100 League Legends.

Barnet

"I had some talent and I wasted it
– I was the has-been that never was."
Manager Barry Fry laments his squandered playing days...

There was a time in the early nineties when Stan Flashman and Barry Fry provided the best entertainment in town. Flashman was the king of the ticket touts; he preferred "broker" but that fooled no one. Ascot, Wimbledon, Frank Sinatra, Princess Anne's wedding, you name it, Stan "two together?" Flashman could sort you out. A heavy gambler and a larger-than-life character, he bought Barnet in 1985 for £50,000 when the club was one week from going under.

Fry had already had a seven-year spell managing the club and returned for a second stint in 1986. A precocious schoolboy footballer, he was signed as a teenager by Manchester United, where boss Matt Busby told him he could be the next Jimmy Greaves. But Fry was also a gambler, addicted to dogs and horses – nightclubbing whenever he wasn't at the bookies or on the racetrack. His career stats tell a sorry story of promise unfulfilled. Four league clubs, 19 games, one goal, he was driven to succeed as a manager where he had failed as a player.

Bizarrely, the man touted as the next Jimmy Greaves found himself managing the old one. The legendary goalscorer was pushing 40 and frankly running to fat when he joined the non-leaguers and had dropped into midfield by the time he arrived at Underhill in 1978. He hadn't lost it though, finishing top scorer with 25 goals in his first full season.

Between them Flashman and Fry pulled it off – the club was promoted to the fourth division in 1991 after 103 years of non-league football. Their performance on the pitch reflected their flamboyance off it – their first two matches in the Football League produced an astonishing 21 goals, a 7-4 defeat followed by a 5-5 draw.

Then it all got a bit tasty. Behind the scenes Flashman was running into money problems. Fry criticised the boss and was sacked and reinstated. Eight times. Flashman infuriated the fans when he told them he didn't care whether they turned up to watch the club or not. Players went unpaid. Flashman holed himself up in his Hertfordshire mansion and refused to come out for weeks at a time, saying he was sick.

In 1991 builders who were owed money tried to have the club wound up. The following year, the FA banned Barnet from making any transfers, and a few months later the club was handed a £50,000 fine for irregular payments and financial irregularity.

Nickname The Bees
Kit Black and old gold striped shirt, black shorts, black socks
Ground Underhill Stadium – 5,568
Contact Barnet Lane, Barnet, Herts EN5 2DN 020 84416932
Tickets 020 84416325
Website www.barnetfc.com

In 1993, with the crisis getting ever deeper, the Bees somehow managed to get themselves promoted. Fry wasn't there to see it – Flashman resigned a few weeks before the end of the season, Fry knew there was no money left and quit for Southend United. That summer Barnet found themselves with huge debts, no chairman, no manager, and a playing staff of three. No surprise that the club lost its first ten games in the third division.

Believe it or not, Barnet hosted England's first ever live televised football match – the BBC were there when the Bees played Wealdstone in October 1946, although they didn't screen the last ten minutes as it got too dark. And if you thought Barnet was nicknamed the Bees for alphabetical reasons, think again. Apparently there were a number of apiaries around Underhill at the turn of the last century.

Unluckiest Bee? Luckless goalie Ross Flitney. The biggest footballing night of his life should have come in 2005 when the 21-year-old was picked to play in a League Cup match away at Manchester United. Flitney went into the record books but for all the wrong reasons. Mistakenly sent off for deliberate handball outside the box after just 80 seconds, he picked up the quickest red card ever recorded at Old Trafford. The decision was overturned on appeal, but that was little consolation.

Underhill? Has been desperately in need of development for decades. Barnet Council bought the freehold back in 2002, but fans who prayed this might herald the start of a longed-for modernisation programme – or better still a move to somewhere better suited to the demands of league football in the 21st century than their ramshackle home with its comedy sloping pitch – prayed in vain. The on-off saga of when and if Barnet moves home has long been occupying the hearts and minds of Keep Barnet Alive, the excellent if long-suffering fans' pressure group.

Bizarre injury... Barnet midfielder Lee Hodges wrenched his groin after slipping on a bar of soap in the shower.

Believe it or not... Barry Fry, a gambler? In January 1984 he was struck down with a heart attack. Did he have a long stretch in hospital, a lengthy convalescence, decide to take it easy for a bit? Not exactly. Just ten days after the attack, the player-manager picked himself for the team.

Barnsley

"We went for a walk in the town centre this morning and as I was talking a bird dumped right on my head. They say that can be a lucky omen."
Barnsley manager Simon Davey after a pre-match amble around Liverpool. His team did the dumping later that day – despatching the mighty Reds from the FA Cup.

No team gave more pleasure to more people in 2008 than Barnsley. One down to Liverpool at Anfield in the FA Cup fifth round, they turned it round to grab a last-minute winner which left the Kop stunned in what was undoubtedly the biggest upset of the year.

Until the quarter-final when the Tykes did it all over again, knocking out cup holders Chelsea at Oakwell, courtesy of a winner from the least in-form forward in England. You would not have put money on striker Kayode Odejayi hitting a barn door – or even a barn – from five paces, after a run that had seen him ram home precisely zero goals in 28 appearances and be booed off by his own fans after a comically inept performance against Southampton. Yet the 6ft 2in Nigerian was there when it mattered – to nod home the winner past Carlo Cudicini and propel Barnsley to a Wembley semi-final.

For a fairytale cup-run romance there was a lot of excitement and an awful lot of excrement. And the pooping town centre Liver bird was only the start of it. Half-time in the Chelsea game and the facilities at Oakwell were awash with wee, the plumbing simply not up to the job

Nickname The Tykes

Kit Red shirt, white shorts, red socks

Ground Oakwell – 23,009

Contact Grove Street, Barnsley,
S. Yorks S71 1ET 01226 211211

Tickets 0871 2266777

Website www.barnsleyfc.co.uk

of coping with a full house of 22,000 fans who'd been drinking deep from the cup that cheers, pretty much all day. And one can only imagine the scenes in the Chelsea dressing room when they found a sign reading "Sorry, toilets out of order" outside the visiting washrooms – a merry prank from the Barnsley boys to welcome their special guests.

The Chelsea backroom boys certainly had their legs clamped together for 90 minutes during the match – or was that simply because a preposterous number of them were pressed together like pilchards in a dugout that could only be described as cosy?

They scarpered pretty quickly when the full-time whistle went and Barnsley fans invaded the pitch. On-loan keeper Luke Steele (so new to the side he later confessed he didn't know the names of his own teammates for the Anfield game) was carried shoulder-high around the pitch by adoring fans so eager for their own souvenir of that special day that they tried to steal the shirt off his back and rip the gloves from his fingers.

Success has been a long time coming to a club that spent most of its time firmly ensconced in the second division and whose finest moment came when they beat West Brom to win the FA Cup way back in 1912. In 1997 they had the whole country enthralled during their one season in the Premier League. It was always going to be a tough year for a small club playing with the big boys, but the fans were clearly determined to enjoy every second of it. Five-nil down at home against Arsenal, Oakwell reverberated to the strains of "It's Just Like Watching Brazil", and they weren't talking about the Gooners. Similarly, six down at home to Chelsea was the cue for "We're going to win 7-6".

There were glorious moments too – an away win at Liverpool and an FA cup victory over Manchester United among them. And plenty of entertainment off the field, particularly when star import Georgi Hristov made headlines slating Barnsley girls as beer-swilling ugly dogs and found himself a media celebrity.

The Macedonian claimed he had been misquoted – and what happened next was so very English. Outraged Barnsley folk organised a beauty pageant to teach Hristov the error of his ways, insisting he be a judge. Hristov, who didn't score that often, found himself in bed with Miss Barnsley – even waking up one morning to find himself the subject of a classic tabloid kiss-and-tell. According to brunette Tina Powers: "He loved me giving him a massage – he said I was better with my hands than the club physio."

Barnsley paid a high price for their year in the Premier League. Relegated

> **Bizarre injury...** Barnsley midfielder Darren Barnard needed an operation for torn ligaments in 1999 after slipping on a puddle of pee in the kitchen deposited by pet puppy Zack.

the following season but saddled with high-earning players on long contracts, they sunk into administration by 2002, £3.5m in debt and losing £50,000 a week. The administrator threatened to turn Oakwell into a retail park or supermarket. After months of fundraising and a number of false dawns, the club was saved when it was bought by a joint venture company which included the local council.

Cradle-snatchers? In October 2008, Barnsley fielded the youngest player ever to appear in the football league. Reuben Nobel-Lazarus was just 15 years and 45 days when he made his debut at Ipswich. Too young to be paid, his reward was a slice of pizza and a ham sandwich.

Greatest player? Tommy Taylor's reputation should be higher than it is. The scorer of 26 goals in his 44 games for Barnsley, he was sold to Manchester United aged 21 in 1953 for the unusual sum of £29,999 and spearheaded United's back-to-back title wins, scoring 112 goals in 166 league matches and netting 19 times in his 16 appearances for England. He was just 26 when he died in the Munich plane disaster.

Don't mention the war... to Lars Leese, Barnsley's German keeper during their solitary season in the Premier League, who was surprised to find himself the target of Nazi jibes by opposition supporters and dumbfounded by the sight of 3,000 Leeds fans welcoming him with chants of "Sieg Heil! Sieg Heil!" That's not to mention the time he was confronted at a fancy-dress do by a man in German military uniform festooned with swastikas and a comedy moustache, who greeted him with "Heil Hitler!" – and turned out to be one of his team-mates. His verdict? "On the whole, I think I preferred shouts of 'You fat bastard', which was more normal."

Birmingham City

"On one occasion a player said to me as I got on the team bus, 'I can see your tits from here'. I retorted: 'Well, you won't be able to see them once I've sold you to Crewe.'"

Karren Brady

Karren Brady was just 23 and knew nothing about football when Birmingham's porn baron chairman David Sullivan shattered the glass ceiling in 1993 and made her the first woman to run a football club. It looked like a cheap publicity stunt and the newspapers treated it as such. At her first press conference one hack even asked for her vital statistics.

It didn't take long for her to prove them all wrong. Hard as nails, she sacked all but two admin staff shortly after taking charge, and soon a club that had been in administration when she joined was showing a profit.

She boasted she could drink, smoke and fight better than any man. And tell better jokes. She was intimidated by no one. Incensed when manager Barry Fry criticised the chairman on TV, she charged into the dressing room and

Nickname The Blues
Kit Royal blue shirt, royal blue shorts, white socks
Ground St Andrews – 30,016
Contact Birmingham B9 4NH 0844 5571875
Website www.bcfc.com

dragged him out of the shower to give him a dressing-down.

She fell in love with a footballer, Paul Peschisolido, but did she let her heart rule her head? No, she sold him. Twice. And she built up the club's commercial side with an array of innovative schemes to generate cash while widening the club's fan base through a number of cheap deals aimed at bringing in families. She sacked Fry – but not before he'd urinated on all four corners of the pitch. Why? Because St Andrews is the only club in the country under the spell of a gypsy curse.

Formed in 1875, the club has spent well over 50 years in England's top division without ever finishing higher than sixth – their only silverware coming in 1963 when they beat Aston Villa to win the League Cup. St Andrews stands on what was once a dumping ground next to the railway line, and the story goes that gypsies encamped on the site put a curse on the ground when they were turfed off to make way for it in 1906.

Cursed? The club cut costs building the ground by charging locals to dump their waste – the resulting mound became the Kop End. But that backfired when Birmingham came to redevelop the ground in the nineties. The waste turned out to be contaminated and the club had to spend a quarter of a million pounds cleaning it up.

More bad luck in 1942 when an overzealous wartime fireman decided to extinguish a brazier with the contents of a bucket. Unhappily, the bucket contained petrol and the main stand burned down along with the club records, so the team had to decamp to Villa Park to play wartime fixtures while the ground was rebuilt.

Manager Ron Saunders certainly took the curse seriously – back in the eighties he stuck crucifixes onto the pylons of the floodlights – and compelled the players to have the soles of their boots painted red – in an effort to lift the curse.

Club hero? Has to be Trevor Francis. Birmingham's youngest ever debutant, he scored four goals in a match when just 16 years old and lit up the Blues for eight years before becoming the first million-pound transfer man when sold to Nottingham Forest. He later returned for five years as manager, reaching the play-offs but was unable to get the club back in the Premier League.

The future?... Birmingham City were relegated to the second division in 2008, owner Sullivan putting the blame fairly and squarely on the players – namely, the "pile of rubbish" bought in the summer of 2007.

Married him once, sold him twice

Blackburn Rovers

"I've played my last match, scored my last goal and elbowed my last opponent."

Rovers striker Martin Dahlin announces his retirement.

Can money buy you happiness? Sometimes. Steel magnate Jack Walker's millions transformed his home club in the nineties, taking them from also-rans to champions in just four years.

All wealth is relative. When multibillionaire Roman Abramovich bought Chelsea, a financial analyst remarked that it made the house that Jack built at Blackburn look like a bungalow. But when Walker bought the club in 1991, it had a glorious history receding further and further into the distance. Twice champions, FA Cup winners no fewer than six times, the Blue and Whites had won nothing worth talking about since 1928.

One of the founding clubs of the Football League, the club battled for supremacy in its early years with near neighbours Preston North End. Friendly rivals? In 1888 Preston refused point blank to fulfil a fixture against Rovers in the Lancashire Cup due to the "offensive way in which North End players have beforetimes been received in Blackburn... by a limited number of uncouth and unmannerly onlookers".

In the eighties the club went close to going bust, attendances as low as 5,000 and the players' wages paid only thanks to the generosity of Irish pig-dealer and superfan Niall Malone. Rovers had no training ground, the club so impoverished that it had to ration milk for the players' tea. Balls were in short supply too – on one bleak morning manager Bobby Saxton had to be pulled out of the Darwen, swept away while swimming to retrieve a precious ball kicked into the river.

For a small town with a population of around 100,000, it looked like their best days would always be behind them. Jack Walker changed everything. His first statement of intent was to install Liverpool legend Kenny Dalglish as manager in October 1991. That season saw Blackburn triumph in the play-offs, defeating Leicester City 1-0 in the Wembley final and returning to the top division for the first time in 26 years.

Shortly afterwards Walker pulled off his masterstroke, paying £3.3m and smashing the British transfer record to bring in 22-year-old Southampton and England centre forward Alan Shearer – Manchester United wanted him, but Walker's money won out. More expensive signings were to follow and in 1994 he broke the transfer record again, shelling out £5m to buy striker Chris Sutton from Norwich City. Shearer and Sutton – SAS – formed a lethal attacking partnership, scoring 47 goals in their first season together and bringing the title back to Blackburn for the first time in 81 years.

Skipper of the side was Scot Colin Hendry, a defender who blocked balls with his bollocks on an unfeasibly large number of occasions. Though it was Hendry's posterior that for some reason fired the

Nickname The Rovers
Kit Royal blue and white split shirt, white shorts, white socks
Ground Ewood Park – 31,367
Contact Ewood Park, Blackburn, Lancs BB2 4JF 0871 7021875
Tickets 0871 2221444
Website www.rovers.co.uk

imagination of the Ewood Park faithful, his appearance regularly greeted with cries of "Colin, Colin, show us your arse".

Since then, the club has seen relegation but bounced back after two years and been a consistent top-ten finisher in the Premier League, while in 2008 it set a first when appointing Paul Ince, the first black British manager to take charge of a top-flight team.

Little love is lost between... Blackburn and neighbours Burnley. A crunch fourth division play-off match in 1991 against Torquay United at Turf Moor was distinguished at half-time by the sight of a plane flying overhead trailing a banner reading: "Staying down 4 ever, luv Rovers, Ha Ha Ha."

Disastrous signing... Kevin Davies. Blackburn smashed the club record in 1998 to sign the £7.5m striker from Southampton. Scored once.

Blackpool

"You look like a bunch of pansies."

Floral tribute or homophobic jibe? It's the Duke of Edinburgh giving the once-over to the Blackpool team parading before the 1953 Cup Final in a fetching tangerine and satin shorts combo...

A colourful strip, and a club with a colourful history. Blackpool FC is owned by a convicted rapist. Magazine mogul Owen Oyston was aged 62 and club chairman when he was jailed for six years for rape in 1996. A spell in the slammer doesn't appear to have harmed the fortunes of him or his family. Come 2008, son Karl was club chairman; his dad a director; the pair together worth in excess of £100m. While Latvian banking tycoon and club president Valeri Belokon is worth twice that.

Blackpool fans want to see more of that money invested in the club. For the last five years Bloomfield Road has been an eyesore. The east stand is a ghastly temporary structure, the sort of thing that goes up on Horse Guards Parade on the Queen's birthday and comes down the next day. While for half a decade there's been nothing on the south side of the ground at all since the south stand was bulldozed.

That may be about to change. When the local radio station announced in May 2008 that work on the new south stand was finally starting in the summer, the club was swift to issue a sniffy denial: "The story about the South Stand developments is a complete fabrication." Fast-forward several, er, days and suddenly Belokon was singing a different tune: "It gives me great pride and pleasure to announce the new South Stand and South-West Corner will go ahead immediately." Fans have been living with this sort of uncertainty for years. Back in 2006 the club announced that building work on the south-west corner of the ground was about to start. Only, it didn't. While in the nineties there was much excitement at the news that the club was planning to move to a 40,000-seater stadium at Whyndyke Farm. Planning permission was granted. That didn't happen either.

Now it's crunch time for Blackpool. A fabulous run at the end of the 2006-07 campaign saw the Seasiders win ten games on the spin, the last and by far the most important against Yeovil in the Wembley play-off final and with it promotion to the second division for the first time in 29 years. The following year they clung onto their status, just, with a draw in the final game against Watford securing safety by a mere two points. Now where? The club, like the town, reached its zenith back in the fifties. There were legends everywhere. Ol' Blue Eyes Frank Sinatra stayed at the Clifton Hotel; at the Imperial, Liz Taylor's suite was redecorated in violet to tone with her eyes. While at Bloomfield Road, the two Stans, Matthews and Mortensen, provided the best show in town. It was a golden period for the club. Blackpool were genuine title contenders, finishing second to Manchester United in 1956, their best per-

Nickname The Seasiders
Kit Tangerine shirt, white shorts, tangerine socks
Ground Bloomfield Road – 9,491
Contact Seasiders Way, Blackpool, Lancs FY1 6JJ   0870 4431953
Tickets 0871 6221953
Website www.blackpoolfc.co.uk

formance to date. And they made three FA Cup finals in six years, losing to Manchester United in 1948 and to Newcastle United in 1951 before the glorious triumph in 1953, when 38-year-old Stanley Matthews conjured an improbable comeback from 3-1 down, tormenting the Bolton defence and setting up three goals for Blackpool in a match where Mortensen bagged a hat-trick.

Were Blackpool not a holiday resort, England may have missed out on winning the World Cup. Alan Ball, just 5 ft 6 in, had already been rejected by Wolves and Bolton for being too small, but his grandfather was having none of it. They were together on a family holiday in Blackpool when his granddad yanked him off the beach and dragged him to Bloomfield Road for one last trial. A fortnight later the pint-sized midfielder was in the team to face Liverpool. A portrait of the late World Cup winner now hangs in the club reception.

Club legends – Matthews, obviously, and Mortensen, the club's leading goalscorer nine years in a row with 197 goals in 317 league games: his statue stands behind the north stand which bears his name, and was unveiled by his widow. Not to forget Jimmy Armfield, best known these days as a Five Live radio pundit who spent his entire career at Blackpool, making a total of 569 league appearances for the club as well as winning 43 England caps and captaining his country 15 times.

Did you know?... Many Continental teams took their strips from colours sported by English clubs. Juventus borrowed from Notts County; Athletic Bilbao were inspired by Sunderland. With Blackpool it worked in reverse. Referee Bert Hargreaves was mightily impressed by the Dutch strip after officiating an international game between Holland and Belgium and passed on his top fashion tip to the club.

Bolton Wanderers

"I miss it, of course, but as a club we had to move on. We've moved from a two-up, two-down terraced house with an outside toilet into a mansion. But when you move into that mansion you never, ever forget your roots, do you? It's just a pity you can't be Doctor Who now and again; jump into your time machine and go back for just one game."

Club secretary Simon Marland misses Burnden Park.

Bolton's caterers got into a flap the day Burnden Park was chosen to host the 1901 FA Cup final replay. The prospect of having to feed William "Fatty" Foulke, United's man mountain 24-stone goalkeeper, was, of course, daunting. But not as scary as the news that the final, seven days earlier at Crystal Palace, had attracted 110,820 fans.

Contingency plans for ticketing, policing and stewarding the replay have been lost in the mist of time. But what is known is that the bakeries of Bolton produced approximately 100,000 pies more than was strictly necessary to feed a crowd of 20,470 – the lowest ever for a final. Afterwards the club cut its losses and gave them away, entire families feasting on thrice-daily pies for days.

The club settled in Burnden Park in 1895 but had been homeless for the previous 18 years, hence, Wanderers.

Bolton have spent 70 years in the top division without once winning the title, although their FA Cup record is a glorious one, appearing in seven finals and winning four.

Three of those finals have passed into legend. The 1923 match against West Ham was the first to be played at Wembley. No one knows how big the crowd was – estimates vary between 150,000 and 300,000 – because no one was counting.

Fans were so eager they burst through the gates and spilled onto, or rather swamped, the pitch, delaying kick-off for 45 minutes, until a sole mounted policeman on a massive white horse somehow cleared the ground.

It says a lot about the British that the name of the horse, Billie, has been remembered and immortalised – the walkway at the new Wembley is called White Horse Bridge following a public vote – whereas hardly anyone remembers his heroic rider, PC George Scorey.

The crowd had a hand in Bolton's opening goal. Hammers defender Jack Tressdern took a throw-in and was promptly engulfed by the massed fans packing the touchline – and swallowed up by the crowd. By the time he'd battled his way back onto the pitch, his team were behind – David Jack put Bolton one-up with a piledriver which knocked out a fan who had his nose pressed against the back of the net.

Bolton came agonisingly close to glory in the legendary 1953 final, 3-1 up with 22 minutes to go before 38-year-

Nickname The Trotters

Kit White shirt, navy shorts, white socks

Ground Reebok Stadium – 28, 723

Contact Reebok Stadium, Burnden Way, Horwich, Bolton, Lancs BL6 6JW 01204 673673

Tickets 0871 8712932

Website www.bwfc.co.uk

old Stanley Matthews weaved his dribbling magic to conjure an unlikely 4-3 victory for Blackpool. They won their last significant trophy in the 1958 final against a Manchester United side that had just lost eight first-team players in the Munich air disaster.

Soon afterwards the club's fortunes went into sharp decline and at one stage they slid into the fourth division. The footballing public sat up and took notice again in the early nineties when second division Bolton reinvented themselves as FA Cup giant-killers and knocked out the holders in successive years – Liverpool in 1993, Arsenal in 1994.

Fast-forward to Sam Allardyce. As a player, he was a hulking great brute. But when he returned to manage the club in 1999, he surprised everyone by revealing himself to be light years ahead of rival managers in his understanding and application of sports science and he revolutionised the club with his views on training and diet.

He also proved immensely astute in the transfer market. His Bolton had a reputation for playing tough, uncompromising football, which was true, but the team was also studded with ageing international stars who added undreamed-of class to the side. Trotters

THE FOOTBALL ASSOCIATION CHALLENGE CUP COMPETITION

FINAL TIE
BLACKPOOL v BOLTON WANDERERS

SATURDAY, MAY 2nd, 1953   KICK-OFF 3 pm

EMPIRE STADIUM

WEMBLEY

Chairman and Managing Director : SIR ARTHUR J. ELVIN, M.B.E.

OFFICIAL PROGRAMME · ONE SHILLING

fans were thrilled to find legendary Real Madrid European Cup-winning captain Fernando Hierro marshalling the defence, French World Cup winner Youri Djorkaeff bossing the midfield, and former Nigerian captain and sublimely skilful Jay-Jay ("so good they named him twice") Okocha dribbling for fun.

Allardyce left for Newcastle in 2007 to win some silverware – a dream that lasted a few weeks before he got the sack. His Bolton replacement Sammy Lee lasted about the same length of time, although the club avoided relegation in 2008, despite losing their best player Nicolas Anelka to Chelsea.

Club legend? There's only one Nat Lofthouse. A one-club man who scored 285 goals, he later had spells as club scout, manager, executive manager and president. His England career was equally impressive. With 30 goals in just 33 games, he held the England goalscoring record and his single-handed destruction of Europe's then top team Austria saw him dubbed "The Lion of Vienna", a moniker that stuck. There's a stand named after him at the newish stadium the club moved to in 1997. And a pub.

The Trotters?... In their wandering years, the club played on a pitch uncomfortably close to a piggery. Balls were regularly hoofed into the pens and could be retrieved only by wading through swill and slurry.

AFC Bournemouth

"This football club doesn't own as much as a napkin."
Club chairman Jeff Mostyn gives a full and frank assessment of Bournemouth's assets.

The more fan involvement in football clubs, the better. In principle. But it can all go horribly wrong. When the AFC Bournemouth Trust Fund rescued the club from extinction back in 1997, it was hailed as a blueprint for the future of smaller clubs. And when the trust handed over its golden share in the club to a fan organisation in 2005, there was jubilation marked by a pitchside ceremony.

But a ten-point penalty for going into administration saw them relegated from the third division by just two points in 2007-08, and the Cherries kicked off 2008-09 with a 17-point penalty because they failed to follow Football League rules on insolvency.

With hindsight, there was trouble on the horizon. Unlike rich owners, trust funds don't usually takeover with oodles of cash to spare. In Bournemouth's case, they inherited well over £2m of debt, and with a fortune needing to be spent renewing the ground, it was always going to be an uphill struggle. Ten years on and the club no longer owns the ground or is in charge of its own catering. The club shop has been sold. In 2008 ground staff were made redundant, the manager's mobile was cut off and companies dealing with the club started to demand cash upfront before they would do business.

The Cherries' heyday came in the early eighties when Harry

Redknapp took his first management job with Bournemouth and stayed for nine years. He took the club into the second division for the first time in their history and masterminded their greatest triumph, a 2-0 victory over Manchester United in the FA Cup third round.

How long is a lifetime? For Ian Leigh, goalkeeping hero of the triumph over United, not that long. Italian restaurant Di Luca's offered the keeper a lifetime supply of free pizza if he kept a clean sheet in the cup tie. But when the restaurant changed hands the new management told Leigh it wouldn't honour the deal. The new proprietor? Harry Redknapp.

Club hero? Has to be Ted MacDougall. He banged in 103 league goals in just three years in his first spell at Bournemouth in the early seventies, while his record in the FA Cup was just astonishing. In 1970 he bagged six against Oxford City; the following season he scored five in the first half in a first-round tie against Margate. At half-time Margate manager Gerry Baker jokingly suggested to Cherries boss John Bond that he substitute MacDougall. He didn't and the Scot knocked in four more in the second half as Bournemouth ran out 12-0 winners. MacDougall's nine remains an all-time FA Cup record.

The Cherries? Maybe because the club played in cherry red; possibly because there were cherry orchards close to Dean Court. The club rebranded itself AFC Bournemouth in 1971 –

Nickname The Cherries

Kit Red shirt with black trim, black shorts and socks with red trim

Ground Fitness First Stadium – 10,700

Contact The Fitness First Stadium at Dean Court, Kings Park, Bournemouth, Dorset BH7 7AF 01202 726300

Tickets 01202 726338

Website www.afcb.co.uk

until then it was called Bournemouth and Boscombe Athletic Football Club, which was a bit of a mouthful.

The future? Bournemouth's supporters have worked tirelessly for ten years to keep the club afloat. Cherryshare, Cherries Hotshots, Playerpledge, Playershare, the Community Mutual, Cherrychange... the number of fundraising initiatives has been heart-warming, the fund of goodwill from the town has been massive, but a club with no assets is a club on a slippery slope.

So near, yet so far... Richard and Mary Hayter were at Dean Court in 2004, the night their son James scored the fastest hat-trick in the history of English football – and missed the lot. The couple left early to beat the traffic, their son came on as a late substitute and rattled in three goals against Wrexham in two minutes and twenty seconds.

Bradford City

"I had a word with the foreman about it and he reckoned this is what our fans would like to see this season – a great view of the car park."

Club chairman Geoffrey Richmond laughed it off in 2000 when workmen erected six corporate boxes at Valley Parade facing away from the pitch. But maybe the foreman knew what he was doing. Hospitality boxes at sporting occasions are a must-have for many corporate bods wanting to wine and dine their clients. Watching the football really can get in the way.

Is your season ticket burning a hole in your pocket? In the Premier League, they're up on average 7.2 per cent for 2008-09, well above inflation, with a mid-price average of £590. At Barcelona the best seat costs just £560 and the cheapest comes in at just £66. Bradford City co-chairman Julian Rhodes was astonished when he realised just how cheap it was to be a regular at the Nou Camp and was inspired. In 2007 the Bantams slashed prices to £138 – the cheapest in the league – working out at just £6 a game. Under 11s got in free. The result – crowds at Valley Parade were three times the size of any other club in the fourth division.

Other clubs have been watching, amazed. In 2008 Port Vale and Huddersfield Town are following a similar route. Fans who had been priced out of football have returned. Kids who may have ended up as glory hunters "supporting" a top side in a remote city have ended up

Nickname The Bantams/the Citizens
Kit Amber and claret striped shirt, black shorts, claret socks
Ground Coral Windows Stadium – 25,136
Contact Valley Parade, Bradford, W. Yorks, BD8 7DY 0870 8220000
Tickets 01274 770012
Website www.bradfordcityfc.co.uk

cheering on their local team. Programme sales have gone through the roof. Many pies have been eaten. Advertisers are reaching loads more fans. And a team that was playing to an ever-dwindling crowd is now being roared on by a large support.

This season Bradford tried to go one better, offering a buy-one-get-one-free deal that would have come into effect if 9,000 adults had renewed in time, but fell just 700 short of their target. But it's heartening to see the Bantams on the up and up after a decade in which they reached for the moon, only to slide into the gutter.

Until recently Bradford City's sole spell in the first division was between 1908 and 1922, during which time the club had its highest league finish and won its only major honour. The 1911 FA Cup final against Newcastle United went to a replay with club captain Jimmy Speirs scoring the winner and lifting the trophy. That was the year a bantam hitched a ride on the team bus – hence, the Bantams.

In 1994, there was widespread scepticism when chairman Geoffrey Richmond took over – with Bradford in the third division – and promised top-flight football in five years. Five years and four managers later City pulled it off, with Paul Jewell steering the club to second place behind Luton in 1999 and taking City into the top division for the first time in 77 years.

But this was where the problems began. City's squad in their first season back was very experienced – old would be another way of looking at it – and the team looked destined to go down from the start. They pulled it out of the bag on the very last day, beating Liverpool 1-0 – becoming the first team to stay up with just 36 points.

The following season was madness. The Bantams went on an insane spending spree in a doomed attempt to avoid relegation. Reckless signings included gifted Italian Benito Carbone, who arrived on wages of £40,000 a week, a fortune then – actually, quite a lot now – and completely unsustainable. The club plummeted through the divisions – three relegations in seven years. Bradford went into administration in 2002 with debts of £13m, and Valley Parade had to be sold the following year along with the club shop, its offices and its car park. It took another spell in administration back in 2004 before the club finally found its feet again.

Supporters throughout the land play a huge part when their club is in financial trouble and none illustrate this better than the Bradford City supporters' trust, which played a massive role when the club was on its uppers, rattling tins, organising the £100,000 appeal, holding vigils and lobbying the council to help because of the vital role the club plays at the heart of the community. Nowhere does that appeal resonate louder than at Valley Parade, hit by tragedy in May 1985, when fire ripped through the wooden roof of the main stand and killed 56 spectators. The Disaster Appeal Fund raised £3.5m and the club has incorporated black into its strip since the tragedy in memory of the victims. The Bradford fire disaster led to the Popplewell Report, published the following year, which made a number of recommendations on ground safety which have since become standard practice.

In 2007 Stuart McCall returned to manage the club where he spent two spells as a player, one as captain. His family were present on the day of the disaster and his dad suffered burns which put him in hospital for a month. You'll never hear a bad word said against McCall in Bradford. His tireless work with the victims of the fire and their families in the aftermath of the tragedy earned him the respect of the city and won't be forgotten.

Strange but true… Bradford City were elected to the Football League before they'd played a single game of football. In 1908 the league was desperate to establish the round-ball game in an area dominated by rugby league and elected rugby league team Manningham FC. Four days later Manningham changed its name to Bradford City, and its code from rugby league to association football. Unlucky losers in all this were Doncaster Rovers, chucked out of the league to make way for City.

Brentford

**"I'm very confident I'll be given more time here.
The people above me have backed me 100 per cent,
both privately and publicly."**
*How much more time? Three days... Bees boss Terry Butcher was on his bike in
December 2007 after a run that included five games without scoring and a seven-goal
hammering at the hands of Peterborough.*

London boasted three big clubs before the war – Arsenal, Chelsea...
and Brentford. With three consecutive top-six finishes and gates nearing 40,000, the club looked like it was going places.

Since the war, not so good. Brentford's biggest battles have been to
retain its ground. There was a close-run thing in the late sixties when
the club was almost swallowed up by Queens Park Rangers. And just a
few years ago, former chairman Ron Noades seemed set on flogging off
Griffin Park and ground-sharing with Woking while looking for a new
home. Brentford fans, fearful the club would end up homeless, protest-
ed loudly and in the end Noades packed his bags and sold the club to
the supporters' trust for £1.

Fanatical fans have played a big part in ensuring the Bees' survival
during assorted cash crises. In 2005, with the club in peril, supporters
walked 268 miles to an away match in Hartlepool to raise money –
since then they've done similar fundraisers to Stockport and Brighton.
Childhood fan and former BBC boss Greg Dyke was roped in as club

Nickname The Bees

Kit Red and white striped shirt, black shorts, black and red socks

Ground Griffin Park – 12,763

Contact Braemar Road, Brentford, Middx TW8 0NT 08453 456442

Website www.brentfordfc.co.uk

chairman, and in 2007 fan Matthew Benham gave the club an interest-free loan for five years to make sure it didn't go under.

Unusually, the club has named one of its stands after a stalwart supporter. Bill Axbey was born shortly before the club moved to Griffin Park in 1904. At the age of 95 he finally fulfilled every schoolboy's dream by running out onto the pitch as club mascot. And he was present at every home game right up until his death in 2007, just short of his 103rd birthday. The club has renamed the New Road stand in his honour. But Griffin Park may not be around for much longer. A shame for beer drinkers, as it's the only club in the country with a pub at all four corners of the ground. After years of dithering and false dawns, it's now looking highly likely that the club will be in a new community stadium in Lionel Road by 2012. There's talk that it will be a training facility for the London Olympics, and in 2008 the club strengthened the Olympic connection by appointing Mike Power to the board – he was the chief operating officer behind London's successful Olympic bid.

Records? The Bees won every home match in the 1929-30 season, 21 in total, an unrivalled achievement in English football. But poor away form meant they failed to clinch promotion from the old Third Division South that year.

The last couple of decades have been eventful on and off the pitch. Since 1992 Brentford has been promoted twice as champions, suffered relegation three times and made the play-offs on no fewer than six occasions – all unsuccessful. There have been money-spinning FA Cup runs to match. Quarter-finalists in 1989 before going out to champions Liverpool, the Bees made it to the last 16 in both 2005 and when they dumped Premier League team Sunderland out of the competition, courtesy of two goals from star man D.J. Campbell. It was the young striker's last game for the club. Snapped up from non-league Yeading for just £5,000 a few months earlier, he was sold to Birmingham for £500,000 just three days after his cup exploits, a move which earned the club some much-needed cash but which may have cost them an automatic promotion spot that season.

There has been turbulence too in the manager's chair. When Andy Scott was appointed in 2007, he became the eleventh man to hold the position since 2000.

Hero? Ken Coote's career at Griffin Park spanned three decades in which he captained the side to the fourth division title in 1963. Incredibly for a defender, he didn't pick up a single booking in a club record of 514 league games for the Bees.

Unluckiest Bee?... No contest here. Knocked unconscious when a crossbar collapsed on his head, goalie Chic Brodie survived when a hand grenade was lobbed into his area by a disgruntled Millwall fan in 1965. The ref stopped that match while the offending explosive device was deposited into a bucket of sand. Unhappily, the ref didn't stop the game when a dog invaded the pitch in a match against Colchester United in 1970 and ran amok for two minutes. Brodie kept his eyes on the ball rather than the dog when dealing with a back pass and didn't see the terrier, which cannoned into the keeper, sending him tumbling and shattering his kneecap. He never played again.

Brighton & Hove Albion

"It's like looking up an old girlfriend – you've got great memories but the only problem is I'm greyer and fatter than last time!"

Micky Adams reflects on returning to Brighton for a second spell as manager.

"And Smith must score!"… Four short words that scar the soul of every Seagulls fan. FA Cup final, 1983, extra time, just ten seconds on the clock and Brighton level at two apiece against Manchester United. Michael Robinson hurtles down the left and splits the shattered United defence with an inch-perfect pass to striker Gordon Smith, unmarked in front of goal with just keeper Gary Bailey to beat. And Smith must score… only he doesn't. The shot is scuffed into the ground, ricochets off the keeper's outstretched leg, and with it goes Brighton's first – and to date, last – chance of glory. Things were never to be so good again but they did get worse. A lot worse.

The Seagulls first came to the nation's attention in 1973 when manager Brian Clough and his right-hand man Peter Taylor took charge in a blaze of publicity. Clough had taken Derby County from the depths of the second division to the first division championship, and would do the same again at Nottingham Forest – and more – but his brief time on the south coast was more remarkable for headlines than results. When quizzed on football violence, Cloughie quipped: "Football hooligans? Well, there are 92 club chairmen for a start." What would he have made of Bill Archer?

It was Archer who sold the club's stadium at Goldstone Road in the mid-nineties without telling anyone. Their home for 95 years, the deal was done in secret – no one knew anything until it was exposed in the Brighton *Argus*. Also done on the quiet: a change to the club rules shortly after Archer arrived in 1993. Until then, if the club went bust, any cash raised from selling the ground had to go to a neighbouring club, or charity. Afterwards, not the case. Goldstone Road became a retail park with a drive-thru burger joint. Brighton & Hove Albion became homeless, with no prospect of a new home in sight and the club refusing to pay rent to play elsewhere.

This book is sprinkled with stories of heroic supporters who have battled against the odds to keep their club alive. None have been more heroic or persistent over so long a spell as fans of the Seagulls.

There were demonstrations, pitch invasions, mass whistle-blowing at matches, and a mass walk-out with 15 minutes to go. The fans boycotted a game against Mansfield where less than 2,000 people turned up. Thousands of supporters held up red cards at the ground when the cameras were in. There were petitions. Supporters designed papier-mâché models of the directors with exploding heads. There were demos on the A3 and A4, protests in Brighton, London, out-

Nickname The Seagulls

Kit Blue and white striped shirt, white shorts, white socks

Ground Withdean Stadium – 8,850

Contact (Club) 8th Floor, Tower Point, 44 North Road, Brighton BN1 1YR. (Stadium) Tongdean Lane, Brighton, W Sussex BN1 5JD 01273 695400

Tickets 01273 776992

Website www.seagulls.co.uk

side the HQ of Archer's company in Crewe and outside his home in Lancashire. There was a bizarre Christmas card protest – the chairman received thousands of Christmas cards at his home from disgruntled supporters begging him to bugger off.

Most innovative of all, there was a Fans United day at the Goldstone in 1997 – thousands of supporters from across the country converged on Brighton to show solidarity with Brighton fans in their hour of need.

For a couple of years the club was forced to play "home" matches at Gillingham, almost 70 miles away – attracting crowds as low as 1,000 – before moving to the Withdean, an athletics and county football stadium closer to home. Meanwhile, a protracted planning inquiry got under way as the club – now minus Archer and his cronies – desperately tried to find a new home. And on the pitch: success that was astonishing in the circumstances, with the club winning two successive promotions at the start of the decade.

But at last – an end is in sight. Planning permission was given in 2007 for a new stadium near the village of Falmer on the outskirts of the town and the club hopes to be installed there by 2010. After narrowly failing to make the third division play-offs in 2008, Brighton brought back Micky Adams, their most successful manager in recent years, for a second spell at the club.

Strange but true… You occasionally read about football-obsessed parents who name their kids after entire football teams. Few of them go on to be professional players. Midfielder Anthony Philip David Terry Frank Donald Stanley Gerry Gordon Stephen James Oatway is an exception. Eight years a Seagull until 2007, Charlie Oatway was named after the entire QPR team from 1973. Charlie? When his mum and dad told his auntie what they were planning to call him, she said: "He'll look a right Charlie…"

Bristol City

"I asked the Holy Spirit where they're going to kick. He said 'left' and I said 'thank you'. I went to the left side and I saved the ball, so today I was very blessed."

*Robins' Brazilian keeper Adriano Basso draws on divine
intervention to save a Watford penalty.*

It's a miracle Adriano Basso came to England at all. The Brazilian only came here because his girlfriend Allessandra was studying in Britain and threatened to finish with him unless he followed her. A top-flight keeper in his homeland, Basso found himself plying his trade at St Alban's City and Woking before being snapped up by Gary Johnson at Bristol back in 2005.

Basso wasn't initially popular at City and neither for that matter was Johnson. Recently arrived from Yeovil with the club in a perilous position, the local papers and phone-ins were awash with contributors claiming he was the wrong man in the wrong job at the wrong time.

Just how wrong can you be. The following season City won promotion to the second division, and in 2008 just missed out on making it to the Premier League, beaten 1-0 by Hull in the Wembley play-off final.

Faith played a large part in the turnaround. Johnson invested dollops of the stuff in a pair of lucky underpants given to him by his mum. While ahead of a clash with Sheffield Wednesday, he publicly asked

Nickname The Robins
Kit Red shirt, white shorts, red and white socks
Ground Ashton Gate – 21, 479
Contact Ashton Gate, Ashton Rd, Bristol BS3 2EJ 0871 2226666
Website www.bcfc.co.uk

supporters worldwide to light a candle and offer up prayers for his team. Fans took him seriously – one in Japan emailed Johnson a photo of a Bristol City pennant illuminated at the Shinto Shrine.

The club started the 2008-09 season in a buoyant mood with bumper season tickets sales, a new junior academy under way and a level of optimism the Robins haven't seen since the glory days of Alan Dicks. The former Coventry City coach arrived at the club in 1967 aged just 33 and stayed for 13 years. What looked like being his greatest moment came in 1974 when the nation was in the grip of a miners' strike and electricity was rationed. The Robins travelled to Elland Road for a midweek fifth-round replay against the then mighty Leeds United which kicked off at the unlikely hour of 2pm and ran out 1-0 winners. Leeds romped away with the title that year, City languished in the bottom half of the second division.

But just two years later they met on equal terms after Dicks steered the club to the first division for the first time in 65 years. Star man in the side was former Leeds United hardman Norman Hunter. The Robins survived for four years. Even in relegation there was something to smile about, with Ashton Gate resounding to ever lustier renditions of "Dicks Out!"

Just two years after being relegated from the top flight, the club was bankrupt – the unhappy combination of three successive relegations at a time when a number of squad players were locked into long-term contracts on top wages. The so-called Ashton Gate Eight helped ensure the club's survival, well-paid players who agreed to take redundancy on reduced terms so that the club wouldn't go under.

The club's finest moments came a century ago. In 1907 they were runners-up behind Newcastle United in the first division, and two years later reached the FA Cup final only to lose to Manchester United at Crystal Palace.

Club hero? Has to be John Atyeo, all-time top goalscorer with 314 league goals. He notched up 597 appearances for the Robins, another record, winning six England caps at a time when City were bouncing between the second and third divisions.

Gary Johnson's arse… became a subject for national debate after he rashly promised to bare all in the unlikely event of Liam Fontaine breaking his goalscoring virginity. It all started back in August 2007 when the young defender galloped the length of the pitch in a cup tie against Brentford only to collapse in a heap with the goal at his mercy. "Fonts will never score," declared Johnson… "But if he does I will show my backside in Burton's window." When Fontaine finally broke his duck on his 108th appearance, Burton's were strangely reluctant to allow Johnson to fulfil his promise. But a happy compromise was reached for the TV cameras at City's training ground, where Johnson gave Fontaine the opportunity to lash the ball at his protruding buttocks from just 30 feet away. Fontaine missed again, and again, and again…

Gary Johnson – bared buttocks

Bristol Rovers

"I'm not going to start lecturing the England players because they are at the top of their profession and get paid good money for what they do. But if they need to come down here to Bristol Rovers and get a few penalty lessons, we'll happily give them some."

After despatching Palace, Orient and Fulham in spot-kick shoot-outs, Craig Disley offers to share his expertise with the hapless national squad.

Rovers reached the FA Cup quarter-finals for only the third time in their history in 2008. Back in 1956 the cup provided the Gas with what must go down as their greatest ever triumph.

Most cup giant-killing feats follow a familiar pattern, the underdogs sneaking ahead then holding out against the odds while the favourites lay siege to their goal. But not this one. A full-strength Manchester United destined to win the title that season (and the next) turned up at Rovers' then home, Eastville, in January for a third-round tie and were annihilated 4-0 in front of 35,000 incredulous supporters. Were it not for an heroic performance from United keeper Ray Wood, it could have been more.

Rovers? Never has a team been more aptly named. Formed in 1883 as the Purdown Poachers, in their early days they were the ultimate itinerants, settling briefly at Purdown, Three Acres, Ashley Hill, Ridgeway and Fishponds before putting down roots at Eastville in 1904.

Was money tight in those days? Rovers were so cash-strapped in 1896 that they charged their opponents admission money to get in the ground. And the referee. One of the first clubs forced to sell their ground to ward off a cash crisis, they flogged it to a greyhound company in 1940 and had to pay rent from then on. More heartache was to follow in 1980 when the south stand burned down in mysterious circumstances. Fans had to swallow hard and up sticks across the Avon to Bristol City's home at Ashton Gate until the ground was repaired. While in 1986, the club sickened of paying rent at Eastville and spent the next decade playing all their home matches 15 miles down the road in Bath, where they endured yet another fire in 1990.

Nickname The Pirates/the Gas

Kit Royal blue and white quartered shirt, white shorts, royal blue socks

Ground Memorial Stadium – 12,011 (3,000 seated)

Contact Filton Avenue, Horfield, Bristol BS7 0BF 0117 9096648

Tickets 0117 9098848

Website www.bristolrovers.co.uk

Off the pitch, uncertainty continues. The club's plan to relocate 43 miles to Cheltenham for 2008-09 while their current home at the Memorial Stadium is redeveloped was postponed at the last minute due to the credit crunch.

Whether the revamped 18,500 stadium will be big enough should Rovers ever hit the big time is debatable. In 2007 the club climbed out of the fourth division after beating Shrewsbury in the play-offs at a Wembley filled with at least 40,000 Gasheads – proof that a city the size of Bristol could support two teams at the highest level if the clubs do their stuff on the pitch.

That Rovers should have found themselves in the fourth division to start with was galling to their fans – until recently the club had been in the second or third divisions for their entire Football League existence. Promotion was masterminded by Paul Trollope, installed as caretaker manager in 2005 after predecessor Ian Atkins was sacked. The club was left with little choice in the matter – thousands of fans boycotted matches until he was shown the door.

The club has a history of colourful bosses. Former England captain Gerry Francis had two spells in charge, while Ian Holloway was a veritable boomerang, becoming player-manager in his third period at the club and staying for five years. Charismatic, passionate and a hero to supporters, he rebuilt the club and signed a succession of top-class forwards – Barry Hayles, Jason Roberts, Bobby Zamora, Nathan Ellington – who all went on to play top-flight football elsewhere. Under Holloway the club twice reached the play-offs but the pressure of having to dismantle and rebuild his squads over and over proved too much.

Heroes? The strike duo of Smash and Grab, aka Alan Warboys and Bruce Bannister, terrorised defences nationwide in the early seventies – nowhere more so than at Brighton, where the little and large duo grabbed seven between them in an 8-2 thrashing. Father and son duo Ray and Gary Mabbutt played a total of 500-plus games, with Gary going on to win England honours at Spurs. While Geoff Bradford, who clocked up 260 goals in 511 appearances in the 1950s, remains the only Rovers player ever to have won an England cap. He scored on his debut in an away fixture in Denmark, but was never picked again.

Unforgettable moment? Clinching promotion against Bristol City on their way to the third division championship in 1990.

Dodgy keeper?… Back in the early sixties Rovers bought goalie

Esmond Million from Middlesbrough. Shame they didn't buy his bungalow as well. Unable to sell his home and sinking deeper into debt, Million took a £300 bribe to throw a match against Bradford Park Avenue. It went as wrong as it could do for the bent keeper – he'd barely touched the ball by the time Rovers raced into a 2-0 lead and, despite all his efforts, the game ended up a draw – and Million ended up in deep doo-dah with the betting syndicate, manager Bert Tann, and the FA, who banned him for life.

Burnley

"We have cut out all the chips and stuff like that but you can't watch them 24 hours a day. Me and Jean-Pierre Papin used to have a McDonalds after training. You just hope that players are good pros and when they leave training they go home, they eat sensibly, they stay in and do all that, but English players are a breed of their own."

Player, manager, sports dietician... Chris Waddle had a lot on his plate during his season at Turf Moor.

May 9th, 1987. A date etched in the hearts and minds of every Burnley fan. The day when anyone with more than a passing interest in football focused on the events unfolding at Turf Moor. The hour when it looked like a club with a glorious history – and one of the 12 founding clubs in the Football League – was going very publicly kaput.

It was in May 1987 that the concept of automatic relegation from England's fourth division came into being. Looking back 21 years on, it's difficult to grasp the panic and terror that created. We've sort of got used to the idea that the conference is essentially the fifth division – teams go down, teams bounce back, life goes on.

It didn't seem like that then. To the club, the fans, the press who descended on Burnley in their hundreds, the public at large, relegation and loss of league status spelled extinction. Clubs that dropped out of the league never came back. Lose the match and the club was dead. Or so it seemed.

The average crowd at Turf Moor that season hovered around 3,000 but over 17,000 turned up for the last match against Orient, believing that the Clarets needed to win and that results elsewhere had to go their way for the club to survive.

How had it come to this? As recently as 1960, Burnley were champions of England. In 1974 they came sixth, behind Derby, Ipswich and Stoke. Of today's so-called Big Four, Arsenal came 10th, Chelsea 17th, and Manchester United... were relegated.

It couldn't happen now. As it happens, the seeds that were to scupper the long-term chances of Burnley and all the smaller clubs in England were sown in 1961 when Burnley were champions. The maximum wage was abolished. Until then footballers could earn a maximum £20 a week, wherever they played.

Suddenly the bigger clubs with more fans could attract the best players by paying more. The level playing field began to slope. In 1983 the bigger clubs pushed through an end to the practice of sharing gate receipts – 20 per cent of them used to go to the away team – which made the rich clubs richer, the poorer clubs poorer. In the sixties all TV money was shared

Nickname The Clarets

Kit Claret and blue shirt, white shorts, white socks

Ground Turf Moor – 22,546

Contact Harry Potts Way, Burnley, Lancs BB10 4BX 0871 2211882

Tickets 0871 2211914

Website www.burnleyfootballclub.com

equally between all 92 clubs, but by the mid-eighties the first division had snaffled half the money.

Now, of course, the gap is obscene – each Premier League club gets on average £45m a year TV money, while 66 clubs in the Football League (excluding the relegated Premiership clubs on parachute payments) have to share around £33m between the lot of them. Add in the £102m the Big Four earned in TV and marketing deals from this year's Champions League competition. And factor in the fact that foreign billionaires with bottomless pockets are buying up England's top clubs just to get their hands on the billions of pounds pouring into the game. And you understand why Burnley – and another 45 league clubs – have plunged into administration at some point since the Premier League was founded 15 years ago.

Back in the days when Burnley were champions, they didn't need a billionaire. A prosperous butcher was good enough. And Burnley had one in the shape of Bob Lord, the autocratic and ambitious chairman who ran the club from 1955. In his time he upset just about everyone. He didn't have much time for supporters, refusing to permit an official supporters' association and publicly berating them if they didn't turn up in sufficient numbers. He was forever falling out with the TV companies. He famously refused to allow the cameras into an FA Cup match – the BBC had already paid for the rights – because he didn't think the club was getting enough. He once chucked Fulham chairman Ernie Clay out of the ground at half-time because of a disagreement. He sold players at the height of their popularity because he'd fallen out with them and he didn't give a damn when the fans demonstrated against him.

But – and it's a big but – he laid the foundations for Burnley's success. While other clubs trained players on seaside beaches and car parks, Burnley was the first club in the country to build a proper training ground. They built up the best scouting network in the country, taking boys straight from school and coaching them with a team of specialists.

They were one of the first teams to fly to matches, and one of the first to develop their commercial side to bring in cash when it became obvious after the abolition of the maximum wage that it would struggle to compete. While his policy of hiring only former players on the coaching staff led to the club's greatest managerial appointment, Harry Potts, who led the club to the title, into Europe, and an FA Cup final.

Club heroes? Jimmy Adamson, who arrived as a 17-year-old and stayed for 30 years, captaining the Clarets in their championship-winning year and going on to be coach and manager. Leighton James, the flamboyant Welsh winger who terrorised defences and made over 400 appearances in four, yes, four spells at the club over 19 years. Ralph Coates, short, squat, okay, maybe a bit fat, with an unhappy comb-over reminiscent of Bobby Charlton in his hirsutically challenged heyday, implausibly pacy on the wide left and the crowd hero in the second half of the sixties. And Jimmy McIlroy, the midfielder from County Antrim who was the lynchpin of the team that won the title and arguably the finest player ever to play at Turf Moor. The east stand is named in his honour.

Did you know?… The first recorded case of bribery in football came at Burnley. The club had to win the final game of the 1899 season against Sheffield United to avoid relegation. Keeper Jack Hillman, who had played for England earlier in the year, offered United players £2 each to throw the match. He was caught and banned for a year. Burnley lost 4-0.

Bury

"As Bury weren't involved, I declined."

*Gordon Sorfleet, crowned UEFA's European Fan of the Year, politely turns down
his invitation to attend the Champions League draw.*

Bury are the only team ever to have been drummed out of the FA Cup
for fielding an ineligible player. They're also the only team ever to have
their drummers drummed out of the FA Cup!

Confused? The first unwanted little piece of history came in 2006
after the Shakers carelessly and illegally included on-loan Hartlepool
player Stephen Turnbull in the team that beat Chester City 3-1 in a
second-round replay – a blunder that cost them a third-round tie
against Ipswich and over £20,000 in prize fund payments.

The second came in 2008 when Southampton banned Bury's travelling band of drummers from St Mary's, citing health and safety con-
cerns. The story went around the world – thousands signed an international online petition in support of the Bury drumming boys – forcing
Southampton to put out a statement to the effect that the sound of the
drums dramatically affected the noise levels and acoustics within the
away stand and "rendered the radio systems inoperable".

Obviously the temptation is to brand Southampton as killjoys,
jobsworths and spoilsports; however, bands in grounds is an issue that
divides supporters. For every England fan bellowing lustily to the strain
of the England Supporters Band and their endless renditions of "The

Great Escape", there's another who'll tell you they're an intrusive pain in the arse. One online Bury wag thought the Southampton ban was simply a delayed case of sour grapes: *"You we're scared of us cos we beat you 4-0 over 100 years ago when about 4 teams entered the FA Cup and half the players had rickets."*

This is an unduly modest reference to Bury's first great achievement – beating Southampton 4-0 in the 1900 FA Cup final – and for the record there were 242 FA Cup entrants that year. Just three years later Bury won it again, thumping Derby County 6-0, which is still the biggest winning margin ever in an FA Cup final. And they went the whole competition without conceding a goal.

More than a century has passed, but it never really got better than that. In 1926 they finished fourth in the first division, their best ever position, but two years later were relegated and have never returned. In 2007 they came perilously close to dropping out of the Football League altogether, surviving a tight relegation battle by the skin of their teeth.

The club almost went to the wall in 2002. Three years earlier it transpired that main moneyman Hugh Eaves had been using someone else's money to bankroll the Shakers, and the club found itself in a spiral of debt which ended up in administration. Club press officer Gordon Sorfleet kept the club alive, raising £60,000 via an online auction, an innovative sponsored seat sale, and forming a supporters' trust. He was not alone. Bury Forever formed to save the club, while thousands of football fans from England and overseas chipped in with a tenner to sponsor a seat. Sorfleet may have declined the invitation to the Champions League draw but he did make it as far as Monaco to receive his Fan of the Year award from Pele, be congratulated by Zinedine Zidane and chat to Sir Bobby Robson while his wife chewed the fat with the president of Barcelona.

Forever Bury has excellent links with the club, although one club man they'll be seeing a lot less of is former director Iain Mills – forced out in February 2008 because Bury had apparently received a number of complaints about his fondness for wearing shorts – always. His fellow directors admitted the club would probably have gone out of existence without him, but said his wearing of shorts was "putting the board in an embarrassing position which Iain feels is not to the best interests of the club". As for Mills? "It's ridiculous to think that 12 inches of material below my bum is causing this much of a problem to people."

An unlikely club hero – famous or infamous, depending on your point of view – was David Adekola, who arrived in 1993 in a blaze of publicity. With 16 caps for Nigeria and a glut of goals in French and Belgian football to his name, he turned down an £800,000 transfer to Marseilles in favour of a free transfer to Bury. Was the boy mad? No, in love with an English girl and desperate to be with her. He uttered those words that fall so rarely from the lips of footballers: "There's more to life than money."

Years later it turned out he'd made it all up. The Nigerian FA hadn't heard of him and neither had anyone else. At Bury, they didn't care. His arrival in the team heralded a run of nine wins in ten with Adekola scoring freely including a hat-trick at Scarborough.

The Shakers? Down to J.T. Ingham, the club's first chairman, who in a rousing speech prior to a Lancashire Cup match in 1892 declared of his opponents: "We shall shake 'em. In fact we are The Shakers." It stuck.

Strange but true... There's another club at Gigg Lane. FC United of Manchester, the breakaway club formed by United fans who couldn't stomach the thought of their club being taken over by American Malcolm Glazer, has been based there since 2005. After three promotions in the first three seasons, the team started 2008-09 in the premier division of the Northern Premier League.

Cardiff City
(Clwb Pêl-droed Dinas Caerdydd)

**"I assured my wife it's not for real. She's worried
I might get foot-and-mouth."**
*When Spencer Prior moved to City in 2001, he signed a contract agreeing to
have a physical liaison with a sheep and eat sheep's testicles.*

History has not recorded whether the defender fulfilled all aspects of his
contractual obligations at Ninian Park, if ewe know what I mean, but
within weeks he was devouring testicle kebab in front of 250 supporters at a fans' forum.

The sheep shenanigans were the brainchild of Sam Hammam, the
former owner who bought Cardiff in 2000. The Lebanese businessman
spotted the possibilities of a club with a potentially massive fan base and
wrapped himself in the Welsh flag, displaying newfound enthusiasm for
dragons, daffodils, even the anti-English rebel hero Owain Glyndw^r.
Supporters lapped it up as he transformed a club in the doldrums,
winning promotion twice with an entertaining team that included free-
scoring forward Rob Earnshaw.

Success came at a price. Around £1m in debt when Hamman
arrived, the club owed nearer £25m by 2004 and began to unravel.
Stars were sold, with Hammam forced out in 2006 when the council
refused to pay £40m towards a new ground unless it saw a sensible business plan.

The 26,500-capacity new stadium due to open in 2009 is near
Ninian Park, home to the Bluebirds since 1912 and originally built on

a rubbish tip. Fans cleared the site and were rewarded as Cardiff rose rapidly from the Southern League to the first division. Their best spell came in the twenties, when they were second to Huddersfield in 1924 and FA Cup finalists twice in three seasons. Beaten by Sheffield United in 1925, the Bluebirds returned as underdogs in 1927 and defeated Arsenal 1-0, taking the trophy out of England for the first and only time.

Best excuse for a howler? Hughie Ferguson's winning goal came courtesy of a ghastly gaffe from Arsenal keeper Dan Lewis who allowed the low shot to slip out of his hands then knocked it into the net with his elbow. Lewis later blamed his goalkeeping jersey, so new and greasy it made handling errors inevitable.

The cup victory is the defining moment in Cardiff's history and in 2008 there was the glorious possibility that they could repeat it after a great run took them to Wembley. A gutsy display saw them lose to Portsmouth by a single goal in a game in which the team were acclaimed for their performance on the pitch and the supporters for their behaviour off it – followers of the club have been involved in a number of high-profile hooligan incidents in the past decade.

Nickname The Bluebirds, or City

Kit Blue shirts with yellow trim, white socks, white shorts

Ground Ninian Park – 20,376

Contact Sloper Road, Cardiff CF11 8SX 029 20221001

Tickets 0845 3451400

Website www.cardiffcityfc.co.uk

Cardiff in Europe? Been there, done that. Welsh clubs competing in the English leagues are now barred from the Welsh Cup but before

1995 it offered a route into Europe. City triumphed 22 times and had some great nights in the Cup Winners' Cup under manager Jimmy Scoular, making the semi-finals in 1968 and reaching the quarter-finals twice – including a magical evening in 1971 when 50,000 packed Ninian Park to see Brian Clarke head home the winner against Real Madrid.

Unluckiest Bluebird?... Has to be Len Davies. The key man in City's great side in the twenties was a successful international, scored the club's first league hat-trick and should be remembered for his club record 128 goals. But he isn't. In May 1924 City went into the final game of the season at Birmingham City in pole position to be crowned champions, a point clear of Huddersfield Town and with a superior goal average. A win would guarantee the title; draw and Huddersfield had to beat Nottingham Forest by three clear goals. Huddersfield did, while at St Andrews the match was locked at 0-0... until Cardiff were awarded a late penalty – only for Davies to fire his shot straight at the Birmingham keeper. It was the closest title race in league history, the Bluebirds' goal average just 0.024 worse than Huddersfield. The miss haunted Davies for the rest of his life.

Carlisle United

"I could have signed for Newcastle when I was 17, but I decided I would be better off at Carlisle. I'd had a drink that night!"

Peter Beardsley

It was a magical moment that captured the nation. In the 95th minute of the final game of the 1999 season, Carlisle were staring into the abyss of the conference after 71 unbroken years in the league. Cue on-loan goalkeeper Jimmy Glass, who sprinted the length of the pitch for a corner and cracked home a half-volley that won the match, saved the club from relegation and sparked the mother of all pitch invasions.

To the rest of us it seemed like a fairytale. The goal was replayed endlessly on TV and Glass became an overnight sensation. For Carlisle supporters it wasn't so simple. They carried the team off, but they weren't getting carried away. For they were enduring an ordeal of Biblical proportions in which years of plenty had

Nickname The Cumbrians
Kit Royal blue shirt and shorts with white stripe, royal blue socks
Ground Brunton Park – 16,981
Contact Warwick Road, Carlisle, Cumbria CA1 1LL 01228 526237
Tickets 0844 3711921
Website www.carlisleunited.co.uk

evolved into years of famine. When the euphoria died down, they were still starving.

Owner Michael Knighton publicly declared that he believed in Frankenstein and he believed in God. He also said he believed in aliens, but we don't have time for that here. The Cumbrians thought he might be a god and they certainly treated him like one when he arrived in 1992. By the time he departed nine years later, his name was frequently prefaced by the F-word, and I don't mean Frankenstein.

He was a genius, a visionary, a maverick, and a fool. A genius because he clocked that football was going to generate obscene wealth for the lucky few long before it occurred to anyone else, and in 1989 he came within a whisker of picking up the bargain of the century when Manchester United accepted his £10m bid to buy a club valued in 2008 at £1.2bn. But with the prize within his grasp, he p***ed it away in a very public fashion, playing keepy-uppy and generally making a fool of himself on the pitch at Old Trafford while being introduced to 60,000 fans and shaming the United board into calling off the deal.

He was one of the first to spot that the key to survival was building what he liked to call peripheral profit centres and bought a club that owned acres of land in which to do it. But his dream, the so-called Carlisle Gateway Millennium Project, complete with golf course, hotel and a lake, remained just that – a dream. He never followed through with his initial planning application and his only real legacy is the east stand – comically about 50 feet longer than the pitch, which he planned to move. But didn't.

He had the nous to buy a club with a potentially massive support – both Barrow and Workington lost their league status years ago, leaving Carlisle the only league club in Cumbria. He was one of the first to see his club as a marketable, exploitable brand – Carlisle may have been the first club to sell coffins in club colours – and one of the first to appoint the now fashionable directors of coaching rather than managers. And one of the few to see his club turn in a profit year after year. But he achieved that by selling every player that threatened to be any good – Matt Jansen to Crystal Palace, Rory Delap to Derby County – and it all started to go horribly wrong when he sacked coach Mervyn Day a few weeks after he'd won promotion to the third division and decided to do it himself.

He went in 2001; the Cumbrians plummeted into the conference in 2004, but since then they've been on the up and up. Back-to-back promotions and, last year, almost within touching distance of the second division, but suffering agonising defeat at the hands of Leeds in the play-off semi-finals, despite being two up after the first leg at Elland Road with just seconds to go.

Who knows where it will end? The club had one year in the first division in 1973-74. In those days newspapers thought it pointless to publish league tables until the season was three games in, so the nation was astonished to open their newspapers one Sunday in August to find Carlisle top of the heap. A key man in that team was midfielder Chris Balderstone, who somehow managed to combine careers as a professional footballer and cricketer – after 11 years at Brunton Park, he went on to play Test cricket for England.

The first manager to sell himself?... Ivor Broadis, appointed player-manager in 1946 aged just 23, sold himself to Sunderland in 1949 for £18,000.

Charlton Athletic

"I wore these boots for the first time today, and I have never scored a goal with my right foot before. Today I got all five with my right. Amazing, ain't it."
The greatest footballing comeback of all time? Rewind to the Valley, December 21st, 1957. Charlton, down to ten men, losing 5-1 against Huddersfield. Annihilated? No. Final score? Charlton Athletic 7, Huddersfield Town 6. Five goal hero? Left-footed left-winger Johnny Summers.

The only club whose supporters formed their own political party? In the 1990 local government elections, candidates representing the Valley Party in Greenwich polled a whopping 14,838 votes. Their aim? To return Charlton Athletic to its rightful home.

The Addicks had been homeless since 1985. The Valley, home since 1919, was falling down. The club didn't have the money to bring it up to scratch so ground shared with Crystal Palace (and later with West Ham) – the first time in England that had happened. An innovative scheme to sell off some land around the ground and use the cash to redevelop the stadium had been blocked by Greenwich Council. The Valley Party was formed to reverse that decision. They lost the election but won the battle, returning home in December 1992 after seven years in exile.

The fans were heroic in their fight to keep the club alive. When the first scheme was announced to develop the ground, hundreds of supporters descended on the crumbling Valley to help clear the rubble and junk. In a strange way, history was repeating itself – the Valley could not have been built in the first place had not an army of fans come forward to dig out the old chalk pit where it now stands.

Charlton's origins go back to 1905, when it was founded by a group of teenage boys, but for the first few years it played in local leagues. Things took off in 1913 when near neighbours Woolwich Arsenal decamped to north London, giving the Addicks room to expand. Football fans have long memories – visiting Arsenal teams are still taunted with chants of "Woolwich rejects".

The club's best years came in the thirties and forties. Promoted to the first division in 1936, they finished runners-up to Manchester City the following year. And in 1938, recorded their biggest crowd with over 75,000 turning up to watch a fifth-round cup tie against Aston Villa.

The only team to lose an FA Cup match but end up in the final? Charlton made it to Wembley for the 1946 final despite losing 2-1 at Fulham in the third round. The FA was worried that fans had lost interest in the competition during the war. So, for one season only, all matches before the semi-final were played over two legs, the Addicks triumphing 3-1 in the home tie. They lost 4-1 to Derby that year but returned the following season to win their only major honour to date, beating Burnley 1-0.

The club stagnated on and off the pitch for the next 40 years with dwindling crowds, a crumbling ground and a side that never looked like escaping from the second division. There was a surreal moment in 1982 when one of Europe's finest footballers landed at the Valley. Danish international Allan Simonsen was a star, first with Borussia Mönchengladbach, then Barcelona, won three European trophies and scored in four European finals. In 1977 he beat Kevin Keegan and Michel Platini to become European Footballer of the Year. However, when Barcelona signed Argentine World Cup-winning genius Diego Maradona, Spanish regulations meant they had to offload one of their overseas players. Simonsen was brilliant, scoring nine in 16 matches – but his arrival coincided with Charlton's deepening cash crisis, and after a few months the club could not afford to pay his wages. The spiral of decline continued with average attendances down to a paltry 5,000, the club up before the High Court for bankruptcy and the Valley forced to close.

Manager throughout this period of turmoil was Lennie Lawrence, who steered the homeless Addicks into the first division in 1986 – their first time for 29 years, and kept them there for four. When he left in 1991, the club couldn't afford to pay the going rate for a manager, so they asked two young former players to job-share. Pundits thought they would last a matter of weeks. In the event Steve Gritt stayed for four years, Alan Curbishley for 15.

So just how poor were Charlton? On one occasion, the club coach was stranded in traffic on the Canning Town flyover on its way to West Ham and midfielder John Bumstead had to sprint two miles to Upton Park to hand in the team sheet because they couldn't afford to pay the fine for being late.

Curbishley masterminded two promotions to the Premier League – the first in 1998 following a thrilling play-off final against Sunderland, the Addicks coming through 7-6 on penalties after a 4-4 draw in what many Addicks fans regard as their greatest ever performance.

In 2007 the club was relegated after spending a total of nine years in the Premier League. Best year? 2004 – seventh by the end of a season that had promised a lot more but was destabilised when star performer Scott Parker wanted out in January and was sold to Chelsea for £10m.

Heroes? Clive Mendonca, hat-trick star in the play-off final, scored another one in Charlton's opening home match in the Premier League although his career was cut short by injury not long after. And Addicks fans retain a soft spot for striker Carl Leaburn, their hard-working but famously goal-shy striker, who at one stage managed just four goals in 89 games. "I was there when Carl Leaburn Scored" was a popular T-shirt on the terraces.

The Addicks? The received wisdom is that the club nickname is a corruption of haddock – fishmonger and club vice-president Arthur "Ikey" Bryan used to reward the young team in its early years by feeding the players a post-match platter of haddock and chips. When the club won the Woolwich Cup in 1909, Ikey selected some of the largest haddocks from his shop for the fans to plant on poles then parade around the ground.

First ever substitute in an English league match? That little piece of history belongs to Charlton's Keith Peacock, a one-club man who played over 500 games for the Addicks in midfield. Except on August 21st, 1965, when he came on to replace injured goalie Mike Rose after 11 minutes of an away game at Bolton Wanderers. It took another two years before substitutes could be made for tactical reasons, and another two decades before it crossed anyone's mind to bring on substitutes simply to waste time – or as they like to say on TV, run down the clock.

Chelsea

"Obviously there's a language barrier. The majority of the lads speak Italian but there are a few who don't."
Dennis Wise, born in Kensington, found himself in a minority at Chelsea.

Ownership looms large in Chelsea's history. The first owners built Stamford Bridge – and then hunted around for a team to fill it. When they couldn't find one, they formed their own, back in 1905, in an upstairs room of what is now The Butcher's Hook pub in Fulham Road.

The club was forced to flog the freehold of the ground to property developers back in the seventies after miscalculating the cost of building a new stand, and were fortunate to buy it back when the developers went bust in the nineties.

These days the freehold, the pitch and even the turnstiles are owned by the Chelsea Pitch Owners, a fan group formed to make sure the club never loses its home again.

So the fans own the pitch but the club is very firmly in the hands of Roman Abramovich, the Russian multibillionaire who took control in 2003. A veritable fairy godfather figure, although it's worth noting that, according to the latest accounts published in 2008, the club owes him £578m. Which would have unimaginable consequences if he decides one day to pack his bags and walk away.

It was the previous owner, curmudgeonly Ken Bates, who declared he wanted Chelsea to be the Manchester United of the south, and this year, in one respect, he got his wish. Watching the Champions League final in a pub packed with neutrals, it was striking how Chelsea have replaced United as the team other teams' fans love to hate. Envy of Abramovich's billions plays its part, of course, but it's not just that – which is why the average Chelsea fan worships the shirt, loves the team, but is circumspect about the club.

How will the club treat World Cup winner Luiz Felipe Scolari? He succeeds a procession of managers who have all been treated shabbily in the last decade. First Ruud Gullit, sacked after winning the FA Cup and with his team second in the league. Then Gianluca Vialli, dismissed notwithstanding his five trophies in three years.

Nickname The Blues
Kit Blue shirt, blue shorts, blue socks
Ground Stamford Bridge – 42,055
Contact Fulham Road, London SW6 1HS 0871 9841955
Tickets 0871 9841905
Website www.chelseafc.com

The charismatic self-proclaimed Special One Jose Mourinho was shown the door despite six trophies in six years including back-to-back championships and a stunningly resilient team which remained unbeaten at home throughout his reign. Then there was the unknown Israeli, Abramovich's chum, Avram Grant, sacked after eight months despite a team which challenged for the title until the last day of the season, finally disposed of jinx team Liverpool in the Champions League, and lost the Champions League final on penalties.

Grant's wife Tzofit is a celebrity back in Israel, a controversial TV host who famously bathed in chocolate and drank her own urine. Avram was dumped on from a great height.

Sandwiched in the middle of this distinguished quartet was Claudio Ranieri, a popular figure forever messing about with his starting line-up, but universally perceived as a dead man walking the moment Abramovich took control. Supported by Chelsea fans who launched a "Don't tinker with the tinkerman" campaign, universal sympathy for his plight extended to Arsenal fans, who applauded him off the pitch following Chelsea's Champions League victory at Highbury, and Manchester United fans, following his last away game at Old Trafford.

Ranieri, Mourinho and Grant were despatched by Peter Kenyon, the chief executive and avowed lifelong Manchester United fan who swapped allegiance the moment Abramovich and his billions arrived. He's not a popular man in London – disliked by West Ham fans for poaching all their best players (Frank Lampard, Joe Cole, Glen Johnson), by Arsenal fans for the part he played in "tapping up" Ashley Cole (for which the club was fined) and by the Spurs faithful when

A young Blues fan on cup final day

Chelsea grabbed Frank Arnesen, technical director – for which the Blues eventually had to fork out £5m in compensation.

It rankled with many Chelsea fans that Kenyon led the team to receive their Champions League medals rather than, say, Ron "Chopper" Harris – the Chelsea legend who played a record 794 games for the club and was captain when the team lifted their first European trophy in 1972, beating Real Madrid in the Cup Winners' Cup.

Harris was the tough man in the flair-filled side of the sixties and early seventies that played champagne football on the pitch and quaffed lots of the fizzy stuff on the King's Road afterwards. The mazy trickery of winger Charlie Cooke and the strutting arrogance of striker Peter Osgood made Stamford Bridge a magnet for the in-crowd – Hollywood action hero Steve McQueen used to hang out in the dressing room, while sex bomb Raquel Welch once sashayed down the touchline mid-match to wave Ossie goodbye. These days, of course, she would be restrained by some power-crazed fourth official, patrolling the technical area like a coked-up traffic warden.

Legend?... No need to look any further back than last season. Captain John Terry, demon blocker, has blue blood coursing through his veins and would die for the club. Their greatest leader, on and off the pitch. When his Champions League final penalty hit the post, you knew it was the worst moment of his life.

Villain?... Nicolas Anelka – unforgivably, "Le Sulk" refused to take a penalty in the same match and, when he finally had to take one, blamed everyone but himself for the miss.

Cheltenham Town

"We can't read and we can't write,
but that don't really matter
We all come from Cheltenhamshire,
an' we can drive a tractor
Ooh Arr."
Robins' chant

Imagine if Bradford City's ground was far and away the biggest in the world – over three times bigger than Wembley Stadium – with room for 300,000 fans – and the Premier League turned round and said, sorry, it's not big enough, and you can't join our league.

Bonkers. Obviously. But a similar thing happened to Gresley Rovers in 1997. The parish side from Derbyshire had a miraculous season, winning their league by 11 clear points, and should have been promoted to the conference. They play at the 2,400-capacity Moat Ground, absurdly big for a village the size of Church Gresley, with its population of just 4,000. But after winning the title, the conference refused to accept them because their ground was too small. Which was shattering news for Rovers and a huge stroke of luck for Cheltenham Town who took their place in the conference and never looked back.

Cheltenham has long been a sporting hotbed. England's most famous cricketer, Dr W.G. Grace, carved out his reputation there, hammering a triple century for Gloucestershire against Yorkshire at the

Cheltenham College Ground back in 1876; two years earlier he had famously scored 35 at the same ground batting with a broomstick. Rugby union was established in the town as far back as 1844, and just eight miles down the road is Kingsholm, Gloucester RFC, who topped the English Premiership table in both 2007 and 2008. And, of course, there's the world-famous Cheltenham racecourse nestling in a natural bowl in the heart of the Cotswolds, the home of legends – Golden Miller, Arkle, Desert Orchid.

So let's not forget Whaddon Road, home of Cheltenham Town FC, sitting on the rim of a council estate and pretty much ignored by the footballing world – not to mention the good citizens of Cheltenham – for over 100 years. Much of that time was spent in total obscurity ploughing away in the Southern League. But after fluking their way into the conference the Robins went stratospheric, promoted three times in five years and are currently established in English football's third division.

How did they pull it off? They say good things come in threes. In 1997 Cheltenham got lucky three times. New chairman Paul Baker took over, rescued the club from insolvency and proved exceptionally capable at handling all matters off the pitch, developing the ground, handling the money and masterminding the transition of a team of part-timers into a fully fledged professional outfit. A dynamic young new manager returned to the town where he was

Nickname The Robins
Kit Red shirts, red shorts, red socks
Ground Whaddon Road – 7,066
Contact Whaddon Road, Cheltenham, Glos GL52 5NA 01242 537558
Tickets 01242 224675
Website www.ctfc.com

born in the shape of Steve Cotterill and forged an incredible dressing room spirit with coaching skills to match. And when bigger clubs came knocking he stayed loyal.

Then there was Clive Walker. Steve Cotterill was just 12 years old when the former Chelsea and Sunderland winger with the electrifying burst of pace started his pro career. Twenty-one years later, Cotterill signed him. Walker may have been 40 but what he'd lost in pace was more than made up for in guile and invention. A class act, he scored his 100th non-league goal while at Cheltenham, becoming the first player ever to notch up a ton in both league and non-league football, and steered Cheltenham into the league. Famous for being the first man to miss a penalty in a Wembley cup final back in 1985, he was a Wembley winner four times over in his twilight years, picking up his fourth FA Trophy-winner's medal with Cheltenham. At Whaddon Road he was sponsored by a local funeral parlour. His manager applauded the undertaker's initiative: "These days, you have to speculate to accumulate."

Believe it or not, Cotterill didn't buy a single player in the three years after winning promotion to the league. And while a number of players made the transition from part-time to full-time football, many had to quit when the club gained league status because they couldn't afford to give up their day jobs – the team that won promotion included two accountants and a lawyer.

It's not just the league where Cheltenham have made an impact. There was a fabulous run to the fifth round of the FA Cup in 2002 that ended in a close-run 1-0 defeat away to West Brom. A wonderful performance away at Fulham in 2004, which saw the Robins go down 2-1, thanks to a last-minute goal from Louis Saha. And a televised fourth-round tie against Alan Shearer and the millionaires of Newcastle United in 2006, the biggest match ever played at Whaddon Road. The Robins savaged the Magpies for 40 minutes, to chants of "Premiership,

You're Having A Laugh" before going down 2-0.

After Cotterill left the club in 2002 there was a dip in fortunes, and a relegation, before manager John Ward turned it round and won promotion via the play-offs against Grimsby in 2006. Cheltenham fans made up the majority of a crowd that verged on 30,000. But with average gates still under 5,000, and despite all their success, the Robins still have a long way to go to make Cheltenham a football town.

Club hero?... Has to be Jamie Victory. The defender won four promotions during his 11-year spell at the club and scored the goal that took the Robins into the Football League.

Chester City

"We've seen the lad from Iceland. Where's the lad from Kwik Save?"

Manager Kevin Ratcliffe despairs after yet another international signing turns out to be spectacularly useless.

Many of the world's worst players found themselves unexpectedly in demand at Chester. Inept but hands-on American owner Terry Smith was an early internet shopping addict. A favourable mention in the local rag covering an obscure league in some far-flung corner of the world and they were suddenly on a one-way ticket to the Deva. Many never got a game. Others, like Kamu Laird, a Trinidadian freighted in from the footballing hothouse of Augusta State University, started twice – substituted at half-time in his first match, and after just 27 minutes in his last. That wasn't the half of it. Where do you start with Smith? By 1999 the club was going to the wall, so skint that manager Ratcliffe famously paid a five-grand water rate bill out of his own pocket so the team could at least get a shower. Uniquely, Smith was turned onto Chester via his regular visits to the local zoo – so fond of the animals that he decided to buy the football team – and promised the club would be in the Premier League within four years. In footballing matters he showed the intelligence of a sheep, the survival instincts of a lemming.

His knowledge of football was skimpy, to say the least. He thought Bobby Charlton played for Scotland. That didn't deter him from appointing himself manager within a month and declaring that such sporting knowledge as he had gleaned from gridiron football could be applied at the Deva. He appointed three team captains – one for defence, one for midfield, one for attack. The squad turned up for training to find there

Nickname The Blues or the Seals
Kit Royal blue and white broad striped shirts, blue shorts, blue socks
Ground The Deva Stadium – 5,376 (4,170 seated)
Contact Bumpers Lane, Chester CH1 4LT 01244 371376
Website www.chestercityfc.net

were no balls available – Smith believed they were an unnecessary distraction and players found themselves involved in games of shadow football, more fitting for Alice In Wonderland than Palace and Sunderland. Players were issued with a thick folder before each match outlining precisely that day's game plan, and woe betide anyone who didn't stick to it. You might have thought a distinguished defender and assistant manager with over 400 games under his belt would know something about defending free kicks, but no. Even Paul Beesley was suspended for repeatedly standing in the wrong place while defending against Canvey Island.

After five disastrous months in charge, which saw Chester stranded 12 points adrift at the bottom of the fourth division, Smith finally appointed a real manager in the shape of Ian Atkins, who nearly pulled off a miracle escape – City being relegated only on goal difference on the last day of the season and dropping out of the Football League for the first time in 69 years. Was the four-year plan to be playing in the Premier League on target? On the day the club went down, Smith's optimism bordered on insanity: "We've achieved 10 of the 11 goals I set at the start of the season." When he stepped down as manager the chaos continued. Managers would select their teams for Saturday unaware that their star players had been offloaded midweek. Smith left after two years, but in truth the club had lurched from one crisis to another for decades. In the nineties City lost the TV sets in the bars because they could no longer afford the rental. They were effectively forced to sell their former home at Sealand Road to developers to get out of a financial hole. For two years they ground-shared at Macclesfield, a good 40 miles away, their typically small crowds reduced to pitiful levels. Over 500 supporters coughed up well over £100,000 to support the club in a shares issue, only to have their cheques returned, uncashed, a year later.

The uncertainty never ends – last season the club was rudderless as the owner stepped down as chairman and wasn't replaced – and there were three offers to buy it. There was a cracking sex scandal too – spelled out in lurid detail on the club's website – which saw manager Mark Wright sacked the day before the start of the 2004 season after setting up home with his centre half's fiancée.

Has it been all bad? There was the promotion from the conference in 2004; promotion to England's third division in 1975, the only Football League promotion in the club's history. And that same season, a League Cup run of hallucinatory proportions. Champions Leeds United were thumped 3-0 during a run which took the Blues into the semi-finals before going out 5-4 to Aston Villa.

Greatest player?... Has to be stringy Welsh goal machine Ian Rush. Scored 14 goals in the 1979-80 season before Liverpool stepped in and paid £300,000 for him – a record for a teenager then and nearly 30 years later, still the most Chester have ever received for a player.

Chesterfield

"I told them all – the butlers, the chambermaids, everybody – to have the day off and go and watch the game. I even had to make my own lunch."

The Duke of Devonshire, president of Chesterfield FC and worth £500m, reflects on the FA Cup semi-final against Middlesbrough.

You can wait 120 years for something earth-shattering to happen at Chesterfield and wait in vain. The most interesting thing about the league's fourth oldest club was that they were England's fourth oldest club. Who then could have predicted the ecstasy and the agony that was to engulf them?

In 1997 Chesterfield could have – should have – reached the FA Cup final. Had they got there they would have been the only club from England's third division ever to do so. For the Spireites (the local church has a famously crooked leaning spire – more impressively twisted than the Tower of Pisa, and a lot taller) it was a shot in the arm beyond imagination. The town had been trau-

Nickname The Spireites

Kit Blue shirt, white shorts, blue socks

Ground Recreation Ground – 8,504

Contact Saltergate, Chesterfield S40 4SX 01246 209765

Website www.chesterfield-fc.co.uk

matised by the total destruction of the coal industry in the eighties and nineties. The last thing you would have expected to have united the town in joy was a cup run – not once had Chesterfield ever progressed beyond the fifth round. They were drawn against a Middlesbrough side whose star man Fabrizio Ravanelli could have bought the entire Chesterfield team with six weeks' worth of pay packets.

Two-one up against ten-man Boro in the semi at Old Trafford and with just 22 minutes to go, Chesterfield scored the goal that should have taken them to Wembley. Andy Morris's deflected shot ran across the length of the six-yard line and found Jonathan Howard, who slipped inside the Boro defender and thumped the ball off the crossbar and into the goal. The crowd erupted; the linesman, who was perfectly placed, ran to the centre circle for the restart. Only it didn't count. Should it have? Referee David Elleray finally cleared up the mystery last year when, politely refusing an invitation to a reunion celebrating the ten-year anniversary of that epic tie, he revealed that very game had convinced him that refs should have video technology: "Had such technology been available then, the outcome of that semi-final may well have been very different."

That semi was a 3-3 thriller with a fairytale ending of sorts. Defender Jamie Hewitt, a lifelong fan with over 400 games under his belt, equalised in the last minute. Did he swap shirts with any of Boro's international superstars after the match? No, he thought his cash-strapped club might need them for the replay.

Amid the euphoria distant storm clouds were already gathering over Saltergate. The old ground was crumbling, the Football League was demanding the terraces be upgraded, new investment was needed, and in May 2000 the club was sold to 29-year-old Darren Brown, who became the youngest chairman in the Football League and who has passed down into history as its biggest conman.

A conman, a thief, a liar, a charlatan, and a very quick worker. When he arrived the club was financially sound with more than a quarter of a million in the bank. Just 12 months later it was in administration with debts of £1.5m. Brown had trousered £800,000 of the club's cash to prop up his other businesses and lead the high life. He put down a £55,000 deposit on a new house and stole the money to buy what must have been the most expensive lawnmower in Chesterfield at £2,500. He might have got away with it for longer had he not attempted to flog Saltergate to developers. The Football Association got wind and the whole house of cards came tumbling down. Brown was eventually jailed for four years in 2004 for defrauding Chesterfield. And in 2006 he was jailed for another four years, for a different scam.

Since the demise of Brown the club has been owned by a supporters' trust, formed just a few days before the club went into administration, and it has battled heroically to put Chesterfield back on an even keel. A new stadium on the site of a former glassworks a couple of miles from Saltergate could be ready by winter 2009.

You won't be surprised... to learn that Saltergate celebrated the jailing of former chairman Darren Brown by playing an assortment of appropriate ditties over the club tannoy – fans were regaled with a medley of "Jailhouse Rock" and Judas Priest's "Breaking the Law".

Colchester United

"I've spent the last fortnight dreaming of scoring a screamer like that. It's just a shame we were 7-0 down at the time..."

Customer services clerk and Leamington striker Richard Adams
takes comfort from bagging the goal of the game in a 2006 FA Cup tie as his team go
down 9-1 to the U's.

Football terraces are disappearing. Which is a shame. Like pop concerts, football is quite simply a more exciting experience when you're standing, which is why seated fans jump up at moments of high drama, incurring the wrath of busybody stewards and possible ejection. On the terraces you hug random strangers, stand with all your mates, make more noise, go where you want, have more fun. In a stand, fans smile weakly at their neighbours when a goal goes in, sit in the same spot week in week out, and are quieter – every single all-seater ground is less noisy than it was when the terracing was there – and are forever tipping their seats to make way for thousands of incontinent supporters incapable of going 45 minutes without taking a leak.

Is terracing dangerous? In 2008 a 70-year-old pervert from Ipswich was convicted of sexually assaulting female fans at Layer Road and banned from every ground. The court heard he made the 36-mile round trip to Colchester because it was easier to molest fans on the terraces than in an all-seater like Portman Road. His lawyer claimed it was totally out of character, a surprising submission given that he'd already been banned for life from Cambridge United (a 106-mile round trip from home) for inappropriate behaviour towards women.

The Oystermen left Layer Road in 2008 to take up residence at the community stadium, a 10,000-seater venue which could increase to 18,000 should the need arise. In 2007 there was the astonishing possibility that Colchester could find themselves in the Premier League, a prospect that had star man Jamie Cureton in stitches as he struggled to imagine Chelsea in the Layer Road changing rooms: "They wouldn't have had enough room for their kit boxes, let alone their team." After the worst possible start, losing the first five matches, the club was in contention for a play-off place until the very last day of the season, eventually finishing tenth, their highest ever position despite having the smallest crowds in the division. However, 2007-08 was a disaster – the club were relegated to the third division.

Nickname The U's

Kit Royal blue and white striped shirt, blue shorts, blue socks

Ground Weston Homes Community Stadium – 10,000

Contact United Way, Colchester, Essex CO4 5HE 01206 755100

Tickets 0871 2262161

Website www.cu-fc.com

"There is a no-smoking policy at Layer Road. Anyone caught smoking will be taken to a darkened room, where they will be imprisoned for 27 hours and forced to listen to Will Young records for all of that time. Thank you."

Colchester's PA announcer provides the half-time entertainment.

For a small club Colchester have done well to steer clear of money troubles, getting a massive boost two years ago with an FA Cup run that made them a million, disposing of Sheffield United and Derby before going out to Chelsea at Stamford Bridge – a thrilling game in which the Oystermen took the lead and threatened to cause an FA Cup sensation, before eventually conceding two late goals in a 3-1 defeat.

Chelsea's owner is the second-richest man in Britain, Colchester's the nineteenth richest in East Anglia. Which is not to be sniffed at – chairman Robbie Cowling is one of the few Brits to have made a fortune from the internet, worth over £100m, thanks to his online employment agency. A fanatical West Ham supporter who once splashed out 50 grand on a fleet of 62 coaches to ferry Hammers fans to Sunderland for an FA Cup tie for free, he took control of the club in 2007 with big plans and big price increases planned when the club moved to their new stadium – plans he had to shelve after the fans revolted.

Greatest moment – the unforgettable fourth-round FA Cup tie against Leeds United in 1971. Don Revie's Whites were top of the table, chasing a treble that mad February afternoon; Colchester were languishing in the fourth division with a team so elderly it was dubbed Granddad's Army. The U's went three up, courtesy of a couple of howlers from Leeds keeper Gary Sprake, with 34-year-old striker Ray Crawford scoring twice, gloriously hooking the ball into the net despite being sprawled on his back. Leeds scored twice in a furious second-half onslaught but some desperate defending saw Colchester cling on.

Coventry City

"The bath had more stains on it than my underwear."
Manager John Sillett reflects on his first glimpse of the dressing room at Highfield Road.

The most memorable free kick in the history of the English game –
ever? It came at Highfield Road, October 1970, with Coventry City
2-1 up against champions Everton and about ten minutes to go.
Awarded a free kick in a central position just outside the
penalty box, flame-haired
midfielder Willie Carr stood
over the ball, wedged it firmly twixt heel and ankle and
flicked it up and behind him
for Ernie Hunt to crash home
an unstoppable dipping volley over the gobsmacked wall
into the right-hand corner of
the net.

Nickname The Sky Blues
Kit Sky blue and white striped shirts,
sky blue shorts, sky blue socks
Ground Ricoh Arena – 32,500
Contact Phoenix Way, Foleshill,
Coventry, Warks CV6 6GE 0870
0211987
Tickets 0844 8731883
Website www.ccfc.co.uk

Type Coventry Free Kick
1970 into YouTube if you
weren't around for this pivotal moment, thankfully caught by the
Match of the Day cameras and hands-down winner of their Goal of the
Season in 1971. Two days later every soccer-mad school-kid tried to

replicate the movement, it has to be said, without much success. In playgrounds they tried it with tennis balls, in classrooms between lessons with scrunched-up pieces of foolscap and wastepaper bins for goals, in parks, on training grounds, on street corners – everyone was at it.

It came at a time when the Sky Blues were on a run that saw them spend 34 consecutive years in the top flight. It's fair to say that no club has spent so many years up there and made so little impact. Sixth place in 1970 was as good as it got, although there were at least ten years when Coventry staged glorious fightbacks at the end of the season to escape the drop.

Founded back in 1883, Coventry made little impact on the footballing world until Jimmy Hill arrived as manager in 1961. Best known since then as a football pundit, he was an energetic and innovative manager and transformed the club from top to bottom, starting with the kit. It was Hill who introduced the sky blue strip – most recently, the club had been playing in a predominantly white strip with blue flashes. Coventry became the first club to organise fan trains to away matches, the so-called Sky Blue Specials, and the first to introduce what is now recognised as the first modern match day programme. Hill also understood the importance of PR, encouraging young fans to meet the players and collect their autographs at every opportunity. And he also wrote the club song, to the tune of the Eton Boat Song.

More importantly, he worked wonders on the pitch, and two promotions in three years saw the Sky Blues promoted to the first division in 1967 for the very first time. There's innovation at the Ricoh Arena in 2008/2009, with City becoming the first club in the country to have a cashless stadium – there's a smart card element to the season tickets, which means they can also be used to pay for pies and pints at half-time, the aim being to double the speed of the catering queues. The club itself was cashless in 2007, and came within 25 minutes of going into administration and incurring a ten-point penalty that would have spelled relegation had a consortium not stepped in to save it.

Finest hour – no dispute here – was the 1987 FA Cup final at Wembley when the Sky Blues went behind after two minutes but ran out 3-2 winners in a memorable match against Spurs. Manager John Sillett attributed cup glory to the lucky pair of underpants he donned at every cup tie. Perhaps they were in the wash in 1989 when City faced non-league Sutton United in the third round of the same competition and were memorably dumped 2-1, one of the handful of first division sides to have suffered this ignominious exit.

There were high hopes that the club would bounce straight back after relegation in 2001 – but with 14 managers or caretakers in the last seven years, the club has rarely looked stable on the pitch and has been in trouble off it. Highfield Road, home for 104 years (and the first all-seater stadium in the country), was vacated in 2005 but the club does not own the new ground that bears the name of a Japanese IT firm where it now plays – it has to pay rent. The club escaped relegation to the third division by the skin of its teeth in 2008, with other results going their way despite losing 4-1 on the last day of the season to Charlton Athletic.

Club heroes?... Along with the managers Hill and Sillett, contenders include Clarrie Bourton, scorer of 181 goals in just six years back in the thirties and the club's most prolific scorer by a stretch. And keeper Steve Ogrizovic, a member of the 1987 cup-winning side who made a club record of 601 appearances in all competitions. He's also one of the few keepers with a goal to his name, scoring with a long punt against Sheffield Wednesday back in 1986.

Crewe Alexandra

"When I first saw the club, I thought it was a dump. There were eight players and no footballs and I was definitely only going to stay a year."
Dario Gradi

Times are changing at Crewe. The longest-serving manager in the Football League is no longer the manager. Dario Gradi stepped down in 2007 after 24 years in the Gresty Road hot seat in favour of Steve Holland and is now technical director. A club that developed a galaxy of exclusively home-grown talent in its excellent academy and gave a second chance to young discards from the big clubs in Manchester and Liverpool is now importing young talent from overseas. And the policy of refusing to deal with football agents has now been relaxed.

Friendly, efficient, solvent and with brilliant training facilities and coaching to match, the club has never disguised the fact that its survival depends on grooming young talent and selling it on. Way back in 2002, Gradi conceded that he would never be able to fulfil his dream of producing a team to perform on the big stage because he had to sell, sell, sell. The fans used to be content with that. But now the rumblings of discontent are growing.

Things were as bad as they could be when Gradi arrived. So accustomed was the club to propping up the fourth division, the joke was that they kept their reapplication letter on file so they could photocopy

Nickname The Railwaymen, or the Alex

Kit Red shirt, white shorts, red socks

Ground Alexandra Stadium

Contact Gresty Road, Crewe, Cheshire CW2 6EB 01270 213014

Tickets 01270 252610

Website www.crewealex.net

it when they went for re-election the next year. All told, they had to reapply on 14 occasions – a record.

There was an air of defeatism around the place – in fact, the club used to sell souvenir mugs commemorating their record defeat, a 13-2 loss to Spurs in a 1960 FA Cup replay. A coach load of supporters arriving late at White Hart Lane to discover the score was already 6-1 are reputed to have asked: "Who to?"

In 131 years their only significant silverware has been the Welsh Cup, won in 1936 and 1937, before the Welsh cottoned on that Crewe was at least 25 miles out of Wales and understandably barred the Railwaymen from future competitions.

Gradi revolutionised everything. Graduates from the Gradi academy learned to pass the ball along the floor rather than hoof it and he took a dim view of foul play or cheating – which is why his club picked up the Bobby Moore Fair Play award for the eleventh time in 2008.

And he produced a string of talented players who have gone on to star on bigger stages. Dean Ashton is the latest Crewe youngster to play for England, following a path trodden by Seth Johnson, Danny Murphy, Geoff Thomas, Rob Jones and David Platt.

Gradi's immense contribution to the game was recognised with an MBE, an honorary doctorate, and the Freedom of Crewe. He is feted by his peers, with Steve Coppell describing Gradi's feats at Crewe as "the biggest achievement in football", and two years ago the Alex won the most-admired club gong at the Football League awards. Between 1997 and 2006 the club spent eight years in the second division, an astonishing achievement for such a small, poorly supported and impecunious outfit.

And yet, and yet... relegation to the third division in 2006 – and narrowly missing the drop on goal difference in 2008 – prompted chants of "Sack The Board" and "Where's the Money Gone?" from a vocal minority of disaffected fans. Fed up with seeing their best players forever sold in the January window, supporters looked at Doncaster and Carlisle slugging it out for promotion, remembered both were recently struggling in the conference, and wondered, if them, why not us?

In the end it all comes down to money. In 2008 chairman John Bowler went on record that he didn't believe the club was big enough to attract a wealthy sugar daddy, the sort who could sub the Alex to the tune of £2m a year, which would let it hang onto its best players.

This may be true, but it didn't appease some fans, who accused the club of a lack of ambition and refused to accept that staying solvent and grooming stars for the benefit of bigger clubs is as good as it will ever get. Many of them have started to lobby for fan representation on the board and better information from the club on exactly what it does with its money. The next couple of years will be very interesting.

Big in Bulgaria?... Believe it or not, the Railwaymen have quite a following out there. Bulgarian club owner and Crewe fan Rangel Beberov paid the Alex to fly out to eastern Europe in the summer of 2008 so his team FC Maritsa could take them on.

Crystal Palace

> **"In my opinion, no owner in their right mind would willingly invite an average agent into his academy, any more than a brothel owner would let a syphilitic nutter into his whorehouse."**
>
> *Simon Jordan*

Simon Jordan let rip in 2008 after a transfer tribunal awarded Palace just £700,000 against Spurs for having poached star youth player John Bostock. "He has been sold for a packet of crisps," raged Jordan, who in 2000 became the latest owner of a club founded in 1905 by workers at the Crystal Palace, the giant building erected to house the Great Exhibition in Hyde Park in 1851 and later moved to Sydenham.

After eight years he was looking to sell. Disillusioned? Impossible to tell with Jordan, a maverick owner openly contemptuous of agents, owners and players alike and refreshingly unafraid to say so. Agents? "Scum – evil, divisive and pointless, they only survive because the rest of the sport is so corrupt and because leading football club people employ their sons in the job." Other club owners? "Tossers". He was exasperated by the greed of players, complaining some had tried to wring more money out of him on the strength of a good star rating in the *Sun*.

As for managers... Jordan took legal action against his former Palace manager and won, the High Court deciding in 2007 that Iain Dowie

Nickname The Eagles

Kit White shirt with blue and red diagonal, white shorts, white socks

Ground Selhurst Park – 26,300

Contact Selhurst Park, London, SE25 6PU 0208 7686000

Tickets 08712 000071

Website www.cpfc.co.uk

had lied when negotiating his way out of his contract in 2006. Supporters? "I admire football fans because in what other business can you serve up crap and then have people come back for more?"

Palace fans saw Jordan as a multi-millionaire fairy god-father when he rescued the club in 2000 – it was on the point of going bust. He'd just sold his mobile phone company for £36m. It seemed a fortune then, less so today when even second division clubs need incredibly deep pockets just to compete.

In 2007 Jordan hired Neil Warnock, Palace's eighth manager since 2000. Great expectations? "He told me he wants to be in Europe within 18 months. Whether that means we're all going to Majorca next summer, I don't know," said Warnock, who announced he was pinning his faith in the club's youth academy, a school aimed at recreating "The Team of the Eighties" – the brilliant group of youngsters that came out of Selhurst Park in the seventies and won the FA Youth Cup in consecutive years.

Star man then was full-back Kenny Samson, Player of the Year in 1977 when only 18, a key figure in Palace's rapid rise from the third to the first division and a full England international at 20, eventually winning 86 caps.

Another young man... Steve Coppell, appointed manager in 1984 aged 28 for the first of what turned out to be four spells at the club and the man who came closest to capturing silverware. In 1990 the Eagles drew a six-goal thriller with Manchester United in the FA Cup final, losing the replay by a single goal. Two-goal hero in the first match was Ian Wright, a latecomer to professional football and nearly 22 when signed from Kent League outfit Greenwich Borough. He forged a lethal striking partnership with Mark Bright – the pair firing Palace to their highest ever finish of third in 1991– and scored 177 goals in six years at Palace before moving to Arsenal and breaking the Gunners' all-time goalscoring record.

Nice work if you can get it? Terry Venables pocketed £135,000, just for agreeing to meet new owner Mark Goldberg when he bought the club in 1998. Goldberg may have bought the club but couldn't afford to buy the ground off previous owner Ron Noades; in fact within two years he couldn't afford to buy anything. He took Palace to the verge of extinction, saddled with debts of £20m after an adventure that cost him his personal fortune and his marriage. In a surreally catastrophic episode in the club's history, Goldberg hired Venables as club manager; and by the time Venables left five months later he was owed £6.9m.

Disastrous signing... Valerien Ismael. Crystal Palace paid a club record of £2.75m for the French defender in 2001. Only nine months and 13 games later, the club sold him to Lens for just £1.3m.

Dagenham & Redbridge

"We will be the only league team sponsored by an undertakers!"

Club captain Anwar Uddin struggles to take in the implications of Dagenham's first taste of league football.

They call themselves the pub team from Essex but the truth is not quite so simple. Dagenham & Redbridge were formed as recently as 1992 but the club is an amalgamation of four famous teams with over 400 years of history between them. Dagenham FC won the FA Trophy, Leytonstone FC landed the FA Amateur Cup three times, Ilford won the same trophy twice. As did Walthamstow Avenue, who created their own piece of FA Cup history back in 1952, famously drawing 1-1 with Manchester United in the fourth round at Old Trafford before going down 5-2 at the replay held at Highbury.

It was the FA Cup that first brought Dagenham & Redbridge to the attention of the nation, with three glorious cup runs in successive years. In 2001 they came within four minutes of a famous upset at Premier League Charlton in a third-round tie with the replay going to extra time before Charlton sneaked it. Manager Garry Hill had packed in his day job repossessing cars by the time the cup came round again the following year. Again the Daggers reached the third round, one up against Ipswich at Victoria Road before going down 4-1, but earning £500,000 in the process.

In 2003 they went one better. Fans of the Sky show *Dream Team* tuned in on a Sunday night to watch the fictional Harchester United dispose of Dagenham & Redbridge in a third-round tie. Three nights later and the Daggers were doing it for real, taking on Plymouth Argyle in a third-round replay and emerging triumphant. Landscape gardener Danny Shipp opened the scoring and the team celebrated by clipping him around the ear, echoing an earlier dressing room incident involving Shipp and his manager. Allegedly. There was heartache in the fourth round away to Norwich at Carrow Road, where the Daggers held on until injury time before going out to a late winner.

Nickname The Daggers
Kit Blue and red striped shirt, white shorts, red socks
Ground London Borough of Barking and Dagenham Stadium – 6,000
Contact Victoria Road, Dagenham, Essex RM10 7XL 0208 592 1549
Website www.daggers.co.uk

The cup runs were mirrored by excellent results in the conference. In 2002 it looked like they might go up after being pipped to the title on goal difference by Boston, who were under investigation by the FA for malpractice. In the event Boston were found guilty and docked four points – but the deduction didn't take place until the following season. And the following year a run of 11 straight victories lifted the Daggers to the first ever conference play-offs but they lost agonisingly to Doncaster Rovers via a golden goal.

It looked like just a matter of time before the Daggers went up. But no – in 2004 it all fell apart in the most public way imaginable with a string of poor results, culminating in a 9-0 thrashing at home by Hereford United in a match televised on Sky. It was a result that cost

Hill his job. Former manager John Still returned to the club for a second spell but the results for the next two years were mediocre. So mediocre, in fact, that at the start of the 2006 season you could have got odds of 66-1 on Dagenham & Redbridge winning the conference. In the end they walked away with it by a 14-point margin. For manager Still it meant a return to league football in East London that he never thought he'd see. He had started, and ended, his league career in one match down the road at Orient, crocking his knee so badly on his debut against Torquay United that he never played again.

Captain for the club's first season in the league was Anwar Uddin, whose family hail from Bangladesh, which makes him the first Asian English captain in the Football League.

Strange but true... Dagenham's glorious FA Cup run in 2002 nearly ended before it began. Two-one down in a qualifying game at Basingstoke Town, they were saved by a last-minute equaliser knocked in by goalie Tony Roberts, the only time in the history of the competition that a keeper has scored from open play.

**Pub team from Essex?
You're having a laugh**

Darlington

"The physio came running out like an idiot – I thought he'd actually got someone fit."

Much excitement in Darlington in 1999 when the club won the historic FA Cup "Lucky Losers" draw. Knocked out in the second round, they found themselves playing in the third after Manchester United dropped out of the competition to take part in the FIFA World Club Championship.

The shadow of former chairman George Reynolds is finally lifting from Darlington. A convicted former safe-cracker who smuggled explosives in a Mister Softee ice cream van, he made millions fitting kitchens and breezed into Darlington in 1999 when the club was on its knees. His business card read "Gentleman, Entrepreneur, Adventurer, Maker of Money and Utter Genius" – and he promised Premier League football in five years. Reynolds took one look at Feethams – the quaint picturesque ground in the heart of the town that had been home to the club since

Nickname The Quakers/Darlo

Kit Black and white hooped shirt, black shorts, black socks

Ground Balfour Webnet Darlington Arena – 25,000

Contact Neasham Road, Darlington DL2 1DL 01325 387000

Tickets 0871 8551883

Website www.darlington-fc.net

1879 – and professed he loved it – like a hole in the head. A soulless 27,000-capacity white elephant of a new stadium half an hour's walk out of town is his legacy.

He didn't like a lot of things. He told an industrial tribunal that a barmaid (wrongfully) dismissed for bad timekeeping should have been shot, not sacked. He booted out his commercial manager then had to shell out 60 grand in compensation. He banned the 16-year-old editor of a fanzine whom he likened variously to Hitler, Goebbels and Lord Haw Haw. Actually, he didn't like any form of criticism – the message board on the club website was closed down simply to silence his critics, whom he scornfully dismissed as a small minority of cranks and he declared that he never listened to the fans or the manager because they never got it right.

Reynolds even refused to accept a donation from the club's supporters' trust, while his wife sparked an uproar and a player walk-out at a meeting with the fans, when she announced that it wasn't unknown for games to be thrown towards the end of the season as a way of paying back favours.

Did the players like him? Imagine their discomfort when he released their salaries to the local paper to try and shame them into playing better.

On the pitch the Premier League looked as distant as ever for a club that had spent most of its time in the bottom tier. There were doomed attempts to sign wayward but ageing football genius Paul "Gazza" Gascoigne, as well as the rubber-legged and unpredictable centre for-ward Faustino Asprilla, who once scored a memorable hat-trick for Newcastle against Barcelona. It looked in the bag – the Colombian was paraded before the fans in August 2002 and was due to put pen to paper days later on an £11,000 a week contract. But he got a better offer from the Middle East at the last minute and packed his bags. Fans who flocked to the ground to see the star unveiled were greeted with a brief but to-the-point statement from the club: "Faustino has f*****d off."

By the time Reynolds left in 2004, the Quakers (Darlington was once a hotbed of Methodism) were back in administration – and Reynolds was under investigation for tax evasion, for which he was subsequently jailed. Things have been on the up and up since he left. The club finished in the top half of the table for four years in a row – a club record – reaching the play-offs in 2008 but losing out to Rochdale.

Greatest moment? Undoubtedly 50 years ago in the fourth-round FA Cup tie against Chelsea, a team that had been champions of England just three years earlier. Darlington went three up at Stamford Bridge but the game went to a replay after Chelsea clawed it back. At Feethams it was 1-1 after 90 minutes – but three goals in a delirious six minutes saw Darlington triumph 4-1.

All-time hero – Marco Gabbiadini won the player of the century poll. A prolific goalscorer with Derby and Sunderland, the much-travelled striker looked to be on the wane when he arrived at Feethams, but proceeded to confound everyone with 50 plus goals in his two years.

Top tip?… The new stadium may be lacking in character but the pies are top-notch – beautifully displayed, great variety, and cheap.

"Faustino has f***d off"**

Derby County

"I've got more points on my license. I'm not joking."

Manager Paul Jewell kept his sense of humour as Derby slumped to Premier League relegation in 2008 with just 11 points. Asked if any of his teams had ever been jeered despite winning a match, he replied: "Dunno – I'd just like the opportunity to find out." As did Rams fans who packed Pride Park long after relegation was a certainty, voted themselves player of the season, and staged a beach party at their final game at Blackburn Rovers, the away end awash with Hawaiian shirts and inflatables, a riot of rubber rings and beach balls.

Derby can cope with failure but not with success. Twice winners of the first division, the club reacted to triumph both times by tearing itself apart.

When 32-year-old Brian Clough and his number two Peter Taylor arrived in 1967 the club was languishing in the second division. Charismatic, energetic, opinionated and controversial, the manager electrified the town long before he galvanised the team, which came just 18th at the end of his first season.

He was a stalker. If players didn't want to come to County, Clough followed them home, invaded their living-room, slept on their sofa, and wore them down to get them to sign. His greatest coup was intercepting ageing Spurs hero, Dave Mackay, on his way to Hearts and diverting him to Derby. The Rams won the second division that season on a

114

course that took them to the first division title in 1972.

But Clough's fame drove chairman Sam Longson mad with jealousy. His manager didn't keep him in the loop when splashing out a £175,000 fortune on a defender – the first Longson knew was when he opened a telegram that read: "Just bought another great player, Colin Todd. We're almost bankrupt. Love Brian." Eventually Longson wanted him out and goaded Clough, barring his wife from the director's box, ripping the bar out of his office and banning him from writing for the newspapers without his say-so.

"It wasn't a clash of personalities. Half the people we were battling with didn't have any personality," quipped Clough, walking out and sparking frenzy. For two weeks, Derby was the biggest story in the land, the Baseball Ground mobbed daily by thousands of angry fans demanding his reinstatement, as did the players. To no avail. Just 18 months after winning the title, Clough was gone.

His successor, Dave Mackay, won the title in 1975, but suffered the same fate, shoved out 18 months later by a boardroom deluded into thinking it could tempt Clough back.

Since then – boardroom splits, police investigations, and courtroom battles after the taxman tried to wind up the club. Derby was baled out by the fraudster Robert Maxwell whose family ran the club for six years. Dirty money? Maxwell handed over the rescue cash in the toilets at the High Court.

High points include four years in the first division from

Nickname The Rams
Kit White shirt, black shorts, white socks
Ground Pride Park Stadium – 33,597
Contact Derby DE24 8XL 0871 4271884
Website www.dcfc.co.uk

1987 and six years in the Premier League from the mid-nineties during which manager Jim Smith enjoyed two top-ten finishes and the club moved home to Pride Park

The Rams? The First Regiment of Derbyshire Militia was based in the town in the 19th century and adopted a ram as a mascot after seeing the Welsh Fusiliers parading with a goat.

Greatest player? Steve Bloomer, 365 goals for County in two spells between 1892 and 1914 and top scorer in 14 consecutive seasons. His England record was equally spectacular – 28 goals in just 23 appearances. Never far from the Baseball Ground, he was a star in the summer and led Derby County baseball club to three British championships.

Just how mean... was the Derby board in the sixties? Manager Tim Ward needed authorisation from the board every time he wanted to put a first-class stamp on a letter. And when star striker Kevin Hector went down with jaundice, a director asked, in all seriousness, whether the club had to pay him if he couldn't play.

Doncaster Rovers

"It's demeaning to define a woman by her breasts and it would be belittling Melinda's very real talent."
Glamour model Melinda Messenger owes her prize DD assets to cosmetic surgeon John Ryan. Doncaster Rovers owe him so much more.

Doncaster Rovers has risen like a phoenix from the ashes in the ten years since John Ryan took charge of the club in the autumn of 1998. In this case, ashes means ashes. Previous incumbent Ken Richardson hired a former SAS man to burn down their home Belle Vue in an insurance scam that all went horribly wrong and saw the chairman jailed for four years. The season before that saw the club set an unwanted record, plummeting like a stone out of the Football League after losing an unprecedented 34 games in front of average gates of less than 1,800 fans.

When Doncaster-born multimillionaire Ryan pulled up in his green Bentley outside the ravaged crumbling hellhole that was Belle Vue, the club was stranded at the foot of the conference, a drop to the Northern Premier League a real possibility. There was no kit, no nets, no balls, and only a handful of players. An unhappy feature of early away matches were scheduled motorway stops where the team coach would pick up players they had never heard of, never seen, and certainly never played with just to make up the numbers for that day's game.

Ryan set about transforming every element of Rovers off the pitch, and in a glorious cameo, on it. In 2003 he fulfilled a childhood dream and was immortalised in *The Guinness Book of Records* when he came on as a substitute for the final few minutes of an away game at Hereford, becoming the oldest player ever to play for a British professional team at the age of 52 years and 11 months.

Fast-forward to 2001 – in South Yorkshire the big news was that Rovers, still in the conference, had pulled off a masterstroke by signing Paul Barnes, the 33-year-old former York City hotshot who had just bagged ten goals in nine matches while on loan to Nuneaton Borough. By way of contrast, up the M1 in West Yorkshire, Leeds United had reached the semi-final of the Champions League with a team studded with star internationals including Rio Ferdinand, Mark Viduka, Harry Kewell, Olivier Dacourt and David Batty. Jonathan Woodgate could only make the subs bench. Who in their wildest dreams would have predicted that the two would meet at Wembley just seven years down the line in the third division play-offs? But meet they did in May 2008, and a header from James Hayter secured second division status for the Donny for the first time in 50 years, and their third promotion in five.

Management heroes? Dave Penney, who masterminded the first two promotions, and Sean O'Driscoll, architect of the triumph over Leeds. O'Driscoll had a tough baptism when he arrived – a string of iffy results saw him dubbed O'Dismal and O'Dreadful by the Donny diehard. But the club stuck by him and the rest we know. Success has been aided and abetted by the local council – so often the villain of the piece in football – who stumped up £30m towards Keepmoat, the spanking new stadium the club shares with the local rugby league team.

Belle Vue had been home to the club since 1922, although the team was formed way back in 1879 by a teenage fitter from the railway depot. In the early days they didn't have a lot of luck – while most fourth division clubs over the years have been re-elected as a matter of course, Rovers

Nickname	Rovers, or the Donny
Kit	Red and white hooped shirt, black shorts, black socks
Ground	Keepmoat Stadium – 15,231
Contact	Stadium Way, Lakeside, Doncaster, S Yorks DN4 5JW 01302 764664
Tickets	01302 762576
Website	www.doncasterroversfc.co.uk

were elected and then booted out of the league twice in just four years at the start of the century. And in truth, they haven't had much success ever since, although the club has regularly attracted gates of over 30,000 in the post war years and the town's population of over a quarter of a million could easily sustain a successful team at the highest level.

Greatest player… and without question the unluckiest – Alick Jeffrey. Made his debut in 1954 aged just 15, possessed with rocket shots in both feet and superb passing skills. Stanley Matthews thought him a genius and Manchester United reckoned he was the next Pele and were on the point of signing him. But at 17, in a season where he was averaging more than a goal a game, disaster struck when he sustained a double leg fracture while playing for the England Under-23s putting him out of league football for seven years. He toured the clubs as a singer, emigrated to Australia and broke another leg before returning to Doncaster in 1963 and scoring a phenomenal 95 goals in 191 games. However, his career continued to be dogged by disaster – he was a passenger in a horror car crash that killed club captain John Nicholson and left him in a coma and out of the game for months. A player who never fulfilled his potential, but with an assured place in Donny history.

Everton

"We used to think Liverpool were cocky when they talked about the derby with Everton as just another game. We'd be discussing it for weeks beforehand. But now we know what they meant."

Everton skipper Kevin Ratcliffe has a top-dog moment as the Toffees aim for a treble in 1985.

Everton and Liverpool don't just share a city. The Blues used to play at Anfield up until 1891 when brewery owner John Houlding bought the freehold to the ground and jacked up the rent from £100 to £250. Everton weren't having it and built their own stadium across the park. Houlding needed a team to fill Anfield so started his own.

Nickname The Toffees

Kit Blue shirt, white shorts, blue socks

Ground Goodison Park – 40,569

Contact Goodison Road, Liverpool L4 4EL 0871 6631878

Tickets 0870 4421878

Website www.evertonfc.com

Links between the two clubs are historically close, and for 30 years up until 1932 they used to share a programme. Could they share a ground again? In 2004 there were rumblings about groundsharing at the new stadium planned for Stanley Park but negotiations broke down after the Reds insisted on retaining ownership of any new development. In 2006 Everton unveiled their own plans to leave Goodison for a site six miles out of town in Kirby, funded in part by supermarket cash, and asked fans to vote on the scheme.

The result? An unenthusiastic yes although a sizeable minority of Toffees fans are bitterly opposed and formed a pressure group KEIOC (Keep Everton In Our City) to fight the proposal. There was much hilarity in the KEIOC camp when Everton chief executive Keith Wyness fired off a letter complaining about stuff on the KEIOC website but sent it by mistake to a similarly named dental practice. In Japan.

With Liverpool's Stanley Park scheme now on ice due to the credit crunch and

Bizarre injury... Everton keeper Richard Wright missed an FA Cup tie against Chelsea after twisting his ankle in the pre-match warm-up. He ignored a sign telling him not to practise in the goalmouth – then tripped over it.

Everton's future equally uncertain as the club seeks new and wealthier investors, it would be foolhardy to predict just how the proposed stadium plans for either Merseyside club will pan out.

The Toffees? Possibly derived from Mother Noblett's Toffee Shop, situated just round the corner from Goodison at the beginning of the last century. The Toffee Lady is one of English football's oldest traditions and on match days a young woman walks round the perimeter of the pitch and tosses Everton Mints into the crowd. Shouldn't they be blue? In the early days Everton used to play in black-and-white.

Tradition plays a big part at Everton, founded by Methodists and the only club in the world that boasts a church within its grounds – the hall at St Luke the Evangelist is a traditional spot for a pre-match cup of tea. The club went into 2008-09 playing its 106th year of top flight football, the only one to have passed the century mark, with a record that numbers nine league titles and five FA Cups. Success in the European Cup Winners Cup in 1985 – where the run to the final included a glorious comeback against Bayern Munich at Goodison – is frequently cited as Everton's greatest ever night.

It came during Everton's most successful spell in the eighties under Howard Kendall, when the Toffees romped away with the title twice in three seasons and made it to four cup finals, beating Watford to win the FA Cup in 1984. Since then the club hasn't had the financial muscle to push for the title again although they are the only team in recent years to have interrupted the sequence whereby the Big Four occupied the top four positions in the Premier League, pushing out Liverpool in 2005.

Blue funk? Harry Catterick, manager of the successful Everton side of the sixties and early seventies, was famously paranoid about revealing any details of his team to press or public. When he handed in his team sheet it was always laid out alphabetically to give rival managers as few clues as possible about his formation. Catterick's team was known as the "School Of Science" for their precise passing game, the team marshalled from the back by skipper Brian Labone.

Disastrous signing... Per Kroldrup. Everton knew they'd made a mistake the minute they bought the £5.1m defender in 2005. Signed in the summer, he wasn't picked until Boxing Day, when he made his first – and last – league appearance in a 4-0 thumping at Aston Villa.

All football fans scour fixture lists carefully to ensure they don't commit to any social engagements that could clash with an important match. Not Labone, who turned down the invitation to be a part of England's 1966 squad which went on to win the World Cup... because it clashed with his wedding preparations.

Disastrous signing... Alex Nyarko. Everton's £4.5m signing in 2000 from Lens made just 33 appearances in four years. During a particularly inept performance at Arsenal, an Everton fan invaded the pitch and offered to swap shirts with the Ghanaian midfielder – the implication being he wasn't fit to wear it. Nyarko asked to be substituted and transferred.

Deep-seated groin injury? Goal-scoring legend Dixie Dean, whose exploits include an unprecedented 60 goals in one season, had an unblemished disciplinary record during his career. Defenders kicked lumps out of him every week but the great man never retaliated and played 438 league games without once being booked or sent off. Unsurprisingly, though, he never forgot the reserve game he played as a teenager when he lost a testicle after a particularly savage kick in the nether regions. Seventeen years later he was drinking in a pub in Chester when a stranger bought him a pint and confessed to the crime. Forgive and forget? In a word, no: "I done his face up and they took him to hospital."

Exeter City

"I have entered into a marriage of love, hate and depression with Devon's finest. It helps to talk about it."
Superfan Brian Kennedy

Have you ever fallen in love with someone you shouldn't have fallen in love with? Exeter City's most devoted fan has to be Irishman Brian Kennedy; he remortgaged his home three times and hammered seven credit cards to the max after mysteriously falling for the Grecians the day his cousin invited him to watch Hull City stuff them 5-1. The man from Waterford was smitten with a passion that has cost him tens of thousands of pounds in travel expenses. The emotional cost was, of course, much higher.

Just six years ago things were as bad as it could get. St James' Park, home since the club was founded in 1904, had been sold for a pittance. Exeter City's new owner John Russell had been a disaster at Scarborough – his tenure saw the club relegated to the conference, drowning in debt and insolvent. He was also a convicted criminal, having received a 15-month suspended sentence just three years earlier for his part in a £180,000 hire purchase scam.

There was an Alice in Wonderland air hanging around St James'. With the club on a downward spiral that was to bring relegation to the conference and in debt to the mind-boggling tune of over £3m, Russell announced two new signings that bordered on the surreal.

Firstly, Uri Geller, the psychic best known for his ability to bend spoons, was appointed to the board as vice-chairman; David Blaine turned up at the ground – as did that bloke who played Darth Vader. While secondly Michael Jackson – yes, that Michael Jackson – was

Nickname The Grecians

Kit Red and white striped shirt, black shorts, black socks

Ground St James' Park – 9,036 (3,806 seated)

Contact Wells Street, Exeter, Devon EX4 6PX 01392 411243

Website www.exetercityfc.co.uk

installed as honorary director. If Bubbles the Chimp had been freighted over from the pop star's ranch in Neverland and installed as goalkeeping coach, it would have been a footballing first, but it wouldn't have been a surprise.

Who could have dreamed that life at Exeter could suddenly be that eventful? In 104 years the club founded on the site of a field that was used to fatten pigs for market has won just one trophy – the fourth division championship in 1990. FA Cup quarter-finalists in 1931, the team reached the same stage exactly 50 years later on a run that included their greatest triumph, thrashing Newcastle United 4-0 before going out to eventual winners Spurs. In more than a century the club has produced just one unquestionably great player. Cliff Bastin cut his footballing teeth at St James' en route to becoming the star man in the great Arsenal team of the thirties under Herbert Chapman.

The 21st-century crisis culminated in a police raid in 2003 which saw Russell arrested, and resulted in supporters taking control of the club and responsibility for its enormous debts. It turned out that Russell had been penniless when he bought the club – he didn't even own a chequebook –

and in 2007 he was jailed for 21 months after admitting fraud and deception.

The supporters, meanwhile, had a massive stroke of good fortune. After battling heroically to reduce the club's debt, with hundreds pledging £500 out of their own pockets to meet payments to creditors and keep Exeter afloat, they hit the jackpot in 2005 when the club reached the FA Cup third round and were drawn away to Manchester United. The tie was televised, the crowd was over 67,000 and the Grecians played a blinder to draw 0-0 and earn a replay and another jackpot payout for a televised tie. Together the games raised roughly a million pounds and the club was able to clear its debt later that year.

In 2008 the club regained its league status after beating Cambridge United in the play-offs at Wembley in front of 42,000, the vast majority from Devon. The previous year the team had made the same stage and had gone one-up, before losing to Morecambe.

The Grecians? How and where the club derives its nickname would make a book in its own right. There are a number of rival and contradictory theories embracing classical mythology, Welsh etymology and clerical dichotomy. What we can agree on is that no-one knows for sure.

Believe it or not... the mighty Brazil played their first ever game of football against Exeter City. The five times World Cup winners made their footballing debut during the Grecians' 1914 tour of South America in the Laranjeiras stadium in Rio. The return match took place 90 years later when a Brazilian side played at St James' to celebrate the club's centenary in 2004.

Fulham

"Johnny Haynes is a top entertainer and will be paid as one from now on. I will give him £100 a week to play at Fulham."

Club chairman Tommy Trinder gave his captain an £80 pay rise after the maximum wage was abolished in 1961.

There was a time when Brentford fans regularly taunted their west London rivals with chants of "Flats on the Cottage, they're building flats on the Cottage." Fulham may be one of the loveliest grounds in the country, nestling as it does by the banks of the Thames alongside the green oasis that is Bishops Park, but it is also a prime slab of real estate in an area where a three-bedroom flat can change hands for in excess of £3m.

Almost everyone who has ever owned Fulham has cottoned onto this at some stage and the fate of the club has troubled fans for well over a century. At one stage there was talk of them moving to what is now Stamford Bridge, then a serious plan to merge with Arsenal to

Nickname The Cottagers
Kit White shirt, black shorts, white socks
Ground Craven Cottage – 26,400
Contact Stevenage Road, London, SW6 6HH 0870 4421222
Tickets 0870 4421234
Website www.fulhamfc.com

create a London superclub. And fans still shudder at the thought of Fulham Park Rangers, a planned merger with their west London rivals 20 years ago, which would effectively have finished off Fulham.

Mohamed Al-Fayed tried to flog Craven Cottage. Specifically, he agreed to sell it to a property developer for £50m, subject to planning permission, and pocketed £15m upfront. In the end the deal fell through. But fans have always wondered precisely what motivated the always unpredictable Egyptian business tycoon and owner of Harrods to buy the club. He arrived in 1997 shortly after Fulham had been promoted to the third division – the season before that had been the worst ever, with the club at one stage 91st in the league and threatening to drop out of it – and, like Ken Bates at Chelsea, announced his intention to make Fulham the Manchester United of the south.

He promised top-flight football in five years and delivered it in just four. With a dream team management of Kevin Keegan and Ray Wilkins (who left after a year) and a budget to match, the team stormed up the divisions and joined the big boys in 2001, after running away with the league and racking up 101 points from 46 matches. Al-Fayed always claimed to have got involved out of love for the game rather than

Heroes. Were it not for Fulham's campaigning fans, Craven Cottage would have been bulldozed years ago

as an investment. It's strange to reflect that five years ago he was the only foreign owner of a Premier League team, and with a fortune of £500m, by some way the richest. Soon, the majority of the league will be under foreign ownership, some of them with fortunes that dwarf the Egyptian's. Unlike them, Al-Fayed has lived here for well over 30 years and has embraced all things British, buying Britain's most famous store and battling, unsuccessfully, for British citizenship. And he's certainly been hands-on at the club, falling out with his managers over signings, cajoling the squad with pep talks, and memorably parading his pal Michael Jackson around the ground.

Legends? Johnny Haynes, England's most intelligent midfield player in the fifties and sixties, a superb passer of the ball who captained his country even when his club had dropped to the second division. He won 52 caps and would have won many more were it not for the car crash which ended his international career at the age of 27. He was the face of Brylcreem in the days when the number of grooming products available to men numbered, well, less than two, the first £100 a week footballer, the first to have a sponsored car. A one-club man who played 657 times in his 18 years there, his stature in the game proved invaluable when Fulham were fighting for survival and needed a figurehead in the grim years of the eighties. Another one-club man and a contemporary of Haynes was full-back George Cohen, a World Cup winner in the 1966 England side.

Jimmy Hill was a lesser player but a stubborn leader of the Professional Footballers' Association and responsible for the abolition of the maximum wage in 1961 – he told the Football Association the England team would go on strike unless the £20 limit was raised. He later became football's first celebrity presenter and pundit in a career spanning 30 years, entertainingly provocative if occasionally sanctimonious and, as club chairman in 1987, played a key role in blocking the proposed merger with Queens Park Rangers.

There was a period in the mid-seventies when a handful of great players decided to spend the twilight of their careers at Craven Cottage. Bobby Moore arrived in 1974 and led Fulham, then in the second division, to their only FA Cup final appearance the following year where they lost to West Ham. He was later joined by two of England's greatest entertainers, George Best and Rodney Marsh.

The Cottage? Wembley's twin towers may have bitten the dust but the Cottage still stands in the corner of the ground, a glorious anachronism between the Putney End and the Johnny Haynes stand, a village cricket pavilion standing at the heart of a London football ground. Fans refer to it as the Cottage although the cottage after which the ground is named that once stood on the site burnt down in the 19th century.

Believe it or not... Fulham thrillingly beat the drop at the end of 2008 after scoring twice during the climactic match against Birmingham. But how many players scored after the final whistle? Al-Fayed promised his players Harrods hampers stuffed with caviar and Viagra if they pulled it off.

Gillingham

"We've still got 4,900 standing at the ground and I was beginning to see a lot of undue movement as people were jumping around while singing the Celery Song. Then we began to see celery coming out of the middle of the crowd and on to the side of the pitch. We had to take action."

Club safety officer recalls the moment in 1996 when the Gills became the first club in the country to fine fans caught in possession of a root vegetable.

Kent may be the garden of England but in footballing terms it's a veritable desert. Gillingham is the only team in the county and has no local rivals, not really, although that hasn't deterred the fans for whom it's Millwall and Crystal Palace – neither of them exactly up the road – that come in for terrace abuse.

Recently the club has had a glittering spell. It all started unpromisingly in 1995 when Gillingham went into administration and was perilously close to dropping out of the league. Bought for a song, or more precisely £1, by businessman Paul Scally, he appointed Tony Pulis as manager and he won promotion in his first season. In his second season Gillingham achieved a football first by becoming the first club in the world to ban celery from its ground. Fans used to smuggle it in down their trousers, initially because they sang an obscene chant in which celery featured heavily, but latterly because they liked to chuck it at the portly figure of Gills keeper Jim Stannard, goalkeeping hero in their promotion year. The ban was well ahead of its time – Chelsea didn't follow suit for another ten years, although they have since set up a celery hotline for fans to snitch on anyone wielding an offensive vegetable.

In 2000 they went up to the second division for the first time ever in their 107 years, after beating Wigan in the play-offs. And for a while they looked reasonably solid at that level. But two relegations in the space of three years saw the club kick off 2008-09 in the fourth division.

Priestfield? The stadium either has three splendid new stands, according to the club's website or it's the crappest ground in England, according to a Sunday newspaper survey in 2004. The Gills ran out of money during rebuilding and the Brian Moore stand, named after the late and very great ITV commentator and former Gills director, remains a temporary structure until they can afford to build a new one. Who "they" may be remains a moot point.

Gills fans got nervous when Paul Scally announced plans to sell the ground then lease it back until a new site is found – and even more nervous when they discovered he had sold it to a holding company owned by one P. Scally. He's taken almost half a million pounds off the club in wages in the last three years, which is quite a lot for

Nickname The Gills

Kit Royal blue shirt, blue shorts, blue socks

Ground KRBS Priestfield Stadium – 11,582

Contact Redfern Avenue, Gillingham, Kent ME7 4DD 01634 300000

Website
www.gillinghamfootballclub.com

a club with debts of over £10m and whose overdraft facility has long expired. And a man who publicly announced his intention to build the best stadium in Britain, complete with casino, housing and a hotel, is clearly fed up that he's gone from hero to zero in the eyes of the fans who were delighted when the club clambered from the fourth to the second division and sickened that they're now back where they started.

Famous old boys? Tony Cascarino, capped 88 times for Ireland, was snapped up from Kent non-league side Crockenhill. The price? Nothing as such, although the Gills chucked in 11 tracksuits as a sweetener. And Steve Bruce, of whom it is more or less a cliché to say that he was the best English defender never picked for his country, is a Gillingham old boy. When in the reserves he had the unusual distinction one season of netting 18 goals and being the club's top scorer, despite playing at centre half.

Don't mention... Ken Bates. The Leeds chairman gloated in 2008 when Gillingham were on the point of being relegated, claiming it was poetic justice that the club should suffer the drop. Why? Because the Gills had voted to dock Leeds 15 points after they went into administration. Along with over 60 other clubs.

Grimsby Town

"I remember how insanely I froze that first month. I was used to wearing woollen underwear and long sleeves when the temperature was nearing freezing point. However, that was out of the question in Grimsby."

Norwegian defender Knuts Anders Fostervold suffered from frozen nuts when he arrived on loan in 2000.

Contrary to common misconception, Grimsby Town is not in Yorkshire. Rather more surprisingly, it isn't in Grimsby. Blundell Park can in fact be found in the bracing, aka chilly, seaside resort of Cleethorpes, but the club takes its name and its heritage from the fishing port just along the Humber estuary. That's why they're known as the Mariners, why Grimsby's Wembley appearances – three so far – have been graced by thousands of giant inflatable fishes all called Harry the Haddock and why their excellent and entertaining fan websites include The Fishy and Cod Almighty.

The Cod War was raging in 1976 when Blundell Park welcomed a Cold War veteran and probably its most famous spectator in the formidable shape of US secretary of state, national security adviser and Nobel Prize winner Henry Kissinger. A man with an excellent scoring record – he dated a string of gorgeous actresses including Shirley MacLaine and Candice Bergen – his presence did nothing for the club, who lost 2-0 to Gillingham; nor for the town – Britain capitulated in the Cod

War (against Iceland over fishing waters) and the port, along with the rest of the British fishing industry, went into a decline from which it has never recovered. Interestingly, it was not fish but chicken with which the club made national head-

Nickname The Mariners
Kit Black and white striped shirt, black shorts, black socks
Ground Blundell Park – 9,546
Contact Cleethorpes, Lincs DN35 7PY
01472 605050
Tickets 01472 605050
Website www.gtfc.co.uk

lines back in 1996. A plate of chicken wings, to be more precise, which irate manager Brian Laws found uneaten in the dressing room and chucked at Grimsby's star Italian man, former Juventus striker Ivano Bonetti, following a defeat at Luton. They somehow fractured the player's cheekbone and made sure he'd be on his bike at the first opportunity. This annoyed the fans and especially those who had coughed up £50,000 to help bring him to the club in the first place – the US owners of his "image rights" had to be paid off before he could play.

Another import who played briefly for Grimsby then got on his bike, quite literally, was Norwegian Knuts Anders Fostervold, who arrived in the arctic winter of 2000 equipped with long woollen underwear, only to discover that they don't hold with that sort of thing in Grimsby. He retired months later with an ankle injury which didn't prevent him from developing a second career as a world-class cyclist, competing in the world championships and breaking three Norwegian records. Talking of ankle injuries, club skipper Justin Whittle missed most of 2007-08 after picking up a bizarre injury when Grimsby beat holders Doncaster on their way to the final of the Football League

Trophy – he managed to turn his ankle after the game in some over-exuberant post-match celebrations.

The Johnstone's Paint Trophy was a big disappointment for the club in 2008. In their third Wembley appearance – they'd won the same competition in 1998 and the second division play-offs the next month – they missed a penalty, then conceded one before going down 2-0 to MK Dons. A number of Grimsby supporters were clocked wearing T-shirts showing their hostility to franchise football, and afterwards they presented a cheque to supporters of AFC Wimbledon – the club formed by supporters of Wimbledon FC irate that *their* club had upped sticks and moved 55 miles away to Milton Keynes.

You have to be very long in the tooth to remember Grimsby's glory days, which came in the inter-war period. They didn't actually win anything but came fifth in the first division in 1935 and reached the FA Cup semi-finals in 1936 and 1939. The 1939 semi against Wolves was played at Old Trafford and the crowd of 76,962 remains the record attendance at the ground.

Blundell Park currently accommodates just under 10,000, but plans are finally afoot to build a new 20,000-seater stadium just outside Grimsby, which is supposed to be ready in time for the 2010 season. You can take a virtual tour on the internet and see computer-generated images that have rather portentously been set to the epic music of *Star Wars*.

One-upmanship?... One of the glorious things about English football is the way so many club traditions are rooted in the history of the town. Where else would home fans taunt opposition supporters with a lusty rendition of "We piss on your fish"?

Hartlepool United

"He's a lunatic but at least when the football's bad – which it is quite often – we're entertained."

Fan Robert Meredith defends Hartlepool monkey mascot H'Angus after he's ejected from Scunthorpe United for simulating a sex act with the woman drawing the half-time lottery numbers.

Meat Loaf is a fan. A big sports nut, the soft-rock god told me in 2008 that while his wide range of interests extends to fantasy bass fishing in which he is an avid participant, he didn't support a league team until the day he was invited to appear on a UK football chat show. Under pressure to spin a line, he plumped for Hartlepool, seduced by the story of the townsfolk who famously tried and hanged a monkey washed up during the Napoleonic Wars under the misapprehension it was a French spy. And he's been rooting for them ever since.

Alice Cooper would have been a more natural supporter because at Hartlepool they know all about being elected. And re-elected. In the days

Nickname The Pool

Kit Royal blue and white split shirt, blue shorts, white socks

Ground Victoria Park – 7,787

Contact Clarence Road, Hartlepool, Teeside TS24 8BZ 01429 272584

Website www.hartlepoolunited.co.uk

before conference teams gained automatic promotion to the Football League, the clubs at the bottom of the fourth division had to apply for re-election every season. Hartlepool had to apply on no fewer than fourteen occasions – a joint record – and succeeded every time. Which is itself an election miracle, but not as miraculous as the fate that befell H'Angus (geddit?), the man in the monkey suit who made his first appearance as the club's mascot in 1999. A controversial figure who got himself ejected from more than one football ground for inappropriate behaviour – once with a female steward and once with an inflatable doll – he stood as mayor of Hartlepool in 2002 on a platform of free bananas for every child and won. And was re-elected with a massive majority in 2006, despite failing to keep his promise.

Until recently Hartlepool had little experience of winning anything. For many years the match programme carried an ad for the Samaritans, and where better to target a service for the suicidal than at supporters of a team stranded at the foot of the table more often than any other? There have been so many lows. Twenty years ago there was an attempt to wind up the club when the company that made the Perspex hoods that shelter the dugouts – sorry, technical areas – complained it hadn't been paid. Hartlepool's defence, that the hoods were not fit for purpose and regularly blew off in the teeth of the icy North Sea gales that howled over the Victoria Ground, may have contained an element of truth, but it didn't wash. Even the players cavilled at the cold – back in the 1920s manager Bill Norman was compelled to strip naked and roll around in the snow to persuade players that it wasn't too cold to train.

Their stand was destroyed by German bombers in the First World War. Centre half John Gill played just 41 games for the Pool but bags an unlikely record, scoring no fewer than five times – in his own net. The Luftwaffe had another crack in the Second World War but just missed. While other teams record ill-advised pop songs to celebrate a triumph – winning a trophy, reaching a final – Hartlepool recorded "Never Say Back" in the early seventies to celebrate yet another successful re-election campaign. How many other teams would sing: "We go to the Park and we're full of hope, but some days it seems we just can't cope… we're not very flash and we haven't the cash"?

The fundraising record raised no funds. In the eighties the players went on strike because they hadn't been paid. The taxman tried to wind the club up on numerous occasions. The boardroom was relocated to a Portakabin. The stands were declared unsafe. The goalposts were impounded by bailiffs. What a far cry from the flush days of the twenties when the club was able to lash out £10 to buy a player from Workington and throw in a whole box of kippers.

Brian Clough called it "the edge of the world" and it was here that he began his career as a brash manager in 1965, building a team that won

The mayor of Hartlepool

promotion to the third division for the first time in the club's history in 1968. It was a false dawn. It wasn't until 2000 that things begin to pick up, and how. Since then there've been no fewer than five unsuccessful appearances in the play-offs, two automatic promotions and a relegation. In 2007 the club equalled an all-time Football League record, winning eight games on the bounce without conceding and going 23 games unbeaten.

The Pools? The club used to be called Hartlepools United until the mid-sixties when the borough of West Hartlepool was abolished. It changed its name to Hartlepool AFC. It added United in the seventies.

Best excuse for missing training?... Top scorer Adam Boyd needed hospital treatment in 2005 after being forced to flee half-naked through a housing estate when a car salesman had taken exception to finding the striker in his bed with his former partner.

Hereford United

"To achieve maximum football, the player has to be in an optimal state of arousal."

Bulls trainer Phil Robinson doesn't know whether to train the players, or breed them.

Chairman, majority shareholder, director, occasional coach. And manager. Let's hear it for Graham Turner, who pulled off a minor miracle of sorts in 2008 when he took Hereford to a second promotion in three years, pulling them from the conference into England's third division.

Turner was a reluctant owner. Formerly manager at Villa and Wolves, he arrived in 1995 with the club in the fourth division, led them to the play-offs in his first season, but saw the club relegated to the conference the following year. It wasn't until the last few minutes of the last game of the season that the Bulls occupied bottom place and the big drop stunned the club. So much so that the then shell-shocked chairman told reporters it was the worst day of his life, momentarily forgetting he had lost both his wife and daughter in the previous 12 months. Taylor offered his resignation but it wasn't accepted; and soon

Nickname The Bulls

Kit White shirt, black shorts, white socks

Ground Edgar Street – 8,843

Contact Hereford HR4 9JU 08442 761939

Website www.herefordunited.co.uk

afterwards he bought a majority shareholding to stop the club folding. It was supposed to be a temporary arrangement but he's still there.

Most significant game in the club's history? No, not that one, we'll come to that in a minute. The future of the club would have been so very different were it not for an FA Cup qualifying tie in 2001 against Dover Athletic. The club was in voluntary administration at the time; if it had lost it would have gone under. A win took them into the first round and a tie against Wrexham, televised live on the BBC. The TV payment for that game kept the Bulls afloat.

It was the FA Cup third-round replay against Newcastle United in 1972 that provided Hereford, then in the Southern League, with their greatest moment. The greatest FA Cup upset of all time? Without doubt, the most memorable. There was a huge build-up to the game. The original tie at St James' Park, postponed twice due to bad weather, finally ended in a 2-2 draw, with player-manager Colin Addison scoring the equaliser. Expectation for the replay was huge, the more so as it was postponed three times, with the Magpies travelling down to Edgar Street on three occasions and spending ten days cooped up in a hotel, and their star player Malcolm "Supermac" MacDonald widely reported as boasting he was planning to stuff eight goals past the non-league side.

Supermac scored one and it wasn't enough. The Whites were one down with six minutes to go when carpenter Ronnie Radford scored his wondergoal equaliser, picking up a loose ball in midfield, playing a one-two, then lashing it into the top corner from fully 30 yards. Cue pitch invasion. And a second one in extra time when Ricky George – a substitute for right-back Roger Griffiths, who had played much of the match with a broken leg, stabbed home the winner. It was the first time since the forties that a non-league side had knocked out a first division team and it was watched by a whopping 14 million viewers on *Match of the Day* in a programme that marked the TV commentating debut of

142

the man with the sheepskin coat, John Motson.

Propelled by that dizzying moment of glory, Hereford were elected to the Football League for the first time at the end of that season, and four years later spent a single year in the second division. But the rot set in soon afterwards and the club spent 19 years in the fourth division and a further nine years in the conference before bouncing back three years ago.

Many of the dark years were spent in financial misery, with the Bulls seeming on the verge of losing its home, which had been sold to property developers to stave off debt. For a long time the club feared its home would be flogged off again, but things are much rosier now with club and developers working in partnership.

Believe it or not, Graham Turner bought just two players in his first 12 years at the club, spending a total of £40,000. Whether the club can progress any further from its current standing depends to a large extent on whether it can attract any more fans. Around 8,000 supporters flocked to the ground regularly when Hereford first gained league status and kept coming for the next five years. But despite two promotion years, the crowds are stubbornly stuck at around the 4,000 mark.

Never mind the bullocks… let's hear it for the Swede. Kick-off at Edgar Street is preceded by one of football's most bizarre rituals whereby a humble root vegetable painted in the club colours is worshipped by prostrate fans in a ceremony in the centre circle before being dribbled the length of the pitch and booted into the net.

Huddersfield Town

"It will be quite a contest. We've got a manager who thinks he's the best-looking in the league and so have they."

Peter Jackson v Jose Mourinho? Huddersfield Town assistant manager Terry Yorath assesses the form book when the Terriers draw Chelsea in the FA Cup.

There was a decade when Huddersfield Town was the best side in England. No question about it. Champions three years in a row, runners-up twice, FA Cup finalists four times (one win) and all between 1920 and 1930, the Terriers straddled the era like a colossus.

Yet just a year before this glorious run began, the club was all set to up sticks and merge with Leeds United. Huddersfield Town had already gone bust once in 1912, poor crowds unable to fill or to pay for the new stadium that went up in 1910. But the town revolted at the thought of merger, the chairman sold up and the Huddersfield revolution was under way.

Key to their success was manager Herbert Chapman, who arrived in 1921. It's impossible to exaggerate just how revolutionary Chapman was. Team meetings, physiotherapy, tactics – no-one had thought of any of this stuff before. An advocate of floodlights, numbered shirts, stadium clocks, synthetic pitches, his most important innovation was to insist that he was the boss, ran the club and crucially, picked the team. Previously, sides would often be selected by a bunch of clueless directors.

Chapman's Terriers won the title in 1924 and 1925 and made it three in a row the following year, by which time Chapman had departed to Arsenal – a club that had won nothing so far – and did it all over again.

Hero in his Huddersfield team was left-back Sam Wadsworth, who volunteered for war while playing for Blackburn Rovers, only to return five years later, wounded and shell-shocked, to discover he was surplus to requirements. Shattered and disillusioned, he gave up on football altogether for a while until he was picked up by Huddersfield

Nickname The Terriers

Kit Royal blue and white striped shirt, white shorts, blue and white hooped socks

Ground Galpharm Stadium – 24,500

Contact Huddersfield, W Yorks HD1 6PX 0870 4444677

Tickets 0870 4444552

Website www.htafc.com

1922 Terriers team with their visionary manager Herbert Chapman

in 1921. Three years later, while walking with his wife past a newsagent's, he saw his name scrawled in chalk on a blackboard outside the shop – which was how he found out he was now captain of England.

Another Huddersfield star whose career started inauspiciously was a teenager given a trial by the club in the fifties and dismissed by the manager as a "freak". But not in a good way. According to Andy Beattie: "Never did I see a less likely football prospect – weak, puny, and bespectacled." He forgot to mention the terrible squint, so bad the youngster had to play with one eye permanently shut, until he eventually had an operation. The club took a gamble with him anyway and it paid off spectacularly – two years later they sold Denis Law for £55,000, then a British transfer record, and equipped themselves with floodlights from the proceeds.

When Law arrived in 1956, Huddersfield were on the point of being relegated from the top flight. Since then they've returned just once, for a two-year spell at the start of the seventies. Team captain Jimmy Nicholl celebrated promotion by dining at Downing Street at the invitation of Labour PM Harold Wilson, a lifelong Huddersfield fan, who claimed to hold a record in Huddersfield schools football: "Eleven goals in one match. The only trouble was I was the goalkeeper who let them all in."

Biggest blunder? Arguably in 1999-2000. Looking good for promotion to the Premier League after the first half of a season in which they'd beaten the league's top teams – along with Chelsea, in the League Cup – they blew it by selling star Marcus Stewart to rivals Ipswich Town. Ipswich were promoted, Huddersfield faded away, finishing two points outside a play-off place.

And now? The club celebrated its centenary in 2008-09, kicking off with a friendly against Arsenal in August and slashing season tickets to just £100. With attendances up, no apparent money problems, a fine new stadium and a thriving academy scheme which has seen a host of home-grown youngsters packing the first team, the club celebrates 100 years in reasonable shape.

Don't mention... the 2006 Club Calendar. The Terriers are proud of their so-called Young Guns, the academy kids who make it to the first team, and thought it would be a wheeze to feature them in a calendar decked out in cowboy clobber and Stetsons and pouting moodily at the camera. Unhappily, the calendar hit the shops at the same time as Huddersfield was flooded with remarkably similar posters for the gay cowboy weepie *Brokeback Mountain*. The fans were confused and refused to buy the calendar, despite the club slashing the price from £5.99 to just £1.

Hull City

"People say 'You don't want to go up too early' but that's absolute bollocks."

Five-year plan? Not for Phil Brown. After 104 years he reckoned Hull fans had waited long enough for top-class football.

For decades Hull fans had to live with the knowledge that their city was the biggest in England never to have hosted top-flight football. No longer. The Tigers made a brilliant start in their debut season in 2008, taunting Spurs fans with "Are you Arsenal in disguise?" while recording astonishing back-to-back away wins over North London's finest. It's been a long time coming – 104 years, to be precise. The vast majority of all football supporters are long-suffering, but for fans of Hull there have been so many years of hell.

Based in a major fishing port, the club found itself under the leadership of chairman Martin Fish in the grim early nineties. Disgruntled fans showed their displeasure by stuffing rotting fish through the letter box of their beleaguered leader.

The same decade saw former rugby league player Tim Wilby installed as chairman, and briefly hailed as the club's saviour. That was until he was unmasked in the press as a man with a number of debts and, astonishingly, a full-time job as a council caretaker in Kensington & Chelsea, where he earned £15,000 a year. Wilby's defence was, to say the least, unusual: "I don't think there's anybody in the world who hasn't had a county court judgment against them" – but he was no longer wanted at Hull, nor indeed by Kensington & Chelsea, who had received a number of complaints from tenants wondering why he was always on the telly when he should have been minding their flats.

Surreal, but not as disappointing as the David Lloyd years.

The former tennis player who opened a chain of indoor tennis centres parachuted into Hull in the late nineties promising to build a superb new stadium complete with bowling alley, fitness centre, cinemas, restaurants… maybe even a retractable roof.

He hadn't done his homework. All this was to be funded by selling off Boothferry Park, the problem being that one end of the ground was on a 125-year lease to a supermarket who wanted a lot of money to get out.

The fans turned on Lloyd, and he turned on the fans. At one stage he said: "The people of Hull are living in the dark ages." Too wordy? They were, simply, "crap". No rotting fish heads for Lloyd – fans vented their frustration by disrupting matches with a hail of tennis balls on the pitch. He quit as chairman but held onto Boothferry Park. When the players were locked out of their own ground in a row over unpaid rent, it looked like the end was nigh.

Nickname The Tigers

Kit Amber and black striped shirt, black shorts, black socks

Ground Kingston Communications Stadium – 25,504

Contact The Circle, Walton St, Hull HU3 6HU 0870 8370003

Tickets 0870 837 0004

Website www.hullcityafc.net

And now? Hull have shot from the basement league to the top flight in just four years with a gleaming new stadium that opened in 2002. A club whose greatest legends – Raich Carter, Ken Wagstaff – were so firmly rooted in a bygone era now has some new heroes. None more so than Dean Windass. Born and bred in the city, the striker was already in his twenties when he signed for his home-town club back in 1991. They had to sell him in 1995 to make ends meet, but in 2008, at the grand old age of 39, he was the key man at Wembley in the second division play-offs, blasting home a volley from the edge of the penalty area after a move begun by another Hull-born veteran, 35-year-old Nicky Barmby.

Off the pitch, another hero in the shape of manager Phil Brown. A man who feared he was on the football scrap heap, after spending most of 2006 unemployed, was appointed boss in early 2007 and transformed the club from second division strugglers to Premier League new boys in just 18 months.

And now? A club whose supporters went on a funeral march through the city in 1975 carrying a Hull City coffin after crowds had dwindled to just 2,000 had sold all 20,500 season tickets before the start of the 2008-09 season and will need to expand the stadium considerably if it is ever to come close to the 55,000 crowd that packed Boothferry Road in the forties.

Anyone for anger management?... Hull hero Windass was once banned for six games during his spell at Aberdeen after receiving three red cards in the same match. The first was for a violent lunge on an opponent, the second for subjecting the ref to a volley of abuse, and the third for punching the corner flag.

Ipswich Town

> "It drives us doolally. It conjures up images of carrot-crunching yokels coming out of the tunnel with straw stuck between their teeth. It drives the lads mad. The sooner we lose it the better as far as we're concerned."
>
> *Jim Magilton*

The Tractor Boys? That didn't emerge as a nickname until 2000 and the players weren't happy when it did. They were never going to win this one. For starters, the fans loved it, welcoming every opening goal with a rousing chorus of "One Nil to the Tractor Boys". By the time Magilton made his protests, T-shirt designers were already doing a roaring trade in tractor-based merchandise. Fatally, it was a dream for headline writers everywhere. Tractor Boys mown down, Tractor Boys plough on, wheels come off Tractor Boys, Tractor Boys reap harvest, the possibilities were endless. Manager George Burley pleaded with the press to drop it, saying: "I'm not a tractor lover,

Nickname The Tractor Boys

Kit Royal blue shirt with thin white stripe, white shorts, blue socks

Ground Portman Road – 33,000

Contact Portman Road, Ipswich IP1 2DA 01473 400500

Tickets 0870 1110555

Website www.itfc.co.uk

we're not country boys… we want to be an up-and-coming vibrant town." He woke up the next morning to find his comments reported faithfully in the papers. The headline? "HE'S AN EX TRACTOR FAN".

For many years Ipswich was a footballing backwater. Founded in 1878 as an amateur side, it took another 60 years before it joined the Football League. It spent every year bar one in the third division (south), which is where it was when Alf Ramsey arrived in 1955.

Ramsey had established a reputation as a master tactician with nerves of steel – they called him "The General" – in a distinguished career with Tottenham and England, winning 32 caps and captaining his country. Unusually for a full-back, he took the penalties. In his first season Ipswich won promotion, then spent three distinctly average seasons in the second division. There was no hint of what was around the corner.

In 1961 the club won promotion to the first division and were hotly tipped to go straight back again. It was a team without stars, made up mostly of journeymen and youngsters. But the club astonished the footballing world by winning the title in their first season, with striker Ray Crawford scoring 33 times and becoming the league's joint top scorer.

Ramsey left to take the England job and led the country to the World Cup in 1966. Ipswich suffered relegation and decline after he went, but by 1969 were back in the top flight when Bobby Robson arrived to take charge. He stayed for 13 years during which Ipswich won the FA Cup and the UEFA Cup and twice finished runners-up in the title race. Key players in the team were two Dutch midfielders, Arnold Muehren and Frans Thijssen – it was most

Sir Bobby

unusual to have an overseas player in the side back then; to have two was unheard of.

Club legend? Kevin Beattie. His manager called him the best English player he had ever seen and the defender was star man when Ipswich won the FA Cup. His most troublesome opponent was Andy Gray, now a TV pundit but then a striker with Aston Villa and Wolves: "I never liked playing Andy. He was as brave as a lion but he didn't have the best timing. Ten minutes after you headed the ball, he'd head you."

He suffered a catalogue of injuries in his career, missing the UEFA Cup final and eventually being forced to retire while still in his twenties. Ipswich fans lobbied for him to receive a UEFA Cup-winner's medal for his contribution in the earlier rounds, and in 2008 he was presented with one by UEFA president Michel Platini in a ceremony at the UEFA Cup final.

Since then… mostly second division, although the club was a founding member of the Premier League in 1992 and stayed there for three years. Up again in 2000, Ipswich had a brilliant year, narrowly missing out on a Champions League spot and finishing fifth. But like many other clubs it fell into financial trouble when relegated the following year and spent a spell in administration.

Not a lot of people know… that Beattie doubled for Michael Caine in the prisoner of war football movie *Escape to Victory*, while team-mate Paul Cooper did the business for Sylvester Stallone. In fact, the film is full of Tractor Boys – Kevin O'Callaghan, Russell Osman, Robin Turner, Laurie Sivell and John Wark are all in it, along with Pele and Bobby Moore.

Leeds United

"I have spoken to the players here and I have told them that I want them to be like the Leeds United of before – and they were horrible. I want a bit of nastiness and togetherness."
Leeds manager Dennis Wise

Nastiness, togetherness, but sometimes sublime levels of skill. For ten years Don Revie's side were the indisputable top dogs of English football. Twice title winners in 1969 and 1974, they also won the Fairs (today's UEFA) Cup twice, as well as an FA Cup and League Cup in their glory years. They should probably have won more. Five times runners-up, they also lost three FA Cup finals and two European finals in the same period.

They would have won more had manager Revie been ahead of his time and developed a squad system – the same 11 players started every match if fit, and regularly played 60 or 70 games a year. But he was a pioneer in so many other ways, and brilliant at developing talent – Billy Bremner was an erratic winger until Revie converted him into a star midfield man. Leeds were the fittest team in the country, Revie 20 years ahead of his time in understanding the importance of diet, nutrition and employing ballet dancers to improve the balance of his squad.

His attention to detail occasionally verged on paranoia – he prepared hefty dossiers on opponents ahead of matches, and acted as social secretary to his players, organising endless games of bingo, dominos and carpet bowls to bind them together. He even concerned himself with their sex lives – whenever a player had a new girlfriend, he'd have them covertly vetted.

Nickname United
Kit White shirt, white shorts, white socks
Ground Elland Road – 40,204
Contact Elland Road, Leeds LS11 0ES
Tickets 0845 1211992
Website www.leedsunited.com

But with the flair came a ruthlessness, in an age when football was far more innocent than it is today. Leeds United tackled hard on the ball and were cynical and sneaky off it. Striker Allan Clarke once ambled behind the goal to retrieve the ball, then trotted back to the halfway line to hand it to his opponents waiting to take a free kick. Today he would undoubtedly have been booked for time-wasting. But in the seventies he was applauded for what was perceived – wrongly – as sporting behaviour.

Supporters may have been naive but Brian Clough wasn't. On the first day of his disastrous 44-day reign as manager, he didn't exactly endear himself to the players with his opening shot: "As far as I'm concerned you can throw all those medals you've won in the bin, because you won them all by cheating."

Clough's reign was the start of a long and steady decline at Leeds. Allan Clarke, Billy Bremner and winger Eddie Gray all had spells managing the club without success in the eighties.

In the early nineties, the club bounced back, winning the first division in 1992 under Howard Wilkinson. Under David O'Leary, a top-five finish every year and a young attractive team that made it to the Champions League semi-final in 2001. It was Leeds's undoing. The club assumed it would qualify for the Champions League every year and borrowed heavily against future earnings. The team failed to make it, the club couldn't repay its loans and the wheels came off. Just three years later Leeds were relegated, all of the star players sold, Elland Road and the training ground flogged off. And three years after that the club went into administration, and down to the third division.

Believe it or not... Leeds supporters may have a long history of hooliganism going back to the seventies, but they have been remarkably loyal during the club's recent decline – in 2007-08 the club was still averaging over 26,000 for home games.

Bizarre injury... Rio Ferdinand was out for a month in 2001 after picking up an injury watching television. The Leeds United defender had his foot up on the coffee table for several hours and managed to damage a tendon behind his knee.

Leicester City

"I was watching TV when it flashed on the screen that my mate George had scored in the first minute at Birmingham. My first reaction was to ring him up. Then I remembered he was out there playing."

Striker Ade Akinbiyi is foxed by the box

The only club in England with its own manager of the month competition? It certainly seemed that way at Leicester City where five managers in seven months was a no-brainer recipe for disaster. The Foxes needed a win at Stoke on the final day of 2007-08 to avoid relegation to English football's third division for the first time in the club's 124-year history.

"We've got to go there and tweak the nose of fear and stick an ice cube down the vest of terror," declared manager Ian Holloway, defiant to the end. A drab draw and they were doomed. Ironically, the club went down with one of the best defensive records in the league – only one team conceded fewer goals at home, and just two had a better away record. The problem was at the other end.

It had all seemed so much more promising five months earlier when Holloway parachuted in from Plymouth on his abortive rescue mission. One of football's more colourful characters with a vocabulary to match, he felt he'd landed a plum job and had stepped up, in footballing terms, from *EastEnders* to *King Lear*. Did no one tell him *King Lear* was a

Nickname The Foxes

Kit Royal blue shirt, blue shorts, blue socks

Ground Walkers Stadium – 32,500

Contact Filbert Way, Leicester, LE2 7FL
0844 8156000

Tickets 0844 8155000

Website www.lcfc.co.uk

tragedy? Leicester's particular tragedy goes back to 2002 when the club went into administration, crippled by the costs of their move from Filbert Street to their new £37m stadium and the loss of expected income when ITV Digital collapsed. The club was rescued by a consortium headed by famous old boy Gary Lineker, and was subsequently bought in 2007 by former Portsmouth owner Milan Mandaric. He announced a three-year plan to turn the club round, however relegation wasn't part of it.

A few years earlier and it was all so different. Martin O'Neill, the key midfield man in Brian Clough's two times European Cup-winning Nottingham Forest team, took over as manager at the end of 1995. He impressed everyone, including his former mentor, who famously remarked: "Anybody who can do anything in Leicester but make a jumper has got to be a genius." In his first year the club were promoted to the Premier League and achieved four consecutive top-ten finishes, reaching the League Cup final three times and winning it twice – two trophies to add to their only other silverware of note, a first League Cup in 1964.

They weren't a pretty team – there were some who compared them, rather unfairly, to Wimbledon – but with Muzzy Izzet, Robbie Savage and Neil Lennon patrolling midfield, the inspirational figure of Mattie Elliott at the back, and a little and large combo of Emile Heskey and

Tony Cottee upfront, they were well organised and difficult to beat.

The Foxes (Leicestershire was big on hunting – and the team still take to the pitch to an old hunting tune) have had their share of disappointment over the years. Four FA Cup finals and four defeats to date, they have never been champions, though they came second in 1929. There was a brief fantasy period in the seventies when Leicester was one of the most entertaining teams in the land. Manager Jimmy Bloomfield took it upon himself to bring some of London's more flamboyant entertainers to the Midlands and suddenly the Foxes were feasting on a diet of Keith Weller, Jon Sammels and Alan Birchenall – remembered fondly as the man who collided with Sheffield United's Tony Currie and kissed him.

They were joined by the gloriously flamboyant genius that was Frank Worthington. Unashamedly selfish – he never made any bones about the fact that playing well himself mattered more than the team's performance – and a notorious womaniser who famously seduced both a Swedish nymphet and her mum, he played with panache, extraordinary hair and a regular hangover. On an international trip he accompanied his suited and booted England colleagues onto the plane dressed in full cowboy attire. His goals pop up too rarely these days in a TV world that mostly ignores anything that happened before the Premier League, but there's one on YouTube during his spell with Bolton where he takes the ball on his head with his back to goal on the edge of the penalty area, plays keepy-uppy, wrong-foots five defenders by flicking it backwards swivelling and volleying a shot past an incredulous keeper.

Talking of keepers – England's two best ever keepers played for Leicester, at the same time. World Cup hero Gordon Banks was allowed to leave for Stoke because the young Peter Shilton was waiting in the wings.

Booked for sarcasm?... Doesn't happen that often in football, although Paul "Gazza" Gascoigne (who else?) famously picked one up during his time at Rangers when he showed the yellow card to a ref who had dropped it. Leicester's Neil Lennon fell foul of the man in black in a match against Coventry in 1999. Unhappy at some of the decisions given by a linesman, he seized his moment when the official was knocked to the ground following a touchline collision and offered to escort him from the pitch in an empty wheelchair he'd grabbed from the disabled area.

Leyton Orient

"Drugs? Who needs them? Just come to Leyton Orient. I'm flying. We are going to drink from the elixir of life here at Brisbane Road, the centre of the universe."

Barry Hearn, Orient chairman, after beating Hull City in the 2001 play-off semi-final.

Leyton Orient were going to the wall in 1995. The club was owned by a coffee grower whose business had gone bust due to war in Rwanda and no longer had a bean. Famously available for a fiver, it was sold to sports promoter Barry Hearn at a knockdown price of £2.43.

Fans heaved a collective sigh of relief. Here was a successful man who had stood on the terraces of Brisbane Road as a child and made a lot of money promoting frankly unpromising sports. He'd taken snooker out of the clubs and made it into a national TV obsession and had managed to make a virtue of the fact that his greatest star, six times world champion Steve Davis, was also one of Britain's most boring men. He'd branched out into tenpin bowling, poker, boxing, darts and pool. Hell, he'd even persuaded Sky to screen several hours of live fishing from Doncaster (this year, Stoke) which, in a genius marketing move, he dubbed Fish O'Mania. Fans sang his name and some dreamed of the Premiership.

The O's then embarked on a stretch of 11 years in the fourth division – their longest spell ever in the basement. It was a run punctuated by a couple of unsuccessful play-off final defeats, but if there was

Nickname The O's

Kit Red shirt, red shorts, red socks

Ground Matchroom Stadium
(affectionately known as Brisbane Road)
– 9,271

Contact Brisbane Road, London, E10
5NF 0871 3101881

Tickets 0871 3101883

Website www.leytonorient.com

a consistent theme, it was caution. Or lack of ambition. Or realism. Hearn may have promised players a trip to the gambling paradise of Las Vegas if they won promotion in 2006, and they did, but he's been too canny to gamble with the club's future when so many lower league clubs have been drowning in debt and plunging into administration.

In the early years he paraded sports stars and glamour girls to the fans before kick-off in a bid to increase the crowds – which are still among the lowest in the league. He cunningly sold off the four corners of the ground to a property developer, banking over £7m in the process.

But fans who banked on him buying success have become used to his wheeler-dealing in the market place. At any given time the O's are likely to be fielding a bevy of YTS kids, youngsters on loan from London's Premier League clubs and talent bought on the cheap. In 2007, unfathomably, the O's managed to mislay an entire team – manager Martin Ling released six players at the end of the season, and five out-of-contract players upped sticks. But the club has an eye for the wily signing. Former Hartlepool hotshot Adam Boyd's career went on the slide after he picked up an infection during a knee operation, not to mention the damage he did to his feet running naked through an executive estate after being disturbed by his lover's boyfriend. Ling snapped him up last year and was rewarded with 17 goals.

In the 127 years since the club was founded by a bunch of cricketers looking to have some fun in the winter, Orient have appeared in the first division just once, in 1962. In the seventies they gained a reputation as cup giant-killers and had a glorious run to the FA Cup semi-finals in 1978, disposing of Norwich, Middlesbrough, Blackburn and Chelsea before succumbing 3-0 to Arsenal. Some great players have passed through Brisbane Road, usually at the latter stages of their careers – the great entertainer Stan Bowles for one, while record-breaking goalie Peter Shilton played his 1000th match during a short spell at Brisbane Road before retiring at 47. Laurie Cunningham is the most famous home-grown talent – his exploits in east London kick-started a career which saw him win six England caps and become the first English player to move to Real Madrid before his untimely death in a car crash aged just 33.

Believe it or not... Andrew Lloyd Webber wrote the hit album *Variations* for his cellist brother Julian after losing a bet with him over the outcome of the Orient's final match of the 1977 season against Hull City. The O's stayed up, on goal average. And Melvyn Bragg, Arsenal supporter, got a tune for the *South Bank Show* which he's been using ever since.

Lincoln City

"The club said they wanted someone with a bit more stature and presence. That is not something I can work on. Not unless I buy a rack off eBay and stretch myself another three or four inches."

After a club record of 351 league games as goalie, Lincoln decide Alan Marriott (5ft 11in) is too small.

The play-offs. Penalty shoot-outs. Golden Goals. Sudden Death. Love it for its intensity, drama, all-or-nothing significance of the matches, the millions of pounds at stake, the joy of victory, numbing misery of defeat – all make for an extraordinary, riveting edge-of-the-seat, gripping spectacle. As if the climax of *X-Factor*, *The Apprentice*, *Pop Idol* and *Big Brother* had all been condensed into 90 spine-tingling minutes, plus extra time, plus a penalty shoot-out if we're really lucky.

And loathe it, because the play-offs are exactly like the climactic moments of *X-Factor*, *The Apprentice*, *Pop Idol* and *Big Brother*. Ordinary players, put in an extraordinary and totally artificial all-or-nothing situation – it is football repackaged as reality TV, manipulated to guarantee maximum pleasure and maximum pain, solely for our entertainment. Nothing to do with football and fairness – otherwise the team in third place after 46 matches of a gruelling season would be automatically promoted – and everything to do with money and TV ratings, with the play-offs providing the broadcasters with 20 money-spinning do-or-die matches every season and giving eight lucky clubs a lucrative day out at Wembley.

Lincoln City endured the agony of the play-offs – in 2003, 2004, 2005, 2006. And 2007. A record. Every year the Imps (their nickname derives from a pair of Imps that terrorised Lincoln Cathedral in days of yore, allegedly) were tantalised by the prospect of lifting themselves from the fourth division. Every year they missed out. The Imps have a dismal history of failure in knock-out competitions – they've never gone further than the last 16 in the FA Cup. Don't ask grandfather to tell you all about it – the last time they got that far was back in 1902.

They may not have won promotion on any occasion, but just being contenders was something the Imps could not have envisaged at the start of the decade when it looked like they were going to the wall.

Mired in administration and over a million pounds in debt, they were saved when the outgoing chairman gave away all his shares and the supporters took over the club, making Lincoln the first club in the country to be owned by its fans.

There's not a supporter in the land who doesn't think they could do a better job if they were running their club, but one fan lived the dream. Rob Bradley, fanatical supporter and formerly editor of Lincoln fanzine *Yellow Belly*, became chairman. Did it change his life? Obviously – although he continued travelling to away match-es with his mates in a

Nickname The Imps

Kit Red and white striped shirt, black shorts, red socks

Ground Sincil Bank – 10,130

Contact Sincil Bank Stadium, Lincoln, LN5 8LD 0870 8992005

Tickets 0870 8991976

Website www.redimps.com

minibus. In 2002 he had to sack manager Alan Buckley because he couldn't afford to pay his wages, and the new and much cheaper incumbent Keith Alexander was given just three grand with which to rebuild the side. By the end of the season they were in the play-offs.

There have been two other promising spells in modern times. Graham Taylor, later to manage England, became the youngest manager in the league when he took over in 1972 aged just 28. After a terrible start – he came within hours of being sacked after failing to win any of his first 11 games – he went on to enjoy five excellent years at Sincil Bank, most notably in 1976, when Lincoln were runaway champions with a record number of points (74 – there were just two for a win in those days) and scoring 111 goals.

In the early eighties the club again flirted with success – in 1982 they missed out on promotion to the second division on the very last day of the season, and the following year they topped the table for four months. But then, disaster. The manager wanted more money, the board said no, the fans got cross, the board received death threats, and every one of them resigned.

The club went into a downward spiral and chalked up an unwanted first back in 1987 – becoming the first team to suffer automatic relegation to the conference. Though on a more positive note, Lincoln has dropped out of the Football League four times in its very long history and bounced back the following season on every occasion.

The future – there were lots of reasons to get excited in the summer of 2008 when the club picked up Stefan Oakes, described by his former manager John Gorman as the best passer of the ball in the country. Not only did he win the League Cup with Leicester, his dad is the guitarist in Showaddywaddy. Chief cheerleader was manager Peter Jackson, who declared: "It's a wonderful, wonderful signing for us. Stefan Oakes' left foot can peel carrots."

Did you know?... The theme from the *Dambusters* movie thunders around Sincil Bank whenever Lincoln score, accompanied by much waving and flapping of arms, aeroplane-style. The reason? Legendary 617 squadron and their bouncing bombs were based just outside Lincoln during the Second World War. There could be a new theme soon as the movie is being remade by none other than (the other) Peter Jackson.

Liverpool

"My son Foster is a fan of soccer. He was a goaltender. His brother was a defenseman."
Liverpool's American owner George Gillett spells out his impeccable footballing credentials.

No one who saw the 2005 Champions League final will ever forget it. When Liverpool trudged off the pitch at half-time they were lucky to be only three down, outclassed and ripped to shreds with humiliating ease by a Milan side at the top of its game. What happened in the second half was a miracle. I watched the match in a city centre sports bar with 2,000 Liverpool fans and a usually excitable Scouse mate who retreated into shock as the second half unfolded and the Reds staged their outrageous comeback. Pint untouched, jaw hanging, eyes glassy, senses unable to absorb the enormity of what was going on, opening his mouth just once to enquire in a gently confused way what the score was, unable to believe that Steven Gerrard had picked Liverpool off their arses in so dramatic a fashion or that the 3-3 score seared in the corner of the giant TV monitor could be real.

The success has been a long time coming. A generation ago Liverpool were the undisputed top dogs. Between 1973 and 1990 they won the title 11 times, the FA Cup three times and four back-to-back League Cups. And were kings of Europe four times in eight years.

Continuity was the key and the architect of it all was manager Bill

Shankly. When the Scot came to Anfield in 1959 the club was languishing in the second flight, the ground was dilapidated, the training facilities appalling. Obsessed with football, he became obsessive about Liverpool. It was his idea to hang a sign above the stairs that go down to the pitch bearing the legend "THIS IS ANFIELD" – the aim being to intimidate opponents. His idea of a good time was watching the reserves play Rochdale – which is exactly what he arranged as an outing for his wife as a special birthday treat.

Shankly had little time for referees, taking the view that they knew everything about the rules but nothing about the game. And he never missed an opportunity to put down other teams in general, and neighbours Everton in particular. Addressing the mourners at the funeral of Toffees goalscoring legend Dixie Dean, he said: "I know this is a sad occasion but I think Dixie would be surprised to learn that even in death he could draw a bigger crowd to Goodison than Everton on a Saturday afternoon."

The continuity continued in his backroom boys. When Shankly retired 15 year later after winning three championships, two FA Cups and the UEFA Cup, his successors included three men who had been key members of the Liverpool boot room, the place where the coaching staff traded tips, swapped stories and drank a lot of tea – namely Bob Paisley, Joe Fagan and Roy Evans. Paisley was in his fifties when he took the job, clocking up six championships and three European Cups in his

Nickname The Reds
Kit Red shirt, red shorts, red socks
Ground Anfield – 45,362
Contact Anfield Road, Liverpool, L4 0TH 0151 2608813
Tickets 0870 2202345
Website www.liverpoolfc.tv

nine years at the helm, and has an excellent case to be regarded as the most successful English manager of all time.

I have a vivid memory as a kid of Paisley giving a rare extended TV interview. He fidgeted in his chair with the uneasy smile of a man well out of his comfort zone, unused to being the centre of attention, surrounded by lights, cameras and crew, looking for all the world like my own granddad and dressed the same – I think a deeply unfashionable cardigan, with toggles, may have been involved. And when asked to explain the secret of his success, he explained patiently, in his gentle Geordie lilt, that football was a very simple game, and as long as a team passed the ball to one another and kept it and didn't allow the opposition to have it any longer than strictly necessary, success would come. I remember thinking at the time, it can't be that simple. But maybe it is. It worked for him.

Liverpool have been involved in two major tragedies. At the 1985 European Cup final at the Heysel Stadium in Belgium, 39 fans, mostly Juventus supporters, were killed when a dilapidated wall collapsed on them as they tried to escape a charge by Liverpool fans. There has never been an official inquiry into the disaster, although it is clear that poor stewarding, inadequate segregation and the poor construction of the stadium all played a factor – great chunks of the stadium were simply ripped out of the ground and used as missiles by warring fans. As a result, four years later, 14 Liverpool supporters were sentenced for involuntary manslaughter, while English clubs were banned from European competition for five years.

And in 1989, 96 fans were killed at the FA Cup semi-final against Nottingham Forest, played at Sheffield Wednesday's Hillsborough ground after police opened gates at the rear of the ground to ease a bottleneck of fans outside the stadium. This caused overcrowding in the central pens, crushing fans who were pressed up against fencing at the front of the terraces. The tragedy led to the Taylor Report and the compulsory introduction of all-seater stadia. A memorial to those who died stands at Anfield alongside the Shankly Gates.

It was another 15 years before Liverpool won their fifth Champions League and although the club has enjoyed eight cup successes in that period, it has never mounted a serious title challenge – runners-up in 2002 under Gerard Houllier was as good as it got.

Liverpool supporters may have been baffled by the crazily inconsistent team selection policy of manager Rafa Benitez, but they got right behind him when he criticised the club's transfer policy and found his position threatened by American owners Tom Hicks and George Gillett, who bought the club in 2007. Last season saw Benitez trying to keep his head down as much as possible, most notably at a press conference when, on being quizzed about internal politics at the club, he replied: "As always, I am focused on training and coaching my team." Nine times.

Will he still be at the club when it moves 300 yards down the road to a brand new stadium at Stanley Park? More to the point, when will the club move? When Hicks and Gillett bought the club they told the shareholders Liverpool would relocate to a new stadium as soon as possible. But in the summer of 2008 the plans went on ice with the owners blaming the credit crunch. With the club already £350m in debt and needing to borrow the same again to fund a new ground, the future is looking decidedly unsettled.

Legends? Too many to list. Ian Rush's 346 goals in all competitions is a club record; that 25 of them came against Everton made them all the sweeter. Younger readers who only know Alan Hansen as a curmudgeonly TV pundit moaning endlessly about defensive frailties should know he was the backbone of a team that won eight league championships and three European Cups.

Emlyn? A legendary name in the Kop where the late Emlyn Hughes dominated in the seventies and captained Liverpool to two European Cups. There must have been a lot of confusion in the Hughes household in those days. His son was also called Emlyn. His daughter? Emma Lynn.

Believe it or not... there's a Kop shrine beneath the swimming pool of Manchester United captain Gary Neville. A pair of crafty Scouse builders buried a tube containing a Liverpool scarf, fanzine and match programme below the foundations.

Bizarre injury... Do real men do the ironing? Liverpool keeper Michael Stensgaard had a go and it finished his career. The 21-year-old Dane tried to put up an ironing board in 1996 and crocked his shoulder.

Luton Town

"She should not be here. I know that sounds sexist but I am sexist, so I am not going to be anything other than that. We have a problem in this country with political correctness and bringing women into the game is not the way to improve refereeing. It is absolutely beyond belief. It is bad enough with incapable referees and linesmen but if you start bringing in women, you have big problems."

A bumper bag of hate mail winged its way to manager Mike Newell after his attack on assistant referee Amy Rayner. He apologised.

Giants led by pygmies? Arguably. The unluckiest fans in England? Definitely. Turn your eyes to Kenilworth Road, home of Luton Town and their ill-starred supporters. The Hatters shot out of the blocks in the 19th century, the first professional club in the south. Elected to the Football League as long ago as 1897, they blew it spectacularly. Financially mismanaged on an epic scale, the club was in such a bad way that when the Hatters finished bottom of the league just three years later, they didn't even bother to apply for re-election. It took another 20 years to win their place back.

Inept? Fast-forward to Luton's first chance to win serious silverware. The omens were looking good when the Hatters reached the 1959 FA Cup final against Nottingham Forest, a team they had trounced 5-1 just a few weeks earlier.

But preparations were a shambles, with the club owners on some crazed ego trip. Chairman Percy Mitchell picked the side and omitted all-time record goalscorer Gordon Taylor. Director Tony Hodgson led the team onto the Wembley pitch following a protracted row with the FA over whether he could wear his favourite hat. Half-time team talk? There wasn't one. Where was the manager? The club appeared managerless on the greatest day in its history? It was. Luton had actually appointed one but kept it a secret and told him not to start until the Monday after the final.

The Hatters were enjoying the first of their two spells in the first division at the time – captain Syd Owen won the Football Writers' Footballer of the Year award that season, the only time a Luton player has ever won it. By the time they reached their second major Wembley appearance against Arsenal in the 1988 League Cup final, they were in their second spell. Nevertheless, they were still a small club battling against big boys, and famously supported by the most popular man in Britain, comedian Eric Morecambe, who lived long enough to see his beloved team return to the top flight in 1982, two years before his death.

So the whole country was rooting for the Luton underdogs in the final against Arsenal (which they won, 3-2) and the following year against Nottingham Forest (lost, 3-1)? Er, no. By 1988 The Hatters were unquestionably the most loathed team in the land.

Whose fault? David Evans, right-wing MP for Welwyn Hatfield, devoted follower of the football-hating PM Margaret Thatcher and chairman of Luton Town Football Club. Travelling football fans hated him because he banned all away supporters from Kenilworth Road, a move which saw Luton booted out of the 1987 League Cup after he banned travelling Cardiff City supporters. Most football fans hated him because he was a staunch supporter of the batty compulsory football ID card scheme Thatcher was set on bringing in (and would have done had not the Taylor Report into the Hillsborough disaster not condemned it). The artificial pitch wasn't too popular either.

Since then the club has been in administration three times and Kenilworth Road is still as much a dump as it was in the fifties when they first talked about moving home. A barmy plan to build a stadium on stilts over the M1 has been explored and abandoned. Nuttier still… Mike Newell was appointed manager in 2003 after the club conducted a phone poll. Former chairman John Gurney was declared bankrupt in 2008. Chairman Bill Tomlins had to resign in 2007 after admitting making illegal payments. And the club, docked ten points in 2007-2008, started 2008-2009 in the fourth division on minus 30 points after failing to reach a voluntary agreement with creditors and as a result of the illegal payments row.

The future… Luton 2020, a new consortium fronted by TV presenter Nick Owen, is the latest consortium looking to turn things round at Kenilworth Road.

Roy of the Rovers?… Couldn't hold a candle to Joe Payne. The striker signed from a colliery side couldn't get a game in the first team and spent two wretched years in the reserves playing out of position at centre half. Until one freezing afternoon in April 1936, when a rash of injuries

forced the Hatters to pick him for the senior team in his favoured position for a home match against Bristol Rovers. A hat-trick in the first half,
another seven in the second; ten goals to his name in a 12-0 win makes
Payne the only man ever to have reached double figures in a Football
League match.

Macclesfield Town

The Football League always looked after its own. Year upon year the best non-league teams applied to join the big boys and were almost always kicked in the teeth, while the four sides propping up the fourth division applied for re-election, almost always successfully.

You'd have thought this might have changed for ever from 1987 when the league grudgingly gave in and offered a promotion place to the top team in the conference – but no. In the mid-nineties no fewer than three consecutive conference winners – Kidderminster Harriers, Macclesfield Town and Stevenage Borough – topped the table only to find their dreams in tatters because their grounds were, apparently, not up to scratch.

Did the league give

Nickname The Silkmen

Kit Royal blue shirt, white shorts, blue socks

Ground Moss Rose – 6,335 (2,599 seated)

Contact London Road, Macclesfield, Lancs SK11 7SP 01625 264686

Website www.mtfc.co.uk

Macclesfield a chance to improve Moss Rose in the close season prior to taking up its rightful place in the league? Of course not. The ground had to be improved by January 1st in the season before promotion. It was a classic catch-22. Clubs with coppers in their accounts didn't want to splash the cash needed to compete at the top level if they weren't promoted. But once they won the league it was too late to upgrade. For Macclesfield Town to be denied their chance in this way was particularly galling, given that fourth division Chester City had used Moss Rose as their temporary home for two years in the early nineties and the Football League hadn't had a problem then.

Macclesfield Town's eventual promotion was down to two men, although one tragically didn't live to see it. Chairman Arthur Jones was devastated when the club's promotion was blocked and he diverted money from his commodity-broking business into building two new stands to ensure it never happened again. When he committed suicide in September 1996, it was revealed that his business was on the point of going bust. His love of Macclesfield Town had cost him everything.

Sammy McIlroy was the man who steered the Silkmen into the league. The former Manchester United star had captained Northern Ireland at the 1986 World Cup and played in the team that sensationally beat host country Spain in the 1982 finals. He galvanised the club when appointed in 1993 and his reputation attracted players like former England international Peter Davenport, who ordinarily might have turned their noses up at conference football. The Ulsterman left to manage his country's team after Macclesfield had been promoted twice, in 1997 and 1998.

Crowning moment of their story so far – probably January 2007 when they took on Chelsea in the third round of the FA Cup at Stamford Bridge in front of 40,000. John Murphy sent supporters delirious when he equalised following Frank Lampard's opener. The day did not end happily – defender David Morley had to keep goal for most of the second half after Tommy Lee was sent off for bringing down Andriy Shevchenko, and the Silkmen were down to nine men for the final quarter of an hour when Murphy was unable to carry on and Town had used all three substitutes.

At a time when black managers are noticeably struggling to win appointments at league clubs, Macclesfield has had two in two years. Former Manchester United midfield man Paul "The Guvnor" Ince arrived in 2006 when the Silkmen were seemingly doomed to return to the conference – the first 12 matches had yielded a paltry four points – and guided them to the cup run that culminated at Chelsea and to safety, albeit just, before departing to MK Dons. And early in 2008 Keith Alexander stepped in. His predecessor Ian Brightwell had complained days earlier that Macclesfield were not ruthless enough on the pitch. Off the pitch it was a different story – the board sacked him after a run of five straight losses. Alexander's first act as manager was to sign former international sprinter Fola Onibuje; his second was to release him after just one appearance from the subs bench. Why? "Fola can play like Maradona, but he can also play like Mrs Maradona."

Did you know?... Wayne Rooney's car was a familiar sight outside Moss Rose in 2008, but he is unlikely to be signing in the near future. Younger brother John has successfully come through the youth team ranks, coached by club legend John Askey (700 plus games), and made his full debut at the end of in 2007.

The Silkmen?... At one time there were 72 silk mills in Macclesfield.

Manchester City

"England did nothing in the World Cup, so why are they bringing books out? We got beat in the quarter-finals, I played like shit, here's my book. Who wants to read that? I don't."
Joey Barton, then at City, speaks for the nation in 2006.

Manchester City is the richest club in the world. Manchester City is the richest club in the world. It's there in black and white but it still beggars belief.

On the morning of September 1st, 2008 every self-respecting football fan was where all football fans are on the last day of the transfer window – hunched over a computer screen, all day, eyes glued, eyes glazed, keeping tabs on every rumour, whisper and half-truth about who's going where, praying their team will sign someone half-decent and that the star man upon whom every hope and dream for the season depends isn't going to bugger-off before midnight.

At 10.17am, a rumour circulated that Robinho shirts were being run off in the Chelsea club shop. Four minutes later, reports that the Abu Dhabi United Group was taking over City. At 18.44, the first indication that City were after Robinho. Five minutes after midnight, confirmation. Robinho was a Citizen. It didn't really sink in until 12 days later, when the little Brazilian stepped up to crash home a wonderful free kick against Chelsea.

Just a few weeks earlier the previous owner, Thai multimillionaire

Thaksin Shinawatra, had pulled off the seemingly impossible and made the whole country feel sorry for Sven-Goran Eriksson. The generally unloved former England coach had been a success for City, winning ten home games on the spin in his first – and what turned out to be his last – season in charge and pulling off the

Nickname The Blues, or the Citizens
Kit Sky blue shirt, white shorts, blue socks
Ground City of Manchester Stadium – 48,000
Contact Sportcity, Rowsley St, Manchester M11 3FF 0870 0621894
Website www.mcfc.co.uk

double over the Reds, but still got the sack. City-mad Oasis leader Noel Gallagher branded his dismissal as "beyond a joke", adding: "he has turned it around and given us a bit of style, dignity and grace and restored the fans' pride in the club."

It had taken a long time. Forty years ago the future looked sky blue. At least it did when the BBC started televising matches in colour at the end of the sixties. Champions in 1968, City took the FA Cup the following year, the year after that both the Cup Winners' Cup and the League Cup. With England's most talented midfielder Colin Bell running the show, Mike Summerbee terrorising defenders down the right flank and pugnacious Franny Lee with his torpedo boots upfront, City in full flow was an awesome sight.

They did all this despite having a goalie remarkable for his total lack of interest in football. Harry Dowd was a qualified plumber, never happier than when he had his arm curled around a u-bend, entirely unapologetic about finding the business of football a total bore. According to Summerbee, coach Malcolm Allison once ended a dressing room team talk with the words: "Harry, we are playing Arsenal today and they're in red and white."

City should probably have won the title again in 1972 – the club was four points clear at the top in March in an era when teams earned two points for a win – but their challenge ebbed away after the club signed Rodney Marsh, the flamboyant if unpredictable England international whose presence threw the whole team out of kilter.

Marsh himself admitted as much. A classic English maverick, he famously scuppered his England career after just six matches during the team talk given by Sir Alf Ramsey before the 1973 World Cup qualifier against Wales. When Sir Alf promised to pull him off at half-time unless he worked harder, Marsh shot back with: "Bloody hell, boss! At City all we get is a cup of tea and an orange."

City's rise coincided with the decline of their rivals United – the Reds went 26 years without winning the title – and in 1974 it was City that despatched United to the second division. United needed to win their last game of the season at Old Trafford to be certain of beating the drop but went down 1-0, with former United hero Denis Law scoring the winner with a cheeky back heel that turned out to be his last kick in league football.

Noel was once the richest man at City

The club traces its history back to 1880 and, unusually, it was founded by a woman. Anna Connell was a vicar's daughter looking to give the local youth an alternative to the traditional pursuits of boozing and fighting. It's had its fair share of highs and lows – more than its fair share, City fans might say. In 1904 they nearly pulled off a league and cup double, beating Bolton in the cup and finishing runners-up in the league. But then City went on to hand the title to rivals United – no fewer than 17 of their players were banned from the club after receiving illegal payments in 1906-07, and many of them went on to sign for United, who promptly won the title the following year.

In the thirties, another unlikely upset. Winners of the title in 1937, the club was relegated the following year – the only champions ever to be relegated – and went down despite scoring 80 goals, the highest total in the league. That season only 16 points separated first and last place (with three points for a win, the gap would have been 18 points). What a contrast with 2007-08 where the gap between first and last was a yawning 76-point chasm.

Other highlights include the 1956 Cup final where City triumphed 3-1 against Birmingham, despite keeper Bert Trautmann playing the final 15 minutes of the game with a broken neck. The former German paratrooper played 545 games for the club and eventually ended up with an honorary OBE for promoting international co-operation through football. That didn't look likely when fans first got wind he was about to sign in 1949 – a 20,000-strong mob took to the streets waving banners that read "Off With the German", and worse, and the club was deluged with hate mail.

A German with a sense of humour, Trautmann was twice sent off: once for booting a ball up the referee's backside, the second time for telling the ref who'd booked him that his name was Stanley Matthews.

Ten years ago, City created another unwanted record, becoming the first side to have won a European trophy to be relegated to the third division. Since then there's been the Keegan era – the manager mastermind promotion to the Premier League, breaking all sorts of club records along the way; an ultimately unsuccessful spell under former full-back Stuart Pearce; and yet another unwanted record, scoring just ten goals at home all season. City fans are counting on all that being behind them now. If we're talking dollars, their club is in the hands of football's first trillionaire.

Welcome to... the Bell End. City bosses made fools of themselves when they invited fans to name the new west stand at the City of Manchester Stadium after a club legend. Midfield hero Colin Bell would probably have won anyway. He won by a landslide after rival fans thought it would be fun to vote for a Bell End. The club refused to recognise the result, declared Joe Mercer was the winner, upset their own fans, outraged Colin Bell's family, then launched an investigation before announcing that the winner was... the Colin Bell stand. It's a fabulous erection.

Bizarre injury... Goal celebrations were especially hazardous for Manchester City striker Shaun Goater. In 2003 he kicked an advertising hoarding in a frenzy of excitement when team-mate Nicolas Anelka scored and damaged his knee. While in 1998 he leaped on the turf to celebrate a strike in a game against Stoke City – and broke his arm.

Manchester United

"Supporting Manchester United will become a criminal offence for anyone born south of Crewe."
Monster Raving Loony Party election manifesto, 2001.

When Elvis Presley exploded into the charts in the fifties he was both worshipped and hated. His hustler manager Colonel Tom Parker made a fortune selling I Love Elvis merchandise. I Hate Elvis? Parker had it covered, flogging thousands of badges and making another mint.

Manchester United have been the biggest club in England for over 50 years and for the last 15, the most successful. Also, the most hated.

Why? They say that an American respects a neighbour with a bigger house; an Englishman would rather burn it down. Historically, we've always put heroes on pedestals, then wanted to knock them off. United's consistent success has undoubtedly bred envy, jealously and dislike from opposition fans.

But the hatred of United runs much deeper than that. When Liverpool was the overwhelmingly dominant team in the seventies and eighties, their relentless consistency commanded respect. When Nottingham Forest were in their pomp, winning successive European Cups, they were universally popular, everyone's second team. Back then any English club competing in Europe could count on the support of the vast majority of English fans. It's only since the Reds started to dominate that pubs throughout the land have been packed on match nights

Nickname The Red Devils

Kit Red shirt, white shorts, black socks

Ground Old Trafford – 76,100

Contact Sir Matt Busby Way, Manchester, M16 0RA 0870 4421994

Tickets 0870 4421999

Website www.manutd.com

with fans supporting ABU – Anyone But United. Even when they're playing Germans.

How has it come to this? The club was formed as a railway works team in 1878, joined the Football League in 1892 and nearly went bust in 1902 – their ground was closed down by bailiffs. Ironically, it was a payments scandal at Manchester City that gave United their first big break. The cream of the City team defected to United after 17 of them received life bans from playing for the Citizens and formed the nucleus of the side that won United's first title in 1908. An FA Cup followed and a second title came in 1911, but after that the club went into decline, eventually dropping into the second division and going without a title for 40 years.

Three titles in the fifties established United as a major force, but it was the Munich air disaster in 1958 that brought the club to the attention of the world. The media was far less interested in football than it is now. There was no football on television – not that many people had televisions – and a fraction of the coverage in the newspapers that there is today. Suddenly United were on the front pages at home and across the world and newsreel footage of the tragedy was seen by hundreds of millions.

It was a tragedy that played out in public for months. After the shock of the crash, the tales of heroism emerged – goalkeeper Harry Gregg dragged Jackie Blanchflower, Bobby Charlton and Dennis Viollet to safety. Two weeks later, more tragedy with the death of Duncan Edwards, the youngest player in the history of the first division and the youngest to play for England. When the club reached the FA Cup final three months later, the whole world was watching. Manager Matt Busby, who had spent two months in hospital and had twice received the last rites, returned to work on the day of the final.

The sympathy and goodwill felt in England and all over the world towards United was enormous, and over the next decade they built on it by assembling a team that won the first division twice, playing entertaining and thrilling football. When they became the first English side to win the European Cup in 1968, it contained no fewer than three European Footballers of the Year – Bobby Charlton, Denis Law and George Best. The boy from Belfast played a huge part in expanding United's appeal. The first footballer to be feted like a pop star, and one of the few to live like one – his sexual conquests included no fewer than three Miss Worlds – he single-handedly brought Manchester United into the lives of millions of people, especially women, who until then knew little about football and cared less.

Bizarre injury... Manchester United goalie Alex Stepney hollered at his defenders in a match against Birmingham City in 1975 and dislocated his jaw. Midfielder Brian Greenhoff had to take over.

United then went 26 years without winning the title, and for most of those didn't even come close. In a strange way it didn't seem to matter. They were the biggest club in England and were treated as such. Money talked. When the TV companies started showing live football in the eighties, it felt as though United were on every week, TV bosses calculating, correctly, that they would draw more viewers and attract more advertising if they constantly showed England's most popular team. This became a self-fulfilling prophecy – the more United was on the box and constantly sold as England's biggest side, the more converts they made. For anyone who wasn't a United supporter the commentaries then, as now, were skewed towards them, the games presented as challenges for United to overcome.

The goodwill United had enjoyed for so long began to ebb away. True, they made thousands of converts, including a little boy from east London called Beckham who grew up in an era when United was the only team he could guarantee to watch regularly. Little surprise he had his heart set on joining them from an early age. But fans of other clubs grew resentful at seeing parks and playgrounds increasingly packed with children sporting United shirts. Nowhere more so than in Lancashire, where fans of clubs with glorious histories – Burnley, Blackburn, Preston – grew accustomed to the sight of hordes of fans wearing red making their way to the station on match days.

And United came to appear more brash and arrogant. They had bigger crowds and more money and they flaunted it. Eighties manager Ron Atkinson came to symbolise this. Dripping in bracelets and medallions, forever supping champagne and rarely out of the headlines, he was the public face of a new United that had more to do with power and money than the traditions of Busby and Edwards, Charlton and Best. Just weeks after the Heysel Stadium disaster, which resulted in British teams being banned from European competitions, United went to the High Court to try and get the ban overturned. It was crassly insensitive and smacked of a club obsessed with money, as did the decision to sell club hero Mark Hughes to Barcelona for a record £2m when he didn't want to go.

In the nineties the club began to exploit its brand with massive intensity, forever bringing out new strips and putting immense pressure on parents to fork out for a new one every few months. Since then, of course, most clubs have followed suit, but as the first out of the blocks United took most of the flak. They made more enemies in 2000 when, under pressure from the FA and the committee organising England's 2006 World Cup bid, they opted out of the FA Cup to take part in the FIFA World Club Championship in Brazil.

The irony is that since Alex Ferguson took charge in 1986 he has produced a succession of wonderful teams playing fast, attractive and entertaining football, and has ten Premier League titles, five FA Cups and two European Cups to show for it. But in 2008, Manchester United is officially the seventh most hated brand in Britain. Then again, it's also the 28th most loved brand.

The future?... The next couple of years are going to be very interesting. A club that for many years was the wealthiest in England is no longer the wealthiest in Manchester, and in 2008 was paying £60m a year in interest payments related to the debt the controlling American Glazer family incurred when they borrowed the money to buy it.

"I hope they all get bloody diarrhoea."

United's decision to opt out of the FA Cup in 2000 did not go down well with former Nottingham Forest boss Brian Clough.

Middlesbrough

"He carried everything, then went to fetch the car. Where do you find blokes like that? I could tell he wasn't from Middlesbrough."

A supermarket shopper is stunned after spotting midfield man
Christian Karembeu and his wife in a Teesside supermarket.

Boro have spent all but two years of the 20th century in the top two divisions of English football. A remarkable record of consistency, especially given that in all that time they won precisely nought worth mentioning. Which made the eventual moment of triumph when it came all the sweeter. One hundred years of woe ended at the Millennium Stadium in 2004 when Boro went two up against Bolton inside seven minutes and went on to lift the League Cup.

When Boro first joined the Football League in 1899 they were so strapped for cash that manager Jack Robson refused to travel to away games – it was a way of saving a few pennies. Fast-forward just six years and it was a very different story – questions were raised in Parliament over the "immoral" purchase of striker Alf Common from neighbours Sunderland for the mind-boggling, record-breaking sum of £1,000 – one parliamentarian plaintively asking: "Where will it all end?"

There was some success before the First World War, with Boro recording their highest-ever finish in 1914 when they came third. In the twenties and thirties a goalscoring phenomenon, George Camsell, rattled in 345 goals in 453 games for the Boro. In his first season he notched up 63 in all competitions and went on to become the club's leading scorer for the next ten seasons. He rates highly in the pantheon of Boro legends, which include left-back and England captain George Hardwick and inside forward Wilf Mannion. Both men are immortalised in statues outside the Riverside Stadium, the club's home after leaving Ayresome Park in 1995. Brian Clough's managerial exploits have over-shadowed his career on the pitch, so it is worth pointing out that his strike record of 197 goals in 213 matches at Boro is the best goals-per-game ratio in English footballing history. He too has a statue, not outside the ground but in Albert Park, close to the house where he was born. Unveiled in 2007, it shows him striding to Ayresome Park with his boots slung over his shoulder.

Nickname Boro/The Smoggies
Kit Red shirt, red shorts, red socks
Ground Riverside Stadium – 35,100
Contact Middlesbrough, Cleveland TS3 6RS 0844 4996789
Tickets 0844 4991234
Website www.mfc.co.uk

The latest chapter in Boro's history began in 1986. The club came within ten minutes of being booted out of the league. The FA was going through one of its tough-guy phases, with secretary Graham Kelly threatened to throw the book at the club if it didn't sort itself out. Middlesborough was wound up, a provisional liquidator was appoint-ed, the gates to the ground were padlocked, phones cut off, staff sent home. Steve Gibson, a young local entrepreneur who had made a for-tune from the haulage business, got a consortium together to rescue the club and registered it just before the deadline expired. He was the man who subsequently masterminded the move to the Riverside, lured Italian goalscoring legend Fabrizio Ravanelli and Brazilian midfield genius Juninho to the club, and saw them lose three Wembley finals in 12 months prior to the triumph in 2004, the same year he was given the freedom of the town.

Implausible moments? They say lightning doesn't strike twice but Boro staged two of the most astonishing comebacks in European football history during the 2006 UEFA Cup run which took them to the final. In the second leg of the quarter finals they were three down to Basle with less than an hour to go, needing to score four to stay in the competition. And did, with substitute Massimo Maccarone slotting home the winner in the very last minute. The delirious scenes at the Riverside were repeated in the semis where, three behind to Steaua Bucharest with less than an hour to go, they again banged in four with Maccarone, again a substitute, popping up with a last-minute header to take them through. Sadly, there were to be no miracles in the final where Boro lost heavily to a very classy Seville side.

Equally implausible? Former Boro star Bernie Slaven publicly promised to bare his bottom in the window of Binn's department store should the team overturn 68 years of history by winning at Manchester United in 1998. They did. And so did he – a huge crowd thronged the shop to see Slaven displaying the 3-2 score emblazoned on his cheeks.

The Smoggies?... It started as an insult from rival fans but many Boro supporters have come to embrace the nickname, a legacy from the not-too-distant past when the town was permanently blanketed with a yellowish fug of pollutant that reeked of rotten eggs and cats. Until 2003, away fans from north-east neighbours Newcastle United and Sunderland would turn up at the Riverside wearing dust masks and chemical suits but Boro had a sense of humour failure when the Iran war broke out on the grounds that they were "inappropriate, given the world situation".

Millwall

"At 6.45pm the Millwall supporters were taken under escort towards the stadium. As they passed a public house, a group of 30-40 males came out and bottles and glasses were thrown and pub windows smashed. After a short while it became apparent that both groups were from Millwall and each thought the other were City supporters."

National Criminal Intelligence Service report, March 2001, on Bristol City v Millwall.

Let's get the hooliganism thing out of the way. Yes, Millwall had problems with hooligans years ago. Most football clubs did. There was trouble at Millwall, as there was at many other London clubs – notably West Ham and Chelsea. In 2002, a sickeningly violent clash following an end of season game against Birmingham left 47 police officers and 24 horses injured after they were bombarded with bricks, paving stones, thunder flashes and flares. The club reacted by banning away supporters from the New Den for the next two years and introducing a membership scheme for home fans.

But… hooliganism as it existed in the seventies and eighties has all but disappeared. In 2007 Millwall topped the arrests league for the third division, but 57 arrests over a year averages out at well under two per match. Which is not very many. Even the word hooligan has an old-fashioned ring to it these days. Strict fan segregation, sophisticated

Nickname The Lions

Kit Royal blue shirt, white shorts, blue socks

Ground The Den – 20,146

Contact Zampa Road, London SE16 3LN 0207 2311222

Tickets 0207 2319999

Website www.millwallfc.co.uk

police intelligence, surveillance cameras everywhere and all-seater stadia have all played a part in reducing trouble, as have family initiatives and community schemes run by many clubs. Millwall has been particularly hot on anti-racist initiatives, pioneering a text service for fans to report racist abuse.

So why do Millwall get singled out? Perhaps because there's always been something warrior-like about the club. They've been singing "No One Likes Us, We Don't Care" (to the tune of Rod Stewart's "Sailing") for at least ten years but the roots of defiance go right back to the beginning of the last century. Early on the club adopted the lion emblem along with the motto "We Fear No Foe Where 'ere We Go" and on the day the Den opened in 1910 a brass lion bearing the inscription "We Will Never Turn Our Backs To The Enemy" was presented on the pitch.

The fans were equally defiant. Most of them worked in the docks – until the sixties, Millwall was the only ground in the country where Saturday games kicked off at 3.15pm, to allow workers time to finish their shift and walk to New Cross – and there were thousands of them, the club regularly attracting 40,000-plus gates when in the third division and generating an intimidating atmosphere. Back in those days it was common to applaud good play by your opponents. Not at Millwall.

The Lions made an early impact, reaching the FA Cup semi-final in 1900 and 1903 although they weren't admitted into the Football League until 1920. What success they had was confined to the cup – in

1927 they defeated Huddersfield Town, champions for the previous three seasons, and ten years later became the first third division side to reach the semi-final, disposing of three first division clubs in the process.

For many years Millwall was the only London side never to have played in the first division. In 1988 they cracked it, thanks largely to a strike force of Teddy Sheringham and Tony Cascarino – the pair struck 135 times in their 325 league appearances for the club. Footballers, generally speaking, do not do interesting autobiographies – deadly dull, most of them – but Cascarino is a glorious exception and his story *Full Time* is one of the most revealing football books ever written.

The promotion-winning side lasted two years in the top flight – Millwall's only time there to date – with its midfield skilfully marshalled by one of football's all-time hard men, Terry Hurlock. Was he as aggressive as Dennis Wise, player-manager in 2003? Wise spelled out his philosophy early on: "Bookings for getting stuck in are OK. Even the odd red card is all right, as long as it is for giving your all. I want my team to be horrible. I want opponents to hate playing us".

Under Wise the club found itself in the unfamiliar position of being the nation's favourite when it reached the FA Cup final in 2004. The English always like an underdog and Millwall were rank outsiders in a match against Manchester United, putting up a spirited fight in the first half but eventually going down 3-0.

Nightmare season? In January 1996 Millwall topped the second division and looked a good bet for an automatic promotion to the Premier League. But a 6-0 hammering by Sunderland had a devastating effect on morale. It all turned sour and by May the club had slid to the foot of the table and were relegated.

Did you know?... Many managers complain they don't get long enough to prove their worth. Steve Claridge has a stronger case than most. The much-travelled striker was appointed player-manager in June 2005 but fired 36 days later, after a boardroom power struggle, before the Lions had played a single competitive match . The newly reinstated chair Theo Paphitis rubbed salt in the wound afterwards by telling everyone that the club would be relegated unless Claridge was removed – though in the event Millwall went down without him.

Milton Keynes Dons

"I've stood and watched Wimbledon since 1979 and now I don't have a club to support any more. I won't be going to Milton Keynes. It has to be the death of our club."

Marc Jones, spokesman for the Wimbledon Independent Supporters' Association, following the decision to relocate to Milton Keynes.

Have MK Dons served their time? Are we ready to forgive them? Those are questions that have been troubling football fans over the last couple of years. Their crime was a heinous one. Built in 1967, the town didn't have a league football team of its own. So they stole one. A lot of bollocks has been written about this over the years, so let's spell it out. They nicked a team. They were always going to steal one. As it turned out they stole Wimbledon FC, but if it hadn't been Wimbledon it would have been someone else. Your team. Mine. Anyone they could get their hands on.

The idea was the brainchild of current club chairman, millionaire music mogul Pete Winkelman. Obsessed with the idea that a town the size of Milton Keynes deserved a Football League team, he wanted a quick fix. So he set out to prey on the weak and the vulnerable.

There was no shortage of candidates. Billions of pounds have poured into the game in the last few years, but the vast majority of league clubs have been existing on pence. Most of them have lived through financial crisis, half of them have been in administration. Winkelman stalked clubs that were having trouble redeveloping their grounds. He sized up Luton Town. He sniffed around QPR. He eyed up Barnet. He courted all of them. He was a wolf in search of a Red Riding Hood. At Wimbledon, he hit the jackpot.

In a bizarre way, Wimbledon were the victims of their own extraordinary success. A Southern League team as recently as 1977, they soared into the top flight in just nine incredible years and two years later defeated the then all-conquering Liverpool to win the FA Cup with a tough, direct, no-nonsense style of football that regularly embarrassed more illustrious opponents.

Their ground at Plough Lane was quite posh for a Southern League team. But following the Taylor Report into the Hillsborough disaster published in 1990, it clearly wasn't up to the safety requirements of top-flight football. From 1991 Wimbledon ground-shared with Crystal Palace. Dons' owner Sam Hamman huffed and puffed about how Merton Council was thwarting his attempts to build another ground – although in reality they bent over backwards to help in all sorts of ways and actually granted him planning permission for a new stadium which he never pursued.

Villains of the piece include Hamman, who sold Plough Lane for £5m (originally to Safeway, who sold it on for flats) and pocketed another £25m when he sold his stake in the club; the insanely naive Norwegians Kjell Inge Rokke and Bjorn Gelsten, who squandered £50m under the delusion that the Irish FA would allow them to move the club lock, stock and barrel to Dublin; the independent commission appointed by the Football Association which, unbelievably, swallowed Wimbledon's line that it could no longer exist in London, even though the club failed to produce any audited accounts to back up their case; and the Football League, which had nothing in its regulations to stop a club being ripped out of its community and transported 60 miles up the road.

Nickname The Dons	
Kit White shirt, white shorts, white socks	
Ground stadium:mk – 22,000	
Contact Denbigh, Milton Keynes, Bucks MK1 1ST 01908 622922	
Tickets 01908 622900	
Website www.mkdons.co.uk	

So it came to pass that MK Dons swallowed up Wimbledon and in doing so became the most hated club in the land. Universally derided as Franchise FC, supporters' groups nationwide urged fans to boycott their games. Fewer than 200 Wimbledon fans continued to support the club and in 2003 just 13 fans travelled to an away match at West Brom. The Football Supporters' Association refused to admit the club's fans to become members. And the Dons went on a downward spiral, going into administration, selling the entire team and plummeting into the fourth division.

And now? The club has a shiny new 22,000-capacity ground, stadium:mk, attracts healthy crowds approaching 15,000, and took 30,000 supporters to Wembley in 2008 to see them beat Grimsby and win their first silverware, the Football League Trophy. A few weeks later the club topped the table to win promotion to England's third division under manager Paul Ince, who then left to take up the top job at Blackburn Rovers in the close season. The future looks brighter, although in summer 2008 the credit crunch was casting a gloom over the new stadium, with major retail partners on whom its future depends pulling out of the project.

And the fans? The FSA has reached an uneasy compromise with supporters, admitting them into the fold after the club agreed to return all Wimbledon's trophies to the borough of Merton. Do they deserve to be ostracised for all time? Probably not – after all, the theft of Wimbledon was nothing to do with them. Is it better to see kids from Milton Keynes supporting their local team rather than a glamorous Premier League side hundreds of miles away? Definitely yes. But make no mistake: if Wimbledon had never existed, there would still be a league club based at Milton Keynes and a different set of fans would be mourning the theft of their team. And four years on, that still stinks.

Believe it or not... Hats off to AFC Wimbledon. The club formed by supporters of Wimbledon FC is enjoying a meteoric rise through the lower leagues, with four promotions (and two unsuccessful play-offs) in just six years. It starts the season in the Conference South, needing two further promotions to rise to the Football League. It also holds the record for the most unbeaten league games by any senior English side, going 78 matches without defeat.

MK Dons return their ill-gotten gains to their rightful owners

Morecambe

"The inevitable was always going to happen."
Morecambe manager Jim Harvey after the Shrimps get well and truly potted by Ipswich.

A love affair between rival fans is a rare and beautiful thing. For one thing, they rarely meet. Police keep them apart in city centres, many grounds have strict segregation, many pubs are no-go areas for away supporters, rolling up on match day and buying a ticket at the turnstile is getting increasingly difficult, and up and down the land fans routinely refer to their near neighbours up the road as the Scum, or worse.

It's not unusual to see home supporters – typically the ugly, socially inadequate ones – their snarling faces contorted with rage because they think they've clocked an away fan who's had the temerity to sit in the home section, gesticulating wildly for the stewards to eject these inter-lopers.

So how come a posse of Ipswich Town fans were spotted supporting Morecambe in their FA Trophy semi-final appearance back in 2002? Because the previous year the then high-flying Premier League side (they finished fifth that season) had visited the seaside resort for a third-round FA Cup tie, only the second time Morecambe had made it that far in 80 years, and were treated like royalty.

When Morecambe repeated the feat just two years later and drew Ipswich away, it was party time. Hundreds of Shrimps supporters

Nickname The Shrimps

Kit Red shirt, white shorts, red and white socks

Ground Christie Park – 6,400 (1,200 seated)

Contact Lancaster Rd, Morecambe, Lancs LA4 5TJ

01524 411797

Website www.morecambefc.com

swarmed to Ipswich for their first ever competitive match against top-flight opponents kitted out in full Eric Morecambe regalia – macs and caps, pipes and horn-rimmed specs. The late great comedian, whose statue dominates the promenade, took his stage name from his home town and was an occasional visitor to Christie Park, standing on the cinder track at what is now the Car Wash End.

Two third-round appearances in three years were all down to manager Jim Harvey. Football management is a cruel game. Apart from a memorable day out at Wembley in 1974 when Morecambe won the FA Trophy, the club had had nothing much to shout about. Ever. And when he arrived in 1994 Morecambe had been marooned in the Northern Premier League for over 20 years and were going nowhere fast under the long-suffering gaze of a paltry 200 fans.

Harvey transformed them – runners-up in his first season, promoted in the second, and then a run of nine years in the conference, where they finished in the top ten most years, narrowly missed promotion a couple of times, and embarked on their stupendous cup runs.

When Harvey was struck down by a heart attack in 2005, he sent for his old mate Sammy McIlroy – Harvey had been assistant when he managed Northern Ireland – to stand in for him until he got better. But the day he got better and went back to work, he was summoned to an emergency board meeting and sacked – with McIlroy installed as permanent manager. And could only watch as the side he had built went on to win the conference play-offs the very next year, beating Exeter City in front of 40,000 at Wembley.

One year on and things are looking good. Eleventh in their first year and two second division scalps in their first appearance in the League Cup – the Shrimps won away at both Preston and Wolves – there are plans for a new ground, which may be ready in time for the 2009-10 season.

Local hero?... Defender and captain Jim Bentley became a fan idol. Let go by Manchester City as a youngster, it took him over ten years to realise his dream of returning to league football.

Newcastle United

"The only way we will get into Europe is by ferry!"

Kevin Keegan dampens optimism on his return to St James' Park.

At the start of 2008, Newcastle fans dared to hope. A billionaire owner behind the scenes, the legend that was Kevin Keegan back in the hot seat. What could go wrong this time?

Newcastle fans – fans everywhere, actually – would do well to read *The Clown Prince of Football*, the autobiography written by former Newcastle wizard Len Shackleton, and in particular the chapter called "The Average Director's Knowledge of Football". It's one page long. And blank.

Keegan's reign at Newcastle was doomed within days of his return. Leeds manager Dennis Wise was appointed without his knowledge and over his head as some sort of superexecutive, based in London but in charge of transfers, scouting and youth development.

Anyone with any knowledge of Keegan knew instantly this was a time bomb that could detonate at any moment. In the summer it did, Keegan undermined and his position untenable as his own transfer targets were ignored, while players were sold and transfer-listed without his knowledge or approval.

Newcastle fans vented their anger and owner Mike Ashley put the club up for sale. For Magpie fans, Ashley and Wise were the Cockney Mafia – London based and out of touch with what they wanted.

United are a club with proud and passionate supporters and a glorious history. Four titles, six FA Cup wins and a succession of legends who have worn the Number 9 shirt. Wee Hughie Gallagher scoring close to a goal a game, "Wor Jackie" Milburn with his 200 goals, the bandy-legged genius that was Malcolm McDonald. The indomitable force that was Alan Shearer, signed by his home-town club from Blackburn in 1996 for what was then a world record £15m fee and who repaid them by becoming the club record goalscorer. Most recently Michael Owen, finally finding form after years dogged by injury.

Nickname The Magpies/The Toon
Kit Black and white striped shirt, black shorts, black socks
Ground St James' Park – 52,387
Contact Newcastle-upon-Tyne NE1 4ST 0191 2018400
Tickets 0191 2611571
Website www.nufc.co.uk

But the bald truth is that the club hasn't won a major domestic honour since 1955 after close on half a century of chronic mismanagement. The club's fans have been starved, while the club's owners burrowed their snouts in the trough and got fat.

None fatter than former club chairman Freddy Shepherd. He became a nationwide figure of fun when it was revealed he had been whoring around the world at the club's expense with his director buddy Douglas Hall. Geneva, Amsterdam, London, New York: a host of hookers in every town.

Le Mans is famous for its 24-hour road race. Shepherd and Hall set a horizontal endurance record of their own there, forking out for two French prostitutes, two Russians, two Poles, a Serb. And a Chinese. Could the married duo not get what they wanted back home?

Apparently not. According to Shepherd, "Newcastle girls are all dogs. England is full of them. The girls are ugly and they're dogs".

Shepherd was equally contemptuous of club hero Alan Shearer ("Boring – we call him Mary Poppins.") and laid into former manager Kevin Keegan ("Shirley Temple"). What had Keegan done to deserve this? His crime – to say "thanks but no thanks" when the pair tried to drag him into a brothel in Amsterdam.

By the time Shepherd sold up he had trousered around £50m, while former owner Sir John Hall and his family made about £100m from a club purchased in the eighties for just £3m.

Where did the cash come from? The fans. Nearly 10,000 of them lost money when the club floated on the stock exchange, while the directors pocketed millions. They were then victims of another money-making wheeze when the club charged them a £500 bond to "guarantee" their season tickets for the next ten years: a guarantee that turned out to be worthless when the club decided to exploit some of those seats for corporate hospitality. Season ticket holders who'd been paying £400 a year were told they'd have to pay £1,300 a year to keep their seat.

Newcastle fans love the shirt and the club exploited it to the hilt. Sir John, in one of his most preposterous moments, announced: "We are like the Basques. We are fighting for a nation. The Geordie Nation." A Geordie himself, he understood how important the club was to the identity of supporters hit hard in the eighties by the destruction of the industries that had made the city famous, shipbuilding and mining. His replica shirts were the uniform of the Geordie nation – St James' Park is always a sea of black and white. The club strips flying out of the shop at £50 a pop were knocked up by cheap labour in the Far East at five quid a time, a detail Hall and Shepherd let slip when suckered by the *News of the World*'s fake sheikh.

The good times in the last 20 years came courtesy of two managers

– Keegan and Sir Bobby Robson. In his two years as a player Keegan had become a club legend, lifting the side out of the second division and hitting 48 goals in 78 league appearances. As a manager he repeated the trick, winning promotion and transforming the team into the most entertaining side in the land, thrilling going forward but dodgy at the back. This failing cost the Magpies the title in 1996, despite being 12 points clear at the top of the table with just three months to go. Sir Bobby arrived with the club in disarray following the sacking of Ruud Gullitt in 1999 and enjoyed considerable success, guiding the team to three consecutive top-five finishes before being sacked by Shepherd.

What happens to United under new ownership promises to be one of the more fascinating stories of 2009.

Believe it or not... successful players usually spend their teen years eating, drinking and sleeping football rather than, say, studying geography. In Keegan's first spell at the club he was economical with the truth when he persuaded midfielder Rob Lee to join the Magpies from Charlton Athletic: "He nearly went to Middlesbrough but I told him Newcastle was nearer London. Luckily footballers believe things like that."

Bizarre injury... Leeds, Blackburn and Newcastle defender David Batty ruptured his Achilles tendon when he was hit by a child on a tricycle.

"Sorry, son..."
The famous faces that failed to make the team

TV funnyman **Angus Deayton** had a schoolboy trial with Crystal Palace in 1968.

The O's had a look at the footballing skills of actor and singer **David Essex** in 1962.

Bandleader **Billy Cotton** was a regular for Brentford Reserves before the Second World War.

Comedian **Stan Boardman** tried out for Liverpool as a 17-year-old.

Funnyman **Bradley Walsh** turned pro with Brentford in 1976 but had to retire at 20 with ankle problems.

Impressionist **Mike Yarwood** had trials with Oldham Athletic and Stockport County but was better in the boardroom, becoming County's vice-president.

The **Duke of Westminster** – Britain's second richest man – went for a trial with Fulham aged 15. Just as well he didn't get through – his dad disapproved of all that hugging and kissing.

Take That's **Mark Owen** went for try-outs with both Rochdale and Manchester United.

Pop star **Rod Stewart** was a Brentford apprentice at 17.

Comedian **Eddie Large** wasn't amused at getting turned down by Manchester City.

Blow Monkeys front man **Dr Robert** tried out for Norwich City.

Comic **Ricky Tomlinson** turned down a goalkeeping trial at Scunthorpe United.

Out for a duck. England cricket captain **Mike Gatting** went for trials with Arsenal.

A late scorer. **Gavin Rossdale**, former lead singer with Bush and husband of Gwen Stefani, had trials with Chelsea as a lad.

"Rising Damp" and "Reggie Perrin" star **Leonard Rossiter** was targeted by Everton as a schoolboy.

Red Dwarf star **Craig Charles** tried out for Tranmere Rovers.

Northampton Town

"Every Friday we had a glass of sherry in the boardroom as our scout, a lovely old man, would go through our opponents. That Friday, our scout didn't mention George Best at all."
Cobblers' keeper Kim Book.

They say if you can remember the sixties, you weren't there. Flower power, free love, hippies, yippies, the era is now shrouded in a drug-fuelled hallucinogenic haze. Hang on, wasn't there something about the Cobblers... The Beatles, The Stones, Hendrix... Northampton Town? At the start of the sixties the Cobblers were ensconced in their traditional position near the foot of the fourth division where they'd spent pretty much their entire Football League existence. With small crowds, a notoriously grotty ground and no reputation to speak of, it was just about the last place on earth where you'd expect a footballing miracle.

That was before the arrival of Dave Bowen, former Arsenal captain who had already proved something of a miracle worker. He'd skippered Wales to the quarter finals of the 1958 World Cup where they'd battled heroically before succumbing to tournament winners Brazil by a single goal from a 17-year old striker called Pele.

Something very odd started happening. In 1961 the club was promoted to the third division, sneaking into third place behind Peterborough United and Crystal Palace. They won the third division title in 1963. And just two years later they were runners-up behind

Newcastle United and found themselves in the giddy heights of division one.

One of England's least fashionable and unlikeliest sides had completed the most meteoric rise in the history of English football. Manchester City manager Joe Mercer reckoned Northampton Town playing in division one in 1966 was a greater achievement than England's World Cup win that same year. It was about as improbable as a Cobbler making the Number One slot in the pop charts – although two years later that actually happened when former Northampton Town reserve player Des O'Connor outsold The Stones, The Kinks, Diana Ross and Marvin Gaye to top the charts with "I Pretend".

Nickname The Cobblers

Kit Claret shirt, white shorts, white socks

Ground Sixfields Stadium

Contact Northampton NN5 5QA

01604 683700

Tickets 01604 683777

Website www.nufc.co.uk

It was a team with few stars. Barry Lines was a typical Cobbler. When Town came knocking on the amateur's door in 1960, he was reluctant to pack in the security of his job in an accounts department because he was already on decent money, at £4 a week, and deep down wasn't certain he was good enough to be playing against the likes of Barrow, Southport and Workington. Five years later he entered the record books – the first player to have scored in all four top divisions of English football while playing for the same club, and was facing the likes of Liverpool, Arsenal and Spurs.

Signing players of any sort was difficult in those days. Manager Bowen made sure every target signed on the dotted line cocooned in the safety of a motorway service station, terrified they'd turn tail and scarper if they got a glimpse of the County Ground. The Cobblers' home for 97 years, it was without question the worst ground in the Football League. Accommodating both cricket and football, it was unsuitable for either – dilapidated and underdeveloped. Thirty years later it was even worse, club chairman Barry Stonhill declaring: "The place is an embarrassment to everybody. We can't get players even to come and talk to us. I can reel off a list of names of people who wouldn't come near the place."

In 1994, after 60 years of talking about it, the club finally moved to a new purpose-built stadium at Sixfields. There were some dark days before then – Northampton lasted just one year in the top flight and three rapid relegations took them back to the basement. In 1992 the club had to sack ten first-team players and replace them with kids after the administrators were called in.

Just weeks before moving to their new home the Cobblers kept their league status by the skin of their teeth – Kidderminster Harriers should have been promoted from the conference but their ground was deemed not up to scratch. And in 2002 the Devil's Advocate tried to move in. Italian lawyer Giovanni Di Stefano made his name representing some of the world's most notorious villains – Saddam Hussein and Slobodan Milosevic among them – but his move to buy 60 per cent of the club was thwarted when the rest of the board threatened to resign.

Unforgettable memory? Not many fans would count an 8-2 thrashing among their finest hours, but a mesmerising and record-breaking six goal display by George Best in an FA Cup fifth-round tie against Manchester United in 1970 is right up there. Afterwards the Northampton team signed the ball and Best and his team-mates spent the evening in the Northampton dressing rooms cracking jokes and sharing beer with their opponents.

And now? Promoted to the third division in 2007 and recording their best finish for a decade in 2008, the Cobblers are in better shape than they have been for many years.

Walter Tull... was Northampton Town's finest player before the First World War, and a remarkable man. The first black outfield player in English league football, and the subject of horrendous racial abuse from the terraces, he volunteered when war broke out and became the first black man ever to become an officer in the British army – an extraordinary achievement, given that the military law manual at the time expressly forbade "Negroes" from any position of command. Mentioned in despatches for his gallantry and coolness, he was killed in no man's land in 1918 during the second Battle of the Somme. There's a memorial garden named in his honour next to Sixfields.

Norwich City

"I've got to watch Match of the Day now. Trouble is, when I tell my mum I've scored she won't believe me."
Gary "Ginger Pele" Doherty breaks his two-year goalscoring duck at Carrow Road.

The Canaries? You'd be forgiven for thinking the club nickname referred to their distinctive kit, but you'd be wrong. Founded in 1902 and nicknamed the Citizens, Cits for short, the club was booted out of the amateur game in 1905 for alleged professionalism, decided to turn professional and appointed John Bowman as its first manager. In his first interview Bowman confessed he knew little about the Cits but had heard of the canaries – a reference to the pastime of canary breeding popular in those parts – and the name stuck. Within two years the club had ditched its blue and white strip in favour of a yellow shirt with green cuffs – the local paper heralding the change with the headline: "The Cits are dead but the Canaries are very much alive."

The club song "On the Ball" is even older. Sung at Norwich as far back as 1905, it had been knocking around East Anglia for some years before that and may well be the oldest football song still sung regularly by fans anywhere.

In truth, the fans did not have much to sing about for the next 50 years, most of which were spent hovering in or around the basement league. What success there was came in the FA Cup. Back in 1908 when in the Southern League, the Canaries beat cup holders Sheffield

Wednesday in the first round, and in 1954, a mighty upset with Arsenal humbled 2-1 at Highbury. There was humiliation too – a 5-0 hammering by the amateurs from Corinthians in 1929.

At the start of the 1958-59 season there was nothing to indicate that the club was about to hit the headlines. Even by its own modest standards the team were playing badly, so badly that Canaries boss Archie Macaulay ended up barricaded in his own office when angry fans staged a protest about their shocking performances. When the FA Cup got under way, their form was distinctly unpromising. They laboured to get past the amateurs of Ilford, while it took a replay to scrape past Swindon. What price victory against a Manchester United team filled with the likes of Bobby Charlton, Harry Gregg and Dennis Viollet? On an icy day in January the third division side skippered by Ron Ashman demolished Busby's Babes 3-0, courtesy of two goals from Terry Bly. The players awoke to headlines the next day – "Bly, Bly, Babes".

And that was just the start of it. Spurs, Cardiff City and Sheffield United were all swept aside on a run that took the third division team to a semi-final against Luton Town, the Canaries finally snuffed out by a single goal after taking the first division side to a replay. Promoted at last in 1960, in 1962 Ashman, who had hung up his boots after a club record of 662 appearances, managed the team to their first significant silverware, capturing the League Cup against Rochdale. Norwich won a second League Cup in 1985 against Sunderland on an occasion remarkable for the camaraderie between both sets of supporters – every time they've met since then, they compete for the Friendship Trophy.

The very first winners of the Premier League? Only four teams have won it so far, but around about Christmas 1992 the Canaries looked odds-on favourites, a staggering eight points clear of the pack. It was a team that won a lot of games but leaked a lot of goals – by the end of the season they finished third but conceded 65 goals, four more than they managed at the other end. The following year, another sensation with the Canaries beating the mighty Bayern Munich home and away in the UEFA Cup, the only English team ever to triumph at the Olympic Stadium.

Just three years later the club was in a deep financial hole – which was when Delia

Smith and husband Michael Wynn stepped in as majority shareholders. Since then they've kept the club solvent, while Delia's high-profile chef status has kept the club highly visible at a time when many second division clubs have been slipping off the radar because of television's obsession with the Premier League. After 12 years Delia announced in 2008 she was ready to sell to someone prepared to invest heavily in players, sparking controversy among fans divided about the merits of prospective buyer, billionaire Peter Cullum. The controversy spilled over onto Delia's cookery website – the moderator had to step in to remove offensive comments.

Club hero? Goalie Bryan Gunn is probably the pick of the crop. A loveable eccentric in Norwich's best team in the early nineties, he regularly greeted fans at the Barclay End by running up to his goalposts and heading the crossbar. A tireless advocate for the club since his retirement, he also served a spell as sheriff of Norwich.

It's good to talk… "The lads will be having a conversation and he'll write down the words. Five minutes later he's laughing." Darel Russell and the rest of the dressing room did their best to welcome Czech Republic striker David Strihavka when the million-pound man arrived on a four-year deal in 2007. But not speaking the lingo remains a problem for many overseas players. Six months and just 12 games later, Strihavka was back home with his Czech mates.

Nottingham Forest

"The River Trent is lovely, I know because I have walked on it for 18 years... I wouldn't say I was the best manager in the business. But I was in the top one."

Ole Big Head? Brian Clough had a lot to be bigheaded about.

Rocky. The Longest Yard. Field of Dreams. Dodgeball. All are movies where sporting underdogs triumph over impossible odds. Nothing that's come out of Hollywood can rival what really happened at the City Ground.

A big club? It took 90 years for Forest to become the biggest club in Nottingham. Formed in 1865 by shinty players, its success before 1975 was confined to an 1898 FA Cup triumph against Derby and a second against Luton in 1959 where Elton John's uncle Roy Dwight scored the opener, then broke his leg.

When Brian Clough and number two Peter Taylor arrived, Forest were second division strugglers. Welcomed with open arms? No – Clough had been successful at deadly rivals Derby, where he poached Forest's best players, and caused a furore in 1972 by cheekily parading Forest star man Ian Storey-Moore before Derby fans

Clough took a team of misfits, fatties, nutters, guitarists, carpet-fitters, chain-smokers, reserves, and has-beens and transformed them into the most successful and entertaining team in Europe. By 1980 Forest had gained promotion to the first division, been champions of

Nickname The Reds

Kit Red shirt, white shorts, red socks

Ground City Ground – 30,602

Contact Nottingham NG2 5FJ 0115 9824444

Tickets 0871 2261980

Website www.nottinghamforest.co.uk

England, and appeared in three League Cup finals, winning two of them. They won the European Super Cup. And won the European Cup. Twice.

With this lot. Ageing full back Frank Clark, devastated after Newcastle discarded him after 487 games, had been resigned to playing his guitar rather than playing football. Clough got him for nothing but paid £2,000 for carpet fitter Garry Birtles, toiling away at non-league Long Eaton. Larry Lloyd? A defender slipping towards obscurity, let go by Liverpool, unwanted at Coventry, number 42 in the *Times* list of the worst ever top flight players.

It was Taylor who wanted Kenny Burns, a hell-raising striker with Birmingham. Clough was appalled: "Forget it, I don't want a troublemaker, I don't want an ugly bastard like Kenny Burns." Then signed him anyway and played him as a defender. Disagreements? "We talk about it for 20 minutes and then we decide I was right."

Then there was John Robertson, the greatest and unlikeliest of them all. Already at Forest when Clough arrived, the midfielder was short, dumpy scruffy and chronically unfit, more interested in fags than football and had spent five years rotting in the reserves. Clough put him on the wing. Perhaps the slowest professional footballer ever, he'd waddle hesitantly down the left flank like a baby penguin taking to the ice for the first time, looking for all the world like he would tip on his arse at any moment, but with the ball somehow glued firmly to his feet, mysteriously slipping past defenders seemingly hypnotised by his lack of pace only to unleash deadly crosses with pinpoint accuracy. He played 243 consecutive games, provided the cross that won the first European Cup against Malmo in 1979 and scored the winner against Hamburg in 1980. Clough's verdict? "John Robertson was a very unattractive young man. If one day, I felt a bit off colour, I would sit next to him. I was bloody Errol Flynn compared to him but give him a ball and a yard of grass, and he was an artist, the Picasso of our game."

They weren't all misfits – Clough signed England keeper Peter Shilton and paid a record million pounds for striker Trevor Francis. After 1980 they bagged two more League Cups and two Full Members Cups (played when English clubs were banned from Europe following the Heysel disaster). But they were robbed of a place in the 1984 UEFA Cup final – what would have been the winning goal in the semis was disallowed by a bent ref nobbled with a £27,000 bribe.

Clough was ill by the time he quit Forest in 1993. He had battled with alcoholism throughout his managerial career: "Instead of walking on water, I should have taken more of it with my drink." In retirement he occasionally resurfaced, arrogant, acerbic and endlessly entertaining, offering one-liners on anyone from David Beckham ("His wife can't sing and his barber can't cut hair.") to the appointment of Sven-Göran Eriksson as England manager ("At last England have appointed a manager who speaks English better than the players.")

Disastrous signing... Andrea Silenzi – the first Italian in the Premier League, Nottingham Forest paid Torino £1.8m for him in 1995. In two years he made just 12 appearances, didn't score, and returned to Italy on a free transfer.

Since Clough – a couple of brief returns to the Premier League, a disastrous spell in the third division, and plans to move away from the City Ground to a new 50,000 seater stadium in the south of the city.

Stuart "Psycho" Pearce played non-league football for five years before coming to the City Ground in 1985 but wasn't convinced he was good enough to play at the highest level. Which is why the man who went on to win 78 caps for his country took out an ad in the Forest match programme offering his services as an electrician.

Notts County

"I should have stayed at Everton and transferred the wife."

Tommy Lawton's marriage hit the rocks when he moved to Chelsea and his wife turned into a 24-hour party girl. He wanted away from the bright lights of the big city. Chelsea's loss, County's gain.

Notts County is the oldest professional football league club in the world, founded 24 years before the Football League was formed, and ten years before anyone came up with the bright idea of teams wearing different coloured strips so you could tell them apart.

Diego "Hand of God" Maradona and Vinnie Jones would have thrived at this level, when handling the ball and kicking lumps out of your opponents was, as they like to say these days, all part and parcel of the game.

Way back then they'd already devised a system of settling drawn games which knocks spots off the hammy theatrics of today's penalty shoot-outs. It worked like this. There were two sets of posts at each end of the pitch. One pair served as goalposts. The second pair was placed 12 feet on either side. So if a shot went wide of the goal – but within the second set of posts – you scored a rouge. If the game was tied on goals, the team with the most rouges won. Genius. And so it came to pass that, in November 1862, the *Nottingham Guardian* reported that the team we now know as Notts County played its first ever match and won by "two goals and two rouges against one and one."

Nickname The Magpies

Kit Black and white striped shirt, black shorts, black socks

Ground Meadow Lane – 20,300

Contact Nottingham   NG2 3HJ 0115 9529000

Tickets 0115 9557204

Website www.nottscountyfc.co.uk

The history of the Magpies has since been a bewildering cocktail of highs and lows – the club has been promoted or relegated a record 27 times. In 1891 they thumped Blackburn Rovers 7-1 but just seven days later managed to lose to them in the cup final. But three years later they became the first of only eight teams ever to win the FA Cup from outside the top flight when they beat Bolton Wanderers 4-1, a match that also saw the first ever cup final hat-trick, courtesy of Jimmy Logan.

Unquestionably the most astonishing thing they ever did came in 1947 when, playing in the third division, they smashed the English transfer record, stunning the football world by paying a whopping £20,000 for England goalscoring hero Tommy Lawton, then at the peak of his fame and his powers. Because of the war, he played just 23 full internationals, scoring 22 goals. Add to that 24 goals in 23 wartime internationals and he averaged a goal a game for his country.

He was a sensation at Meadow Lane, scoring 103 goals in 166 appearances and in 1950, the Magpies averaged over 35,000 spectators a match. There have been other great moments – ten years ago the club, then managed by Sam Allardyce, won the third division championship before the end of March, finishing 17 points ahead of the pack. And in 1991 County won promotion to the first division under Neil Warnock after winning the play-offs in consecutive years. On their previous visit to the first division in 1981, County went to champions (and soon to be European Cup winners) Aston Villa on the opening day of the season and beat them – probably their most memorable result of the last 30 years.

Recently there have been a lot of lows. In 2000 Meadow Lane was flooded – there were no home games for seven weeks. And in 2002 County were relegated and went into a seemingly never-ending period of administration – 534 days, to be precise – when extinction seemed a terrifyingly real possibility.

The Football League set the club a succession of deadlines to sort out their finances and granted a number of last-minute reprieves before they were rescued by a consortium, which included money from the supporters' trust and saw a trust member put on the board.

County faced extinction of a different sort in 2006, coming within a whisker of being relegated from the Football League. Although they did top one league in 2007– a survey of all 92 league clubs revealed the Magpies had the most stressed supporters in the land. In 2008 they were involved in yet another relegation battle. Their anthem is "I had a wheelbarrow, the wheel fell off." The wheels are still on. Just.

Pretty in pink?… Italian giants Juventus used to play in pink shirts, but in 1903 they decided they needed a new strip. Not because they looked like big girls' blouses, although they did, but because the colour used to run in the wash. Englishman John Savage played for the side and was entrusted with the task of finding a new kit. He had a mate who was a Notts County fan – the rest is history.

Oldham Athletic

"Warhurst was sent off for foul and abusive language but the lad swears blind that he didn't speak to the linesman."

Athletic manager Joe Royle

The Latics haven't won a significant trophy in a history stretching back to 1895. But they pulled off the greatest Great Escape.

No club has ever looked more certain to be relegated from the top flight than the little Lancashire club did back in 1993. Seven days of the season left, nine points adrift of safety, three games to go, strikers injured, they needed to win all three and depended on results elsewhere going their way to stay up. A thousand to one? The manager wasn't exactly confident: "I couldn't see us winning a game of tiddlywinks".

First up was an away match at Aston Villa, second in the table and chasing the title. Oldham won by a single goal, went on to beat Liverpool 3-2 and on the final day of the season scraped home by the odd goal in seven against Southampton. Unlucky losers in all this were Crystal Palace, seemingly safe just a week earlier (barring a mathematical miracle) who lost their last match of the season and went down on goal difference.

That Oldham were in the top flight at all was the culmination of a 20-year journey that started back in 1970, when former player Jimmy Frizzell took charge at Boundary Park mid-season with the club in trouble near the bottom of the fourth division. He immediately turned the team round and went on to win two promotions in the following four years in a 12-year spell at the club.

When Joe Royle took over in 1982, Oldham Athletic were lurching into financial trouble. On stepping into his new office on his first day, the former Everton and England striker was confronted by a bailiff, one of many people chasing the club for money – at the time they were almost a million in debt.

Careful husbandry off the pitch was accompanied by flamboyant play on it. Royle transformed Oldham into a team of crowd pleasers, playing an open style of attacking passing football that was perfectly suited to the even plastic pitch laid at Boundary Park. The club had not excelled in cup competitions since a semi-final appearance in 1913, and in 1988 Royle joked that "a good cup run for us is getting a third-round replay".

Two years later and the Latics had the whole country sitting up and taking notice of their cup exploits. Still in the second division, the club made it to the final of the League Cup and the FA Cup semi-final in the same season. There was an early sign it might be a special cup year when Frankie Bunn scored six times in a record 7-0 League Cup win over Scarborough. And so it proved, with the team disposing of Arsenal, Aston Villa, Southampton and Everton in a run which included a 6-0 destruction of West Ham at Boundary Park.

Oldham's greatest season

Nickname The Latics

Kit Royal blue shirt, blue shorts, white socks

Ground Boundary Park – 10,900

Contact Oldham, Lancs OL1 2PA 0871 2262235

Tickets 0871 2261653

Website www.oldhamathletic.co.uk

but one that was doomed to end in disappointment, when they lost to Manchester United in the FA Cup and did everything but score against Nottingham Forest in the League Cup final at Wembley – a match that even Forest boss Brian Clough conceded they were desperately unlucky to lose. The club's promotion push was undone by the punishing schedule inflicted by their cup run. At one stage the Latics were unbeaten in 38 home games, but 19 cup ties in the season left them exhausted, and with four league matches to play in just seven days at the end of the season, their challenge withered away. However, they were promoted the following year as champions, and spent three years in the top flight, reaching another FA Cup semi – again against Manchester United. 1994 marked the end of the most successful spell in the club's history.

More recently the club has been in serious danger of going to the wall. It came close to bankruptcy in 2003. At one point former Leeds United chairman Peter Ridsdale – in charge when that club drowned in debt – looked to take it over, and a couple of Norwegians tried to move in before admitting they didn't actually have the money. Things looked very bad when the council refused to allow redevelopment at the ground. That's now all behind them and plans are forging ahead for an £80m redevelopment of Boundary Park, which will increase capacity to 16,000, and include 693 homes and a hotel.

Heroes?... Paul Scholes spoke for thousands of Latics fans when he said Andy Ritchie was his all-time hero. The striker was the key man in Oldham's most successful period, bagging 82 goals in the late eighties and early nineties.

Peterborough United

"I've told the players we need to win so that I can have the cash to buy some new ones."

Chris Turner gees up the Posh prior to the 1992 League quarter final.

A fabulous April Fool's wind-up in the Peterborough *Evening Telegraph* in 2008 made out the club had sold its nickname to Victoria Beckham. Scores of outraged supporters rang and texted the paper to complain after it revealed the club planned to employ an army of wardens to ensure fans didn't utter the word Posh during matches – with on-the-spot fines for anyone who uttered the forbidden word.

Far-fetched? Not at all. Back in 1999 Mrs Beckham formally objected to the UK Trademarks Registry when the club attempted to register its nickname, which dates back to 1921, when Pat Tirrel, player-manager of a side that used to play at London Road, announced he was looking for Posh players for a Posh team. It stuck.

Peterborough United was formed in 1934 and when they finally made it to the Football League in 1960, they announced themselves with a bang. Striker Terry Bly scored 52 times in that first season as Posh ran away with the fourth division title, a record for the lower leagues that still stands, and netted 88 times in just 81 appearances for the club.

Since then – a roller coaster: relegated four times, promoted five, most recently in 2007-08. The club's money woes appear to be behind them ever since young Irish multimillionaire property tycoon

Darragh MacAnthony took control in 2006.

The club no longer owns its current ground in London Road, as it was transferred to a holding company in 2003 – a sore point with some fans who would rather see club and ground remain together. Many supporters were openly hostile when Sir Alex Ferguson's son Darren was appointed to his first managerial job in January 2007 – they craved someone with experience – but he confounded them all by steering the club to promotion in his first full season.

Nickname The Posh
Kit Royal blue shirt, white shorts, white socks
Ground London Road
Contact Peterborough PE2 8AL
01733 563947
Tickets 01733 865674
Website www.theposh.com

Barry Fry was director of football during the promotion season, but the rent-a-quote boss entertained us all for ten years prior to that, both as manager and then owner. Never more so than when he invited the cameras to London Road to film *Big Ron Manager*, a fly-on-the-wall show which saw the former Manchester United medallion man Ron Atkinson parachuted into the club to help caretaker boss Steve Bleasdale secure promotion. It all went very horribly and publicly wrong and the cameras were there to capture the aggro, chaos and mayhem that resulted in Bleasdale quitting his job in a dressing room full of stunned players minutes before a vital match against Macclesfield.

Fry bought the club twice, on the second occasion from Pizza Express founder Peter Boizot, who rescued the club in 1997 when it was close to drowning in £3m of debt. They don't get much posher than Boizot. A man for whom sportsmanship was always more important than winning, he wasn't entirely familiar with footballing ways. Before his first game as chairman he asked Fry whether it was customary to give three cheers for the opposition.

Boizot's arrival took some of the pressure off the multidimensional Chris Turner. The man who first joined the club as a defender in 1969 had spells as captain, manager, chairman, chief executive, company secretary, managing director, owner and football co-ordinator before finally bowing out.

Unusual warm-up techniques? Leon McKenzie, a prolific striker with 54 goals in 104 games, had boxing blood in his veins. Dad Clinton was the British welterweight champion, Uncle Duke held three world titles. Leon warmed up for matches by watching DVDs of Rocky movies.

Oddball? Keeper Fred Barber was the man in the rubber mask, achieving iconic status by regularly running on to the pitch as Freddy Krueger. This occasionally got him into trouble at away matches with police, who suspected he was trying to incite the crowd.

England call-up? It just doesn't happen in the fourth division, but in 2008 Fabio Capello summoned keeper Joe Lewis to the England squad for the tour of the US and the Caribbean. Naturally, he assumed it was a wind-up when he got the call, but it wasn't. It was an experience that highlighted the astronomical divide between wages in the Premier League clubs and the rest – it takes Steven Gerrard about three days to earn what Lewis gets paid a year. What did Lewis learn? "Capello's English is better than Barry Fry's."

> **"The only certainty in management is that you'll get the sack. The beauty of this job is, I can't get the sack."**
> Barry Fry reflects upon the benefits of ownership.

Club hero?... Has to be Noel Cantwell. Twice manager, he first arrived in the early seventies when the club was deep in the doldrums, a legacy of being booted out of the third division a few years earlier because of financial irregularities. He transformed the club from top to bottom, winning promotion in his first full season, and stayed loyal despite an offer to manage Atletico Madrid. In Peterborough he is remembered fondly as "The Messiah".

Plymouth Argyle

"We beat Tiverton last week. I don't see why we should be afraid of Real Madrid. They may have won the Spanish league 29 times, but they haven't played us yet. No problem. Besides, we've got nothing against Real Madrid. It's Exeter City we hate."
Diehard Plymouth fan John Greatrex awaits the clash of the titans.

Pies, pasties and pizzas are standard half-time fare these days, but ice cream? Pilgrim's Passion is an unusual tasty treat at Home Park, an apple pie and clotted cream confection mirroring the team's green and white strip. There's been talk of repainting the red and white hooped lighthouse on Plymouth Hoe in the club colours, a sure sign of a town that senses better times are ahead for its club.

The Pilgrims? The club takes its nickname from the Plymouth Brethren who set off for the New World in the 17th century. Their boat, the *Mayflower*, appears on the club crest, and it was the Mayflower terracing that had to close in 2007 after the government turned down

Nickname The Pilgrims
Kit Green shirt, white shorts, white socks
Ground Home Park – 19,500
Contact Plymouth, Devon PL2 3DQ 01752 562561
Tickets 0845 3387232
Website www.pafc.co.uk

the club's request for special dispensation to keep it open. It's a long way from New England, but then Plymouth is a long way from anywhere – their geographically closest league rival in 2008 was Bristol City, a 230-mile round trip away. Following the Pilgrims is a labour of love, but the travelling Green Army is surprisingly large and loyal.

They're a long way in every sense from Real Madrid, but it was the Spanish champions who provided the surprising opposition for Plymouth in a pre-season friendly in 2006, a reward for Plymouth's willingness to give up their luxury hotel in Austria to the nine times European champions and a far cry from Tiverton Town, Plymouth's regular warm-up fare. Could it be a sign of things to come?

The club was a founding member of the third division when it was formed in 1920 and have been solid performers, mostly in the second and third divisions, ever since. They were on a slippery slope in 2000 near the foot of the fourth and staring Football League oblivion in the face when manager Paul Sturrock arrived. Dundee United's record striker – he once scored five times against Morton – he wrought a miracle at Plymouth, securing promotion in his second season and guiding them to the verge of another promotion two years later, leaving for Southampton just before it was secured. And in November 2007 he returned, replacing previous manager Ian Holloway. "Olly" had been a popular figure during two years in the south-west, but his departure to Leicester City left a bitter taste with fans – just days before he decamped he assured supporters he was staying put.

An exodus of star players in the January transfer windows hasn't helped. Because of its location, Plymouth has had trouble attracting players, not to mention wives and girlfriends. Maybe the opening of the new covered shopping centre at Drake Circus will turn the tide. The club was particularly annoyed when it lost top goalscorer Sylvan Ebans-Blake to Wolves in January 2008 – there was a clause in his contract that said he could move if a club offered £1.5m for him. Chairman Paul Stapleton was upset that he didn't get the clause removed and even crosser at how many clubs seemed to know about the get-out clause, given that it came in just a few days before he went.

Don't mention Watford. Plymouth's two finest moments probably came in the FA Cup. In 1984 they made the semi-final, one of the handful of third division clubs to do so, following a run which saw them dispose of West Brom and Derby before losing out to Watford in the semi-final. In 2007 they made it as far as the quarter-finals before again succumbing to the Hornets.

Balti pies have conquered stadia everywhere, but what price a sushi Cornish pasty? Japanese investors took a 20 per cent stake in the club's holding company this year and will help publicise Home Park overseas. The ground itself is in fair shape – home to the club since 1901, it was destroyed by German bombers in the war but has since been rebuilt and the club now owns it outright.

Heroes? Step forward midfielder Kevin Hodges. He had an unsuccessful spell as manager for a couple of years but before that made a club record of 530 appearances between 1978 and 1992, netting 81 times.

It's your (£2,000) round... When the Pilgrims went to Sunderland's Stadium of Light in August 2006 and won 3-2, Holloway celebrated his first away win as manager by offering to get the drinks in for all 700 members of the Green Army who had made the 808-mile round trip. Fans were invited to write to him to get their pint.

Portsmouth

"Where are we in relation to Europe? Not far from Dover."

Manager Harry Redknapp had always been quick to quash speculation that Pompey could qualify for the UEFA Cup...

The jury will be out for some time on the success or otherwise of Fabio Capello. But the FA missed a trick, again, when it overlooked Harry Redknapp for the England job. A brilliant judge of footballing flesh these days, a master tactician, utterly ruthless, a total charmer, unwilling to take nonsense from anyone, and an unashamed patriot – Redknapp has everything it takes to succeed at that most unforgiving of jobs.

Portsmouth and England keeper David James wouldn't disagree – he famously complained that in the unhappy shambles of the McClaren era, all he got off the boss in 18-months was a cheese roll.

As manager of humble Bournemouth, Redknapp masterminded the downfall of FA Cup holders Manchester United back in 1984, and in 2008 he did it again. Since promotion, a row with Mandaric over assistant Jim Smith, another when Mandaric brought in Velimir Zajec as director of football which provoked Redknapp's temporary defection to rivals Southampton. And the 2006 takeover by Sacha Gaydamak which gave Redknapp money to rebuild a club where until recently - according to agent Pina Zahavi: "The changing rooms were only fit for a Third Division team in Afghanistan. However debts of £60m found

Gaydamak considering his options at the end of 2008.

Funny thing, football. When Pompey striker Sulley Muntari hammered home the penalty that knocked out the champions and celebrated by blowing a kiss and drawing a heart for his girlfriend in the stand, the entire country somehow divined that 2008 was destined to be Portsmouth's year. And so it proved with the Blues landing their first significant trophy in 49 years by beating Cardiff City 1-0 at Wembley and taking Pompey into Europe for the very first time.

When Redknapp took charge of Portsmouth in March 2002 the club had been in the doldrums for decades. Three times FA Cup finalists in the ten years preceding the Second World War, they triumphed in 1939, beating favourites Wolves 4-1. After the war, greater success, winning back-to-back titles in 1949 and 1950 with a team that included club the young Jimmy Dickinson, who went on to make 834 appearances for the club and win 48 England caps.

Nickname Pompey or the Blues

Kit Blue shirt, white shorts, red socks

Ground Fratton Park – 20,700

Contact Frogmore Road, Portsmouth, Hants PO4 8RA

02392 731204

Tickets 0844 8471898

Website www.portsmouthfc.co.uk

But by the end of the decade it all started to go wrong. Relegated in 1959, the club spent the next 19 years in the second or third divisions, while a cash crisis in 1978 forced them to sell off their best players and slide inevitably into the fourth division. A revival in the eighties saw Portsmouth clamber back up the leagues, winning promotion to the first division under Alan Ball in 1987. But more money troubles that same year scuppered the club's ambition before the season was properly under way and Pompey went straight back down again.

The club went into administration in 1999 and was rescued by Mandaric who brought Redknapp to the club as director of football in 2001 and installed him as manager the following year.

The transformation was extraordinary. In 2001 Pompey escaped relegation by the skin of their teeth, needing to win on the last day of the season and counting on results elsewhere going their way. In 2003 Portsmouth were champions, and what champions. Most teams have to hoof their way out of the second division; in recent years a few – Newcastle, Fulham, Manchester City – have played some exciting attacking football along the way. But no-one has done it before or since like Portsmouth, who played a classy, incisive, short-passing game, more Continental than second division.

There have been ups and downs since promotion. A row with Mandaric over the future of his assistant Jim Smith. Another one when Mandaric brought in Velimir Zajec as director of football, provoking Redknapp's temporary defection to deadly rivals Southampton. And the takeover by Sacha Gaydamak in 2006 which gave Redknapp more money to rebuild a club, where until recently – according to football agent Pina Zahavi: "The changing rooms were only fit for a third division team in Afghanistan." However, debts of £60m found Gaydamak considering his options at the end of 2008

With a new stadium in the offing by 2011, have Portsmouth got what it takes to move on to the next level? The club is certainly broadening its international appeal. Lauren, Kanu, Papa Bouba Diop, Sulley Muntari and John Utaka have been prominent in the last couple of years, which would explain the unprecedented appearance of Pompey replica shirts at the last Africa Cup of Nations.

Pompey Chimes? Fratton Park – one of the noisiest grounds in the country – has resounded to the chant of "Play up Pompey, Pompey play up!" ever since 1899. It was originally sung by fans of the Royal Artillery football team, many of whom switched their support to Portsmouth after their own side disbanded at the end of the century.

Friends at heart… Portsmouth and Southampton have a long history of unbridled rivalry and hatred? Actually, no. When Portsmouth reached the 1939 Cup final, just 4,000 Saints fans turned up for their home match that afternoon, while the rest of the city tuned in to Wembley on their radiograms. And when Pompey brought the trophy back to Hampshire, they paraded the cup at the Dell and were greeted like heroes.

Bizarre injury… Portsmouth's Alan McLoughlin was out for a month after picking up his baby daughter and tearing tendons in his arm.

Port Vale

"We try to dissuade them from letting their hair grow too long. One wouldn't look too bad, but can you imagine a whole team of them?"

Manager Sir Stanley Matthews lays down a hair today, gone tomorrow policy in 1968.

Getting into bed with a neighbour generally ends in tears. For Port Vale, it would surely have been the kiss of death. In 1926, when the club was skint, the board announced a merger with deadly rivals Stoke City. Uproar. The fans revolted and threatened a breakaway club; the directors retreated. It would never happen again.

Except it did, in 2003. With Port Vale in administration and vulnerable, Stoke City offered to buy it. The Icelandic consortium then running Stoke was upfront about being in football to make money. Had they succeeded, Vale Park would surely have been flogged off and the Valiants would have ground-shared at the Britannia for a bit before being swallowed up by their neighbours. The supporters revolted, again, and eventually the Valiants were rescued by a fans' consortium.

There's rivalry between the two teams but not the hatred often found elsewhere. Fifty years ago many fans would support one team but watch both. Although it is a source of great satisfaction to Port Vale fans that the club record for the fastest goal was the one that beat Stoke City in 1996 – a long-range effort from Ian Bogie that rocketed home after 12 seconds.

Fans of the late DJ John Peel became surprisingly familiar with Port Vale. Peel was a massive football fan and in the eighties banged on entertainingly between records about Liverpool in general and Kenny Dalglish in particular. But in the nineties he began to take a surprising interest in the goings-on at Vale Park, revealing he had been to watch Vale beat Stockport 2-1 in the 1993 Football League Trophy – the club's first Wembley appearance.

Nickname The Valiants

Kit Black and white striped shirt, black shorts, black socks

Ground Vale Park

Contact Hamil Rd, Burslem, Stoke On Trent, Staffs ST6 1AW
01782 655800

Tickets 01782 655832

Website www.port-vale.co.uk

Peel's interest was fired by *The Memoirs of Seth Bottomley*, an unusually brilliant and witty Vale fanzine which, like most of the records he raved about, was almost impossible to get hold of. It was short on stats, big on fantasy, and all the more entertaining for it. Fans hoping for a thoughtful analysis of the squad in the issue preceding the Wembley final would, for instance, have been astonished to read that Mark E. Smith, the curmudgeonly front man from pop group The Fall, was a likely starter after being taken on loan from Notts County.

It wasn't all made up – the Bottomley boys did the country a valuable service with their campaign to ensure football fans ate hot pies, travelling to away games with a giant thermometer and carrying out rigorous pie temperature tests.

For a club formed way back in 1876 – it was a founder member of the second division in 1892 – the big prizes have yet to come. In 1954 they came within a whisker of being the first club from the third division to make the FA Cup final, knocking out holders Blackpool along the way. One up against West Brom at half-time, they were knocked out thanks to a late penalty.

More recently the Valiants prospered for 16 years under the managership of John Rudge, who arrived in 1983 and galvanised the club. Four promotions saw them coming tantalisingly close to making the play-offs for the Premier League in 1997, and there were a number of glorious FA cup runs, highlights of which included the defeat of Spurs in 1988 and holders Everton in 1997.

Astute buying and selling were the key to his success – Robbie Earle, Darren Beckford, Steve Guppy and Jon McCarthy being among the players who flourished and were then sold. A man who collected flat caps the way Imelda Marcos collected shoes, Rudge is to date the only manager in Britain whose sacking has caused a headache for air traffic control. Surprisingly sacked in 1999, supporters unhappy at how the club had treated him let off 843 helium balloons, one for every game in charge, at the next home match against Huddersfield.

Robbie Williams is famously a fan. Many Valiants fantasise that he may be Port Vale's answer to Roman Abramovich, sinking countless millions into the team. In fact, Williams gives most of his spare cash to a nearby children's hospice, although he is a major shareholder in the club.

Darkest hour... came in 1967 when the club became the first in 48 years to be expelled from the Football League, after being found guilty of illegal payments and financial irregularity. A crippling blow? Not at all. By the time the FA had completed its inquiry, the season had finished and the club had completed all its fixtures. In the close season the club applied for re-election to the league and were readmitted.

Delusions of grandeur?... When the Valiants decided to build a new ground after the war, the chairman commissioned madly ambitious plans to construct what he described as the Wembley of the north. Luckily the money ran out before work was complete on what would most certainly have been a huge white elephant. Even then Vale Park was big enough when finished in 1950 to hold 50,000 and had a capacity crowd, once, for a fifth-round tie against Aston Villa ten years later. And the pitch is the biggest in England.

Valiant fan Robbie Williams

Preston North End

"Elvis seems to put everyone in a bit of a depression. I'm not saying we are losing games because of that song. But we have to do whatever we can to generate an atmosphere."

Boss Paul Simpson thought he'd do things his way when he banned "Can't Help Falling In Love" from the traditional pre-match entertainment at Deepdale. Did it work? Soon afterwards he was checking in at the Heartbreak Hotel, fired after a string of poor results.

Imagine Steven Gerrard popping round to remove your mum's lead piping? Wayne Rooney knocking on the door to sort out your granny with his plunger? Or Ashley Cole getting stuck into your u-bend?

Unlikely? Impossible. But it was a common scenario in Lancashire after the war when Preston's greatest ever footballer supplemented his £14 a week wage by keeping his hand in.

Tom Finney, aka the Preston Plumber, was a legend. A one-club man who netted 187 goals in 433 games and was club president 60 years after making his debut, he also won 76 England caps and knocked in 30 goals for his country.

In 1952 he was made an offer that would have transformed his life. Italian club Palermo wanted him for two years and were prepared to offer him a £10,000 signing-on fee – the equivalent of ten years' wages. That's not to mention generous wages and bonuses, a car and a villa on the Med. It's an oft-repeated myth that he declined the offer. Maybe he would have done. But he never had the chance. He told the chairman, the chairman told the board and the board refused to let him go.

Big money played a big part in the early years of Preston North End. They were the first club to import talent from elsewhere on a big scale. Bossman Major William Sudell was determined to make the club the biggest in the country and lured the best players in Scotland to Lancashire with the promise of good money and well-paid jobs. Other clubs grew envious and it all came to a head in 1884 when Upton Park (the London club that represented the United Kingdom at the 1900 Olympics – and won it) came to Deepdale for an FA Cup tie and complained to the FA that their opponents were stuffed with Scottish pros. The FA, still resolutely amateur, chucked Preston out of the competition, but clubs in the north-west rebelled and formed a short-lived breakaway organisation which forced the FA to admit professionals for the first time.

Nickname The Lilywhites
Kit White shirt, navy blue shorts, white socks with hoops
Ground Deepdale – 24,525
Contact Sir Tom Finney Way, Preston, PR1 6RU 0870 4421964
Tickets 0870 4421966
Website www.pnefc.co.uk

When the Football League was formed in 1888, Preston were founder members, and in its first season they won the league and cup double and went unbeaten the entire season. The following year the team dubbed the Invincibles retained the title. They haven't won it since.

Did you know?... The most popular football team in England in the

1920s was a women's team from Preston? In 1920 they attracted 25,000 to Deepdale, where they took on and beat France, and drew the biggest crowd of the year when they played at Goodison Park – 53,000 inside, another 12,000 locked out. Dick, Kerr Ladies was a team of girls working in the munitions factory in town, who went on to become an international phenomenon, playing in France and Belgium and, in 1922, touring the United States, where they played all their matches against male teams – winning three, drawing three. The Football Association set women's football back 50 years when they decreed that, "The game of football is quite unsuitable for females and ought to be barred." Allegedly because it was a health risk to women. Possibly because it was threatening the dominance of the male game. Or maybe they were just misogynists.

Queens Park Rangers

**"QPR isn't a wealthy club.
It's a club that's owned by some wealthy people."**
Bernie Ecclestone

Roman Abramovich was the wealthiest club owner in Britain until Arab squillionaires bought Manchester City? Wrong. Despite the Russian's billions, Chelsea wasn't even the wealthiest team in west London.

That honour belongs to Queens Park Rangers, owned since 2007 by a consortium that includes the world's fifth-richest man, Indian steel magnate Lakshmi Mittal. Not to mention two men who accumulated billions between them via Formula 1, Bernie Ecclestone and Flavio Briatore.

The Italian who spotted the potential of Michael Schumacher and turned fashion house Benetton into a massive global brand has been romantically linked with many of the world's most glamorous women – Eva Herzigova,

Nickname The Superhoops

Kit Royal blue and white hooped shirt, white shorts, white socks

Ground Loftus Road Stadium – 19,100

Contact South Africa Road, London, W12 7PA 0208 743 0262

Tickets 08444 777007

Website www.qpr.co.uk

Heidi Klum, Elle Macpherson, Naomi Campbell, Adriana Volpe and Elisabetta Gregoraci.

Hoops fans hoped his arrival would result in equally glamorous overseas signings – Lionel Messi, Luis Figo, maybe Kaka? The truth has been far more prosaic. While Abramovich has been splashing the cash since Day One, QPR has brought in the likes of Daniel Parejo Muñoz, Samuel Di Carmine and Emmanuel Jorge Ledesma, none of them exactly household names but all part of Briatore's plan to transform QPR into a team that will be in the Champions League in four years.

The takeover marked a turning point in a turbulent decade for Hoops fans which saw them relegated to the third division for the first time in 30 years; there was a rapid turnover of managers, a period in administration, and the club became crippled by debt. Extraordinary stuff was going on behind the scenes as well, including a court case in 2006 which resulted in seven men being acquitted of charges of false imprisonment, blackmail and possession of a handgun after club chairman Gianni Paladini alleged he had been threatened with a gun before a match with Sheffield United.

The club had been hit by real tragedy. In 2006 youth team footballer Kiyan Prince was murdered and the following year teenager Ray Jones, a first-team regular and England youth international, was killed in a car crash.

These days everything seems more stable at a club that maybe should have been called Queens Park Wanderers. Wormwood Scrubs, Notting Hill, Park Royal – Rangers had no fewer than 14 different homes in west London in their first 31 years before trying Loftus Road for size in 1817. Still they weren't sure. The club moved to White City in the thirties, and again in the sixties, before committing themselves to their current home.

It was in the sixties that the club secured its only significant silverware to date, capturing the League Cup in 1967, the first time the match was staged at Wembley Stadium. A thriller that saw Rangers triumph after going two down, it was a game which did a lot to establish the League Cup as a major competition – until then it was viewed as a Mickey Mouse trophy. QPR pulled off a unique double that year, the only side to win a major cup trophy and promotion to the first division in the same season.

The glory days came in the mid-seventies. Former Chelsea manager Dave Sexton took over in 1974 and two years later the club came agonisingly close to winning the title. These days every club plays their final match of the season at the same time on the same day. Not then – QPR completed their fixtures a point ahead of Liverpool but had to wait ten days for the Reds to play their final match against Wolves. A win for Wolves, or a 2-2 draw would have sealed it for the Hoops, and Wolves nearly pulled it off. Ahead for most of the match, Liverpool equalised with just 20 minutes to go and went on to win 3-1. QPR have never come as close again.

Few football fans have the privilege of seeing maverick genius centre forwards play for their team. Lucky Hoops fans saw one flamboyant hero replaced by another.

Rodney Marsh scored 106 goals in 211 league appearances for QPR, firing them from the third division to the first. A daunting task to wear the Number 10 shirt when he left for Manchester City in 1972? Not for Stan Bowles, a signing from Carlisle United, who claimed as a northerner never to have heard of his predecessor.

Capped five times by three England managers and a self-confessed boozer, gambler and womaniser, he stunned fans on April 20th, 1975 when he announced his retirement from football in a Sunday newspaper which paid him £500 for his exclusive story.

Probably the shortest retirement in the history of football, Bowles made his comeback two days later. None of this affected his status at the club – 30 years on, the supporters' football team is called Accrington Stanley Bowles.

Urban myth... "Sir Les" Ferdinand did NOT trash the Blue Peter garden in 1983. The popular centre forward joked that he had been a member of the gang that carried out the dastardly deed and has been quizzed about it in every interview he's done since. Not guilty.

Reading

"Reading play at the Robin Friday stadium in Bennett Road."

Not true, sadly. Friday was a Reading footballing legend. A stunningly gifted ball-player and scorer of 55 often spectacular goals in his three years at the club, he was a hellraiser who made as many headlines off the field as on it. A heavy smoker and drinker with a penchant for mindbending drugs, he was player of the year in his first full season and adored by the crowd.

His antics could (and have) filled a book. Given his marching orders for kicking Mark Lawrenson in the face, he promptly hotfooted it to the dressing room and crapped in Lawro's kitbag, a gag he later repeated in the opposition's team bath. He kissed coppers patrolling the pitch, yanked down the pants of his opponents when they least expected it and regularly had a skinful just before kick-off, which sometimes affected his balance – he staggered a bit – but not his goalscoring prowess. Transferred to Cardiff when 24, he was arrested within minutes of arriving in Wales for fare-dodging.

Reading's ground is not named after any royal legend but after the club owner, a man who gave his name to The John Madejski Fine Rooms at Burlington House, The John Madejski Academy in Reading, The John Madejski Garden at the V&A, The John Madejski Centre for Reputation in Henley and The Madejski Millennium Hotel. It's easy to scoff at this

Nickname The Royals

Kit Blue and white hooped shirt, white shorts, white socks

Ground Madejski Stadium – 24,200

Contact Bennett Road, Reading, Berks RG2 0FL 0118 9681100

Tickets 0844 2491871

Website www.readingfc.co.uk

apparent narcissism, but the fact remains that a man with no real interest in football rescued the club when it was on its last legs, becoming chairman in 1990 and masterminding the new stadium, which opened in 1998.

He also took it to the Premier League for the very first time. In 2006 the club won promotion with a record number of points for the second division – 106. It came agonisingly close to going up in 1995, the only year in living memory that second place didn't guarantee an automatic promotion spot, coinciding as it did with the Premier League reducing from 22 to 20 clubs. The club made it to the play-off final, going two up against Bolton and missing a penalty, only to lose in extra time.

Star man during the promotion surge was the notoriously forgetful striker Kevin Doyle. Unable to remember what positions to take up at corner kicks, he scribbled instructions on his arms.

The first season in the big time was a glorious adventure, the club surprising everyone and emerging as serious challengers for a spot in Europe, before eventually finishing eighth with a squad substantially the same as the one that was promoted. Manager Steve Coppell spent just over £1m on new talent in the close season while rivals were breaking the bank and he won Manager of the Month award twice. Another winner was left-back Nicky Shorey, the first Reading player to be picked for England in almost a century.

The following season, not so good, the club relegated on the final day on goal difference, overtaken by Fulham's phenomenal run-in.

What next? Madejski has never made any secret of the fact that he'd be happy to sell up and get out if a super-rich suitor comes along.

The Royals?... Frankly, a bit of a rubbish nickname, chosen by a newspaper poll back in the seventies and a reference to the fact that Berkshire is a royal county. Who cares? Reading used to call themselves the Biscuitmen, infinitely more interesting, and a reference to the fact that the world's biggest biscuit manufacturers, Huntley & Palmers, were based in the town. The biscuit reference lives on in the unofficial club fanzine, *Hob Nob Anyone?*

Bizarre injury... Reading striker Leroy Lita missed a month after waking up, in bed, having a quick stretch – and damaging a muscle in his leg.

Rochdale

"I've had 28 years of it. You get less for double murder."
Long-serving director Graham Morris looks back fondly on three decades at Spotland.

England's least successful club? Let's start with their most glorious moment, the League Cup semi-final victory over Blackburn in 1962, which was, and remains, the only occasion in 120 years when a team from England's fourth division has made it to the final of a major cup competition. Two-goal hero of the hour was "Little Joe" Richardson, footballer and dog botherer. Unable to get by on the meagre wages paid in those days, he played football by day, and by night prowled the streets of Rochdale kidnapping Alsatians. The unlucky hounds would spend a bewildered night caged in the back of his van before being freighted to Liverpool, where Joe offloaded them for a few quid as guard dogs.

"Who Let the Dogs Out" blares from the tannoy whenever the Dale take to the pitch at Spotland, but for 101 years it's been largely a case of sleeping dogs. Comatose, even. The club has been anchored in the fourth division since 1974, itself a record, and been marooned there for all but five years in its long league history.

Just 25 minutes down the road from Old Trafford, the rare headlines when they come are so very different. Last season manager Keith Hill grabbed the limelight and scandalised radio listeners with his all-too-graphic post-match analysis of a home defeat after going down, so to speak, to Stockport: "You can compare us at the moment to a bit of soft porn – there is an awful lot of foreplay but not a lot going on in the box."

There was an unusual incident of mascot mayhem in 1999 when Halifax Town's Freddie the Fox somehow got up the not-inconsiderable nose belonging to Rochdale's Desmond the Dragon. A flaming fracas ensued.

In September 2000 the announcement of the football pools results was delayed until well after five o'clock when the goalposts collapsed at Spotland – two burly Rochdale defenders sent the whole lot crashing after hurling themselves theatrically into the net following a Southend tap-in. Dognapper Richardson went on to make headlines again but for all the wrong reasons. He quit football to work as a brewery drayman but was crushed to death by a giant beer barrel that toppled off the edge of his cart.

Nickname The Dale
Kit Blue shirt, blue shorts, blue socks
Ground Spotland
Contact Sandy Lane, Rochdale, Lancs OL11 5DR 0870 8221907
Website www.rochdaleafc.co.uk

Such triumphs as there have been need to be heavily qualified. In 1986 striker Steve Taylor won the fourth division Golden Boot award after hammering home 25 league goals that season – nationally, only Ian Rush and Gary Lineker scored more. So a great season for the Dale? No – the rest of the team managed just 16 goals between the lot of them, leaving the club mired as ever in mediocrity.

Were it not for a car crash, Rochdale might have dropped out of the league years ago. Back in 1980 they finished bottom and their bid for re-election appeared doomed. Altrincham had a strong case for league status that year and were near certainties to replace them. But come the day of the vote in London, the chairmen of Grimsby and Luton – both advocates of Altrincham – were involved in a car crash on their way to the election meeting and missed it. Both survived the crash; Rochdale survived by a single vote.

Aside from two good FA Cup runs in recent years which took them to the fifth round, Rochdale have had little – okay, nothing – to shout about until last season when, under the guidance of former player and youth team coach Keith Hill, they reached the play-off final for the very first time and were on the verge of achieving what would have been only their second promotion in just over 100 years, but went down 3-2 against Stockport at Wembley. It may have taken a century but there is every sign that the fog of resigned defeatism that has surrounded the club for so long may, at last, be lifting.

Believe it or not... if it weren't for Rochdale players, the 1966 World Cup would have had a very different outcome. Charles Hurst and Alan Ball Sr may not have made history on the pitch but off it they played a blinder, fathering World Cup hat-trick hero Geoff Hurst and midfield dynamo Alan Ball respectively.

Rotherham United

> "The chairman, Ken Booth, is fully committed to the club for the immediate future and his company will continue to underwrite the overdraft as they have done since 1987 so nothing has changed. Rotherham United have no debts."
>
> *Club Statement 2004. A lot can happen in four years...*

The town of Rotherham used to boast two professional football clubs. Now there are none. United has moved five miles to the city of Sheffield, which already has two teams of its own and it now plays its matches at the Don Valley Stadium, an athletics track never designed for league football – with a yawning chasm separating the pitch from the fans.

Meanwhile Millmoor lies empty. Home to United for 101 years, it's a crumbling anachronism. A visiting West Ham side took one look at the grotty dressing room back in 2003 and famously refused to enter. The main stand is unfinished – the money ran out – and from a distance

Nickname The Millers
Kit Red shirt, white shorts, red socks
Ground Don Valley Stadium
Contact Worksop Road, Sheffield S9 3TL 01709 512434
Tickets 0844 4140737
Website www.themillers.co.uk

the east stand is virtually indistinguishable from the giant scrapyard alongside it. Close up it doesn't look much better. But the Millers would still play there if they could. The tragedy is, they can't afford to.

For a team that has spent most of its existence in England's third division, Rotherham have had their moments. They came within a whisker of winning the very first League Cup in 1961, beating Aston Villa 2-0 in the first leg but losing by three in the return. In 1953 they knocked out FA Cup holders Newcastle United in a run which took them to the fifth round. In 1981-82 they humiliated Chelsea twice in one season, thrashing them 6-0 at Millmoor and 4-1 at Stamford Bridge. There was a great day out at Wembley in 1996 when they returned with the Football League Trophy. And they came within an inch of winning promotion to England's first division in 1955, ending the season with the same points as both Birmingham and Luton but coming third on goal average.

Hard to believe but until recently Rotherham were making headlines for all the right reasons. As a player Ronnie Moore was a larger-than-life striker who once celebrated a hat-trick by snatching a helmet off a pitchside copper. As a manager he cemented his hero status, winning back-to-back promotions in 2000 and 2001 and securing football in the second division for four years.

Now, of course, it has all gone horribly wrong. In administration twice in three seasons, relegated twice in four seasons, the club kicked off the 2009-09 season with a 17-point deduction. Chairman Denis Coleman became the first man to be barred by the Football League from being on the board of a football club for not being a "fit and proper person" which, to an outsider, seemed grossly unfair. From the moment he took over the club, he was fighting impossible odds.

The root of the problem lies in the scrap metal yard next to Millmoor. There's a lot of scrap metal in Yorkshire and the Booth family who own it are multimillionaires. For 17 years they kept the Millers afloat, but in 2004 club chairman Ken Booth wanted out and sold the club for just one pound. But – and it's a massive but – he retained ownership of the ground (not responsibility for its upkeep), as well as the nightclub next to it and the training ground. And he negotiated an unusual package which guaranteed him 30 seats to every game, Cup final tickets, advertising rights and a lot more besides, for the next 70 years.

This left Rotherham like a cast-off bride, searching for a suitor but with no dowry. The strain of paying the £200,000 a year rent on Millmoor sent the club spiralling into administration, and the move to Don Valley has been done to cut costs. There has been talk of moving into a new community stadium, but plans for that are in their infancy and could depend heavily on the goodwill of the council. And the club is unlikely to attract an investor rich enough to turn its fortunes round until it has assets to call its own, which it hasn't. There was a ray of optimism at the start of 2008-09, with the club winning its first three league matches and giving itself a fighting chance of clawing back its 17-point penalty.

Wasted opportunity... Rotherham had one of England's greatest centre halfs on their books – and never noticed. Dave Watson carved out a career as a striker at Rotherham before Sunderland signed him in 1972 for a club record of £100,000. They took one look at him and converted him to centre half where he won the FA Cup for them. He went on to win the first of his 61 England caps at the age of 27.

Scunthorpe United

"Dad, you're going to get hammered."
*Peter Beagrie's son Sam gives his verdict after hearing the Iron have
drawn Chelsea in the FA Cup.*

A lot of people might have done things differently had they but known the age of the internet was looming. When Matt Johnson called his excellent band TheThe back in 1979, he could not have anticipated the challenge he was setting for search engines in the future. A challenge still beyond the capacity of search engines searching for information about the Leeds rockers known only as "A".

Then there's the Scunthorpe problem, a phenomenon that occurs when the internet filth police block search results on words that include a string of letters that could be obscene. Fans wanting to keep up with the latest gen on the Iron were flummoxed to learn that access was often denied, and in 1996 everyone with a Scunthorpe address was barred from signing up with internet provider AOL. A similar problem exists for anyone googling Nwankno Kanu, the Nigerian striker of Arsenal, West Brom and Portsmouth fame. Scunthorpe appears in the Doomsday Book as Escumetorp, coincidentally another of those words that fall foul of sensitive search engines.

The club was formed at the end of the 19th century but didn't gain league status until 1950. For much of that time they played at the Old Show Ground in the heart of the town, but in 1988 became the first club in the modern era to move to a new purpose-built stadium. Money, or the lack of it, was the driving force for the move – Safeway were desperate to buy a city centre site, United were desperate to clear their debts – so the arrangement suited both. For some years there was a plaque inside Safeway marking the spot where the centre circle used to be – next to the deli counter, in fact – but that disappeared when Sainsbury's took over the premises and couldn't stomach a plaque bearing the branding of a rival chain.

Nickname The Iron or the Scunny
Kit Claret shirt, claret shorts, claret socks with sky blue trim
Ground Glanford Park
Contact Doncaster Rd, Scunthorpe, Lincs DN15 8TD 0871 2211899
Website www.Scunthorpe-United.co.uk

The Show Ground also boasted the first cantilever stand in the country, which went up in 1958 after the old one burned down. The club were so proud of it, they tried to take it with them when they moved to their current home at Glanford Park but couldn't afford to.

Who made his debut for the Iron in 1980 and was appointed captain of England the same year? Arise Sir Ian "Beefy" Botham. He made his first appearance for Scunthorpe United in a 3-3 draw at Bournemouth and turned out on a number of occasions for the club over the next few years, attracting a lot of media attention and raising a lot of money. The club made the cricketing legend an honorary vice-president in 1985, though the shareholders chose to bite the hand that fed them by rather ungraciously booting him off in 1994 because he wasn't spending enough time around Glanford Park.

Santa Claus stepped in to solve another severe cash crisis at

Christmas 1967. Manager Freddie Goodwin departed for the States to take charge at New York Generals and paid top dollar to entice his former charges to accompany him to the Big Apple.

Great players? Two future England captains started their careers at Scunthorpe in the sixties, with Liverpool manager Bill Shankly having the nous to snap up both. Keeper Ray Clemence arrived in 1965 and stayed for two years before going to Anfield for an £18,000 fee, becoming an Anfield legend and playing for his country 61 times. Had he not had the misfortune to be an exact contemporary of Peter Shilton, capped 124 times, his own tally could have been so much higher.

Then there was Kevin Keegan, who made 124 league appearances for United and scored just 18 times – about a goal every seven games. Which is why some thought Shankly had paid way over the odds when he lashed out £35,000 for Keegan in 1971 (the British transfer record was then £200,000). The rest, of course, is history – Keegan remains the only Englishman to have won European Footballer of the Year twice and, when Hamburg bought him in 1977, he cost a record £500,000.

Great moments? Two FA Cup runs that took them to the fifth round in 1958 and 1970, the latter occasion after a glorious fourth-round win against Sheffield Wednesday at Hillsborough. A few giddy minutes in 2005 when they were one up against a Chelsea side whose squad was worth £186,950,000 more than the Iron's. Approximately. Two Wembley play-off finals, one successful, at which the entire town appeared to decamp down south for the day. A tremendous run in 1961-62 that took them to the top of the second division when Scunthorpe looked odds-on to break into the first division for the first time in their history. Hero of the hour was Barrie Thomas, who rifled home an amazing 31 goals in the first 24 games of the season but was flogged to Newcastle in January – and the Iron challenge melted away, although the fourth place they recorded that year remains their best ever finish.

And two years ago, a fabulous season when Scunthorpe started out as 66-1 outsiders to win the third division and proceeded to do just that in some style, clocking up 91 points in the process – the highest in England that year – and with record buy Billy Sharp becoming the country's leading scorer with 30 goals. Over the years Scunthorpe have made a habit of going straight back down after a promotion season and last year they did it again.

The Iron in Europe? One day maybe. A surprisingly large number of fans dipped their toes in Continental waters back in 1999 to support Scunny when they embarked on an historic pre-season tour of Belgium (won one, lost two), prompting keeper Tim Clarke to enquire, "Haven't you lot got anything better to do?"

Believe it or not... Kevin Keegan used to sit on the knee of sports reporter Tom Taylor when travelling back from away matches on the club coach. Space issues? No, Taylor used to entertain the squad with a ventriloquist act to relieve the tedium on the long journeys. Keegan was his dummy.

Bizarre injury... Give that man a rubber duck! Kevin Keegan was out for several weeks in the early seventies after getting his toe stuck up a bath tap.

Sheffield United

"Every player was given a tailor-made booklet detailing the things they can and can't do on holiday. Every member of the team has also been weighed and they will be expected to be within certain parameters when they report back for pre-season training."

Blades manager Kevin Blackwell, Summer 2008

Blades? Sheffield United players went on their 2008 summer holidays with the sword of Damocles dangling over their heads. Pig out on pies – or paella – and you're on your bike. Manager Kevin Blackwell promised to sack any player who reported for pre-season training looking too chubby.

Complete madness. Sheffield United's glory days came when they fielded England's porkiest player. With 24-stone man mountain William "Fatty" Foulke in goal at the turn of the last century, United won their only championship and two FA Cups.

He had no truck with diets, or referees. At the end of the first match in the 1902 Cup Final, Foulke was convinced Southampton's late equalizer was offside and went hunting for referee Fred Kirkham. According to linesman J.T. Howcroft: "Foulke was in his birthday suit outside the dressing room and I saw the secretary of the FA, pleading with him to rejoin his colleagues. But Bill was out for blood, and I shouted to Mr. Kirkham to lock his cubicle door. He didn't need telling twice. But what a sight! The thing I'll never forget is Foulke, so tremendous in size, striding along the corridor, without a stitch of clothing."

Foulke would no doubt have enjoyed "The Greasy Chip Butty Song", a rousing reworking of Annie's Song dedicated to the pleasures of ale, fags, snuff and Sheffield United. And fatty food. It's played religiously at Bramall Lane, the club's home since 1879. The ground dates back to 1855, the oldest in the world still used for professional football, and until 1973 United shared it with Yorkshire Cricket Club. The Blades brought the FA Cup home in 1915 and 1925 but have won no major silverware since.

Nickname The Blades

Kit Red and white striped shirt, black shorts, black socks

Ground Bramall Lane – 32,702

Contact Sheffield S2 4SU
0870 7871960

Tickets 0871 2221889

Website www.sufc.co.uk

Big in China? Sheffield United were the first English club to takeover a Chinese team. Chengdu Wuniu have been renamed the Chengdu Blades – their youth team is called Sheffield United – and ambitious chairman Kevin McCabe also bought Hungary's most successful club, Ferencváros. When United were relegated from the Premier League following the Carlos Tevez affair in 2007, over 5,000 protest emails were sent from China.

Tevez. Complicated story, still rumbling on as this book goes to press, Sheffield United maintained West Ham should have been relegated in their place in 2007 for fielding an ineligible player. They appealed against relegation twice, lost, but in September 2008 an independent tribunal decided Tevez's performances kept West Ham up and ordered the Hammers to pay £30m in compensation.

Talking of controversial Argentines... world cup hero Diego Maradona was lined up to be a Blade. Manager Harry Haslam spotted the 17-year-old on a scouting trip to South America and negotiated a £200,000 deal. It fell through when the board refused to stump up the cash... they didn't think he was worth it.

Club heroes? Tony Currie was the great entertainer in the early seventies. Pass, shoot, dribble or crack a looping volley into the roof of the net from 30 yards. He could

Fatty Foulke: 24 stone

do the lot. Before TC – Jimmy Hagan, who came back from the Second World War wanting to go part-time and become a chartered surveyor. Scored 124 goals in 321 appearances, knocked chartered surveying on the head and went on to manage Benefica to three consecutive championships and a European Cup semi.

Fabulous comedy moment – came in the 2-1 FA Cup fourth round tie victory in January 2008 at home to Manchester City. Blades striker Luton Shelton fired home the opening goal after City defender Michael Ball managed to lose the ball in a sea of balloons cluttering the goalmouth, leaving a surprised Shelton free to poke the ball home. City later complained to the Football Association – and lost.

Bizarre injury... Sheffield United keeper Paddy Kenny needed 12 stitches after his eyebrow was bitten off in a curry house brawl in 2006.

264

Sheffield Wednesday

"We had not troubled David Seaman for most of the first half. That was our plan, to try to get him to doze off."

Owls manager Ron Atkinson had a cunning plan....to outwit the Arsenal keeper..

Big Ron did the dirty on Wednesday in 1991. Six days after telling supporters he'd be barmy to leave, he upped sticks to Aston Villa. Owls fans who had just honoured him with a civic reception for winning promotion and beating Manchester United to take the League Cup were unimpressed. When Atkinson returned to Hillsborough with Villa a few weeks later, it was like the miners' strike all over again, the ground reverberating to howls of "scab".

Fans watching the League Cup final on TV saw their team win its first trophy for 50 years but missed the lap of honour. While the rest of the country watched skipper Nigel Pearson parade the trophy, Yorkshire TV screened a US import show instead, which is why Wednesday's most famous fanzine was called "War Of The Monster Trucks".

A Leeds conspiracy? Wednesday fans are convinced the Yorkshire media favours Elland Road and were appalled when manager Howard Wilkinson defected in 1988 believing the Whites were more ambitious. Wilkinson's Wednesday were dull but very fit – new signings struggled to cope with his hill-running regime and former Newcastle striker Tony Cunningham had to be returned to Hillsborough by tractor after a passing farmer found him knackered and disorientated.

Nickname The Owls

Kit Royal blue and white striped shirt, black shorts, black socks

Ground Hillsborough – 39,812

Contact Sheffield, S6 1SW 0870 9991867

Tickets 0871 2301867

Website www.swfc.co.uk

A club with an illustrious history including four first division championships and three FA Cups, Wednesday's roots go back to a cricket club formed in 1820. The football side dates from 1867 and in 1876 it hired James Lang, now recognised as Englans's first professional footballer.

It's a big club, with fervent support and a ground that was once the envy of England. But fans have endured decades of agony and dashed hopes. Fifteen years in the top flight since 1984, the club has been on the slide ever since Trevor Francis was sacked in 1995 after assembling an entertaining team (star man – Chris Waddle) which lost to Arsenal in both the League and FA Cup finals in 1993.

After that, 10 managers in 11 years, a mountain of debt racked up from chronic overspending in the mid-nineties which just won't shift and a history of calamitous signings that damaged morale. Under Danny Wilson, the players hung baby clothes on the locker peg of Italian Benito Carbone. While when Terry Yorath arrived, he discovered his warring players divided into two dressing rooms at the training ground – he had them knocked together in an attempt to restore harmony.

Tragic hero? Derek Dooley scored an unbelievable 63 goals in 63 games for the Owls but had to have his broken leg amputated aged just 23 after it turned gangrenous. Later manager, the club showed remarkable callousness when sacking him out of the blue on Christmas Eve 1973.

Scandal rocked the club in 1964 when Tony Kay, Peter Swan and David Layne were implicated in a match-fixing scandal, betting on Wednesday to lose at Ipswich. They were jailed for four months and banned for life. The man who planned the scam was Mansfield Town player Jimmy Gauld, who sold his story to a tabloid for £7,000 but was jailed for four years.

The Boxing Day Massacre? Means little to anyone outside Sheffield but for Wednesday fans, a day to treasure. Bottom of the third division and with relegation threatening, almost 50,000 packed Hillsborough on Boxing Day 1979 to see Jack Charlton's side stuff rivals Sheffield United 4-0.

The hardest shot... ever recorded in England was a 114mph thunderbolt hammered against the crossbar by David Hirst against Arsenal in 1996. The boy had gunpowder in his boots – second-placed David Beckham could only clock 97.9mph against Chelsea in 1997, although his effort did find the net. Hirst played alongside keeper Kevin Pressman who entered the record books in August 2000 after being sent off after just 13 seconds for handling outside the area in a match against Wolverhampton Wanderers.

Shrewsbury Town

"It is hoped the name of Shrewsbury as a football town will be purged of the evil repute it required last season – a repute well earned by some of the most blackguardly exhibitions ever presented to the public."
Shrewsbury Journal, 1886.

Football in Shrewsbury was in the doghouse back in 1886. The town was represented by the Castle Blues, a successful side who treated the opposition much as they treated the ball. Both were likely to get a good thumping over the 90 minutes and, according to the *Shropshire Journal*, their hooligan supporters were just as bad. In what may be the first recorded case of a football club obsessing about its brand, the Blues disbanded and reformed as Shrewsbury Town in a bid to shed their bad boy image.

Looking back 122 years later, what do they have to show for it? Six Welsh Cups for starters, although they were always denied the UEFA Cup spot awarded to other winners – Bangor City, Barry Town, Inter Cardiff, Llansantffraid – on the not unreasonable grounds that Shrewsbury is not in Wales.

There have been moments of glory to savour. A footballing fairytale in the League Cup quarter-final against Everton in 1961, when skinny 20-year-old striker Peter Dolby put in a full shift at the Rolls Royce factory, cycled home via Gay Meadow to gawp at the illustrious

Everton players playing cards in their luxury coach, and was accosted by a local butcher who tossed him a huge slab of steak and uttered the immortal words: "Build yourself up, Dolby, and score." He walked to the match with his boots slung over his shoulder and scored, twice, to dump Everton out of the cup.

There was a spell during the eighties when the Shrews excelled themselves in the second division and the small club with the tiny ground in a rural area seriously threatened to break into the first. There was also a day out at Wembley in 1995 that failed to bring the Football League trophy back to Shropshire.

Until 2007 the club was based at Gay Meadow, one of the loveliest grounds in the country, with views of the castle and cathedral – not to mention the River Severn, which flowed along the side of the ground, and quite often ran through it. Just a few weeks after opening in 1910 a game was abandoned because the ball was floating and that happened on a regular basis for the next 97 years. It was certainly the only ground in England where the best view was to be had from the classroom windows of the school that loomed above the Wakeham End. And it was the only club in the country to employ a man in a boat to return balls booted into the river. Fred Davies, known to all as "the coracle man", did the job for decades in his home-made boat and would retrieve up to

Nickname The Shrews

Kit Royal blue shirt, blue shorts, blue socks

Ground ProStar Stadium (also known as New Meadow) – 9,875

Contact Oteley Road, Shrewsbury, Shrops SY2 6ST 0871 8118800

Tickets 01743 273943

Website www.shrewsburytown.com

seven balls a match. When he retired, his son Tom inherited the mantle. Last year the club moved to the ProStar Stadium, a more functional and less floodable 10,000-seater on the outskirts of town.

> **"My investment strategy has been a disappointment ever since I bought a non-controlling interest in the Shrewsbury Shrews, an English football team which for some reason refuses to win."**
> Bassist Derek Smalls sheds some light on why he wears a Shrewsbury shirt in the spoof rockumentary *This Is Spinal Tap*.

Heroes?... The BBC boobed a few years back when it asked supporters to choose their all-time favourite from a shortlist of three made up of Dean Spink, Steve Anthrobus and Austin Berkeley. Which, with the greatest respect to all three, is a bit like asking who is the most important living member of the Royal Family, then giving Fergie, Zara Phillips and the Duke of Kent as the only options. Shrewsbury's greatest legend and record goalscorer also happens to be the most prolific scorer in the history of English football – Arthur Rowley, the player-manager with the dynamite left boot who broke Dixie Dean's record of 379 league goals in 1961 and went on to amass 434 in total. As manager he won promotion and took Shrewsbury into the semi-finals of the League Cup.

Southampton

"We reckon he covers every blade of grass on the pitch, mainly because his first touch is crap. But he has made a big difference."

New signing Carlton Palmer impresses manager Dave Jones.

Carlton Palmer played for England, but he was never captain. Though back in 1982 no fewer than six players who had or were to captain their country turned out for the Saints, namely Kevin Keegan, Alan Ball, Mick Mills, Dave Watson, Mick Channon and Peter Shilton. Add Peter Osgood, Charlie George and David Armstrong to the mix and you have the secret of Southampton's golden era under manager Lawrie McMenemy.

The Saints' squad of the early eighties was perhaps the last case in the history of English football of an unfashionable club of modest means being in a position to assemble a team of the highest quality. At the time they were

Nickname The Saints

Kit Red and white striped shirt, black shorts, red and white hooped socks

Ground St Mary's Stadium – 32,689

Contact Britannia Rd, Southampton, SO14 5FP 0845 6889448

Tickets 01743 273943

Website www.saintsfc.co.uk

the most entertaining club in the land, although they didn't quite climb to the summit, coming closest in 1984 with a second-place finish just three points behind Liverpool.

Their one unforgettable moment of glory came in 1976, early in McMenemy's reign, when the club reached the FA Cup final while in England's second division. Pundits confidently predicted the Saints would get pounded by Manchester United, but Southampton confounded the critics, with Bobby Stokes grabbing the winner seven minutes before time.

Disastrous signing... Ali Dia. Southampton boss Graeme Souness was hoaxed by a phone call from a man claiming to be former World Player of the Year George Weah and signed Dia believing him to be an international footballer who played for Paris St Germain. Souness found out the hard way that Dia was in fact an amateur from Senegal and spectacularly useless – the Southampton boss brought him on as a first-half sub for Matt Le Tissier but had to replace him early in the second half because he was so inept. Le Tissier described his performance as "Bambi on ice".

Southampton enjoyed a lot of success in their early years. Long before they were elected to the Football League in 1920, they'd already appeared in two FA Cup finals, losing to Bury in 1900 and Sheffield United in 1902. The FA Cup runs coincided with a long period of domination in the Southern League: six championships in eight years.

But it wasn't until 1966 that the club finally broke into the first division. The promotion was masterminded by Ted Bates, manager and club legend who served the Saints for an astonishing 66 years. He was 21 when the Second World War broke out and 27 by the time it finished, but either side of it he scored 64 times in 216 appearances and went on to be coach, manager, assistant manager, director and club president, winning the MBE in 1998 and Freedom of the City the same year.

There was a deeply surreal moment in 2007 when the club erected a larger-than-life bronze statue of the great man outside the ground – fans raised over £50,000 towards it – but was shamed into taking it down again days later after furious supporters pointed out, not unreasonably, that it looked nothing like "Mr Southampton" and was comically out of proportion – the arms appeared to be the same length as the legs.

In 2005 the club dropped into the second division after 27 consecutive years in the top flight. In truth, they could have gone down on a number of occasions in the preceding decade but were rescued time and again by the only player ever to have been bombarded by Christian groups requesting that he publicly renounce his divinity.

To a generation of Southampton supporters, Matthew Le Tissier will always be "Le God". A one-club

The Ted Bates statue cost £112,000, stood 16 feet tall, lasted less than a week

man who joined Southampton in 1986 and stayed 16 years, he was a sublimely talented and creative attacking midfielder with a genius for the unexpected – and dynamite in his boots. Controversial throughout his career and variously accused of being lazy, overweight and unambitious, he played only a handful of games for England and occasionally fell foul of Saints' managers. Ian Branfoot was unpopular at the best of times, but never more so than when he consigned Le God to les reserves.

In an era when our enjoyment of football on TV is marred by a spate of meaningless statistics that spew all over the screen – who, honestly, gives a rat's arse about pass completion rates, or if a substituted player has covered 8.62 kilometres of turf in 73 minutes? – one unarguable statistic is that Le Tissier scored 162 times in 442 league appearances, an excellent record by any standards and a phenomenal one for a midfielder playing in a team that regularly struggled for points and goals.

And now? Saints fans thought they had seen the back of Rupert Lowe, club chairman from 1996 until 2006, a successful businessman and hockey enthusiast who confessed to never having seen a football match until six months before taking charge. He put backs up on his arrival – Lawrie McMenemy quit the club as did manager Graeme Souness with a memorable parting shot: "You tell me if there is anyone else in football by the name of Rupert?"

Lowe successfully masterminded the move to the new St Mary's Stadium but relegation in 2005 was nearly followed by a successive relegation in 2006. Lowe courted controversy throughout his time in charge, surprising the football world by bringing in England rugby coach Sir Clive Woodward as performance director then promoting him to director of football. Not to mention hiring Harry Redknapp from deadly rivals Portsmouth in a doomed attempt to stave off relegation. A man not afraid to make the same mistake twice – he unsuccessfully promoted coach Stuart Gray into the managerial hot seat in 2001, then repeated the error with coach Steve Wigley in 2004 – he stepped down in 2006, with fans clamouring for his head.

But then he came back, regaining control of a club in trouble in May 2008 – the Saints staying up by the narrowest of margins after beating Sheffield United on the last day of the season. One of his first acts was to appoint Jan Poortvlieb as manager, a man whose managerial pedigree with FC. Den Bosch, RBC Roosendahl, Stormvogels Telstar and Helmond Sport did not make him an obvious choice.

Do club chairmen have the faintest idea... how the average football fan thinks? Saints fans who packed St Mary's for the final match of the 2005 season against Manchester United knowing that anything other than a win spelled certain relegation found these words of comfort from Rupert Lowe in the match programme: "It is always easy to forget the progress we have made as a club over the past decade when the first team results go badly. Our academy has continued to flourish, our community and educational activities have made progress, our shop is doing well, our match-day and non-match-day catering is the envy of other clubs, our radio station has made great progress and, above all, our match-day staff are all committed to ensuring that our supporters enjoy their match-day experience to the full." You really couldn't make it up.

Southend United

"I have not had my suit cleaned or my hair cut since we embarked upon our great run way back in August. I may look a bit of a mess but I am not complaining. Long may it continue."

Success didn't smell so sweet when Southend won eight games on the bounce in 2005 – deeply superstitious manager Steve Tilson refused to clean his clothes for almost two months.

Every league team that's ever played Manchester United has come off worse in the long run. Liverpool, Arsenal, Chelsea, take your pick, there's not a club in the country that's ever taken on the Red Devils and won more often than they've lost. Except one.

Step forward, the Mighty Shrimpers. Played one, won one. In 2006 they took on Ronaldo, Rooney and the rest at Roots Hall in the fourth round of the League Cup and beat them 1-0, thanks to a 25-yard screamer from Freddy Eastwood, a Romany traveller who'd returned to football after a spell as a second-hand car salesman and was at the time threatened with eviction from his caravan. Was that their finest moment? Maybe.

I say "the Shrimpers" but these days the club's preferred nickname is the Blues. Some time in the eighties owner Vic Jobson removed the shrimp from the club crest, replacing it with a lion-with-anchor motif of which he owned the copyright and presumably the royalties. The shrimp made a welcome return to the crest in 2001.

There was a glorious if implausible period in the early nineties when Southend threatened to be one of the founding fathers of the Premier League, or Premiership as it was preposterously known in those days. Managed by Chelsea legend David Webb, they won two successive promotions from fourth to second division and briefly topped the table on New Year's Day 1992. But Webb quit after a row with owner Vic Jobson and it all went wrong.

Nickname The Shrimpers or the Blues
Kit Royal blue shirt, blue shorts, blue socks
Ground Roots Hall – 12,392
Contact Victoria Ave, Southend-On-Sea, Essex SS2 6NQ 01702 304050
Tickets 08444 770077
Website www.southendunited.com

Fast-forward two seasons and maverick manager Barry Fry, brought in earlier in the year to stave off relegation, again threatened to take the club into the first division, aided and abetted by the awesome if erratic talents of forward Stan Collymore who was banging them in for fun. But the dream was over as soon as it had begun – before Christmas, Collymore had been flogged to Nottingham Forest for nearly £3m – Southend had paid £150,000 for him just a few months earlier – and Fry decamped to Birmingham, taking most of his staff and many of the better players with him – and Southend went on a ten-year downward spiral. Roots Hall – which was bought in the fifties with £74,000 raised by supporters, and built by the groundsman, his mates and some of the players who got paid 3'6 (or 17.5p) an hour for their work in the close season – was flogged off to developers, and the club went within days of going bust in 2000.

Many supporters still blame Fry for the decline – his name opens few doors in these parts – and things only started to look up in 2003 when Steve Tilson got the manager's job. Successive appearances at the Millennium Stadium in 2004 and 2005 in the Football League Trophy have been recent highlights, although the club went down 2-0 on both occasions to Blackpool and then Lincoln City.

Ever taken a penalty... and wondered how come the goal suddenly looks so small, the goalkeeper so big, 12 yards so long? A familiar feeling to Southend strikers in the early nineties – the Shrimpers contrived to miss seven consecutive spot kicks spanning the 1990-91 and 1991-92 seasons.

Stockport County

"People in China tell me that we are already bigger than Manchester United in their country and 30% of our income comes from our interests in China, such as soccer schools."

Stockport County – huge in China? Strange but true – the Hatters under then chairman Mike Baker were trailblazers in 2003. They were the first foreigners to co-own a Chinese club – Liaoning Tiger Star was renamed Stockport Tiger Star – and a touring County team found they drew far bigger crowds in Shenyang than ever came to Edgeley Park. The adventure was short-lived. When County changed hands in 2005, some of its debt was down to its Chinese adventure.

Three years ago Stockport County looked dead and buried, propping up the fourth division following two recent relegations and hurtling headlong to the trapdoor that leads to the conference. Edgeley Park, their home for 101 years, had been sold off because of a mounting cash crisis, and when a supporters' trust took over the team in 2005, it uncovered four million pounds of debt. County had spent the vast majority of their Football League history in the basement division and were unarguably one of England's least successful clubs. The writing was on the wall.

Just look at them now. Promotion via the play-offs in May 2008 was the culmination of three glorious years on and off the pitch. Off it, the supporters' trust put the finances in order. On it, the club got into bed with a ladies' man.

Nickname The Hatters

Kit Royal blue shirt with white hoops, blue shorts, white socks

Ground Edgeley Park – 11,000

Contact Hardcastle Road, Stockport, Cheshire SK3 9DD 0161 2868888

Tickets 08456 885799

Website www.stockportcounty.com

Former player Jim Gannon was helping out with the ladies' team when he was unexpectedly thrust into the manager's role. It was supposed to be a temporary arrangement. In his first year he saved the club from relegation, in his second the club established an all-time Football League record with Stockport winning nine games on the spin without conceding a single goal. In 2008, a 3-2 victory over Rochdale at Wembley and promotion.

Just seven miles away from the massive Manchester clubs, County has inevitably struggled to attract the best young talent, the limelight, and, of course, the fans.

The 1990s were Stockport's most successful era, with the club spending five years in the second division. In 1998 they found themselves looking down on Manchester City for the very first time when the Blues dropped to the third division, although Maine Road still drew half a million more fans through the turnstiles than Edgeley Park that season.

In 2000 County fans were in uproar when it looked like they might end up ground-sharing with City, which would surely have been the first step along the road to extinction. Luckily for County, it was City who scotched the move after deciding the rugby union team Sale Sharks would make better tenants.

Greatest cup success? 1998, again, on a League Cup run that took

County to the semi-finals, claiming three Premier League scalps along the way – Southampton, West Ham and Blackburn – before eventual defeat by Middlesbrough.

Hero? The Hatters have a hat-trick hero in Jack Connor, their all-time record goalscorer whose 140 goals in the fifties included an incredible 13 hat-tricks. Not to mention the two matches in which he scored four times. And a further two occasions where he bagged five. Stockport's 13-0 annihilation of Halifax Town in the 1933-34 season remains an all-time Football League record.

Strange but true… Most lower-league managers would love to be on the telly more often but rarely get asked. So why did boss Jim Gannon refuse to play ball with Sky prior to the 2008 fourth division play-off clash against Rochdale? Believe it or not, he clammed up because he was fed up that a row over his allegedly defective Sky Box was still festering unresolved after nine months.

Stoke City

"The reason for this change is that despite all the good work he has done for the club, he has failed to implement the strategy of exploiting foreign markets for players and it is felt we will again fail to exploit those markets this summer with him in control."

Stoke chairman Gunnar Por Gislason sacks manager Tony Pulis, 2005.

There you have it. In black and white. The first manager sacked for failing to buy cheap foreign players in sufficient quantities. Over 260 foreigners compete in the Premier League and every week about two thirds of starting line-ups are made up of overseas players. Premier League chairman Sir Dave Richards let the cat out of the bag in 2008, admitting the volume of foreigners was damaging the England team

Equally damaging is the number of foreigners in the lower leagues. Clubs are increasingly reluctant to take a chance on homegrown young-sters when they can pick up a proven player from abroad on the cheap. A generation ago the England team was studded with stars developed in lower league football. Kevin Keegan started off at Scunthorpe, David Platt at Crewe, Peter Beardsley spent three years at Carlisle, while Stuart Pearce had five years in non-league football at Wealdstone. When England played Croatia in September 2008, not one outfield player had come through lower league football.

The Icelandic owners may have ditched Pulis but in 2008 he took his side to the Premier League after leading Stoke to second place in the second division. How come? They say you should never go back but at Stoke two men who had taken a lot of stick returned with glorious results. Peter Coates, club chairman from 1989-98, regained control of the club in 2006. The same fans who sang "There's only one Peter Coates" when the team sealed promotion against Leicester City in 2008 must have included many of the same supporters active in the "Coates Out" campaign in the nineties.

Nickname The Potters
Kit Red and white striped shirt, white shorts, white socks
Ground Britannia Stadium – 28,383
Contact Stanley Matthews Way, Stoke On Trent ST4 4EG 01782 592222
Tickets 0871 6632007
Website www.stokecityfc.com

The same with Pulis. Coates brought him back in 2006 but he wasn't everyone's cup of tea and that October a group of disgruntled fans planned a red-card protest against him. Ten thousand cards with "Give Pulis his cards" on one side, "Time to get rolling Tone" on the other were to be handed out before a match against Preston. The demo was postponed, results picked up, the rest is history.

The protest was organised by The 1972 Committee, a reference to Stoke's finest moment when they defeated hot favourites Chelsea 2-1 to land the League Cup. Stoke had a good team in the early seventies and enjoyed a couple of great cup runs, reaching the semis in 1971 and 1972. But in 1976, the roof blew off the Butler Stand at Victoria Park, Stoke's home from 1879 until 1997. The £250,000 replacement cost crippled the club. Star men Jimmy Greenhoff, Alan Hudson and Mike Pejic were sold and the following year the club was relegated.

Club hero? Sir Stanley Matthews, obviously. The right-winger first signed with his hometown club in 1932 and rejoined them 29 years later, playing another four years. The first footballing knight, he inspired the team to the second division title in 1963, winning Footballer of the Year for the second time at the age of 48. He finally hung up his boots in 1965 aged 50, although later regretted it, reckoning he had retired "too early".

What happened... when Stoke sacked Pulis and replaced him with a man ready and willing to buy foreign players? His Dutch replacement Johan Boskamp smashed the club transfer record to bring in Guinea international striker Sammy Bangoura. A success? Not exactly – he kept going AWOL. When he didn't return to Stoke after the 2006 Africa Cup of Nations, Boskamp was apoplectic with fury: "If I was a player, not a manager, I would kick him in the balls."

Sunderland

"It was the masseur's choice of music but what annoyed me was that none of the players had the balls to say 'We're not listening to this rubbish'."

In 2008 Roy Keane revealed that his darkest moment as manager came when he discovered his players dancing in the dressing room to Abba's "Dancing Queen" shortly before a match against Ipswich.

Sundireland? The club was taken over in 2006 by a consortium consisting largely of Irish publicans and property developers who installed club goalscoring legend Niall Quinn as chairman and former Manchester United captain Roy Keane as manager. The result? The Black Cats are now astonishingly popular in Ireland. Keane is mobbed wherever he goes on the club's annual pre-season tour of the country, while some 800 Irish folk regularly make their way to the Stadium of Light for Sunderland home matches.

There's an air of

Nickname The Black Cats

Kit Red and white striped shirt, black shorts, red socks

Ground Stadium of Light – 49,000

Contact Stadium Of Light, Sunderland SR5 1SU 0871 9111200

Tickets 0871 9111973

Website www.safc.com

optimism around the club these days after decades in the doldrums. It's easy to forget Sunderland was once the most successful and wealthiest side in the country. Founded in 1879 by teachers and admitted to the Football League in 1890, the next 50 years saw them crowned champions six times, runners-up five times, and spend an unbroken 68 years in the first division.

Disastrous signing... Milton Nunez. Sunderland paid £1.6m for the Honduran striker in 1999, played him for 44 minutes, then tried to get their money back. Boss Peter Reid thought he had signed a star from Uruguayan first division club Nacional Montevideo. Nunez played in the Uruguayan third division.

But they've been a yo-yo club for the last 50 years and have recently suffered two ghastly seasons, losing 17 consecutive games in 2003 and being relegated with an all-time record low of 15 points in 2006.

The greatest moment since the war by some stretch came in 1973 when the then second division side won the FA Cup at the expense of all-conquering Leeds United after disposing of Manchester City and Arsenal in earlier rounds. Heroes of the hour included goalscorer Ian Porterfield and keeper Jim Montgomery whose double save against Peter Lorimer regularly crops up as a contender for the greatest save of all time.

The win was masterminded by manager Bob Stokoe, who arrived just weeks before the cup run started. He is immortalised in a giant bronze statue outside the ground capturing the moment he ran onto the pitch at the end of the game to hug his match-winning keeper. The players? Every member of the cup-winning team has a bar or food kiosk named after him inside the ground.

The Stadium of Light is a noisy place and Sunderland supporters are officially the noisiest in England, according to a club survey carried out in 2007. The crowd clocked 129.2 decibels – much louder than a rock concert and as deafening as a military jet. At Roker Park, home until 1997, the noise may have been louder – the morning after a fifth-round tie against Manchester City during the 1973 campaign, a London journalist was discovered rooting around inside the ground looking for the hidden amplification system.

Hero? Sixties centre half Charlie Hurley regularly comes up when all-time greats are mentioned: more recently Kevin Phillips captured Black Cats' hearts. A latecomer to professional football, there were many who thought the diminutive former carpet fitter from Baldock would be out of his depth at the highest level when Sunderland were promoted to the Premier League in 1999. Did he sink? No, he ended up the Premier League's top scorer in his first season and also won the European Golden Boot (now mysteriously renamed Golden Shoe), the only Englishman ever to win it.

Giant-killers. Second division Sunderland's goalie Jim Montgomery is hugged by manager Bob Stokoe after his incredible double-save in the 1973 FA Cup final kept Leeds out andgave Sunderland victory after a fairytale cup run

Comedy villain? Former midfield man Lee Clarke. A lifelong Newcastle fan, he was transferred for his own safety in 1999 after being spotted out with his mates wearing a T-shirt calling his own fans sad bastards.

Dud forwards? Every club makes the odd unwise investment from time to time but Sunderland had an astonishing run in the early years of the decade, with Peter Reid lashing out a combined £6.6m on Argentine midfielder Nicolas Medina, Dane Carsten Fredgaard and Honduran Milton Nunez. Just how bad were they? Hard to say... they didn't start a single league game between them. French international striker Lilian Laslandes was equally disastrous, costing over £3m but failing to find the net once.

Don't mention... the Mags. Such is the rivalry with near neighbours Newcastle United, Sunderland fans organised a boycott of Sugar Puffs in 1996 after then Toon boss Kevin Keegan appeared in TV adverts endorsing the cereal. It is a source of immense satisfaction to Sunderland fans that their club holds the all-time record for the biggest away win in the top flight – Newcastle were thrashed 9-1 back in 1908.

**A young Sunderland fan gets
his hands on the FA Cup 1973**

Swansea City
(Clwb Pêl-droed Dinas Abertawe)

"To see Cardiff in the final would be hard to take for Swansea fans. So, to be brutally honest, I think I'm behind Barnsley on this one."

The BBC drop ex-Swansea player Leighton James as a pundit after his all-too-frank preview of the 2008 FA Cup semi-final.

Viva Swansea City! Back in the second division in 2008 after an absence of 24 years, following a season in which all sorts of club records went tumbling. Fourteen away wins, unbeaten in 12 consecutive away games and amassing 92 points, they also boasted the league's top goalscorer in Jason Scotland. While Roberto Martinez won Manager of the Month three times before running away with Manager of the Season.

Martinez spent six years playing for Wigan Athletic and was best known to the footballing public as that personable and knowledgeable Spanish chap who regularly pops up as a studio pundit

Nickname The Swans
Kit White shirt, white shorts, white socks
Ground Liberty Stadium – 20,500
Contact Morfa, Swansea SA1 2FA 01792 616600.
Tickets 08700 400004
Website www.swanseacity.net

when Sky screen Spanish football. Appointed manager last year, he's made it his mission to bring Spanish football to Wales. By August this year there were no fewer than six Spaniards in the Swansea squad and the club has been playing a crisp Continental passing game that has paid dividends.

Is the Premier League within reach? The last time Swansea City made it to the highest level it was – to quote then manager John Toshack – a magic-carpet ride. Liverpool hero Toshack wasn't the obvious man to lead Swansea. His first visit to the Vetch Field was as a striker with rivals Cardiff City and he bagged a hat-trick. Long before then he'd already passed his FA coaching exams – he took them when he was only 18 years old.

Tosh was just 28, the youngest manager in the Football League and a surprise appointment when he arrived at the fourth division club in 1978. In the space of three years he pulled off consecutive back-to-back promotions, and in 1981 the Swans found themselves in the first division for the first time.

It was breathtaking stuff. Four of the team present when Toshack took over were still at the club at the time of their opening match in the first, when they crushed Leeds United 5-1. They went on to beat Spurs, Manchester United and Arsenal and topped the table on several occasions before slipping back into sixth place. The following year they chalked up a record 12-nil victory, annihilating Maltese team Sliema Wanderers in the European Cup Winners' Cup. That Swansea team of the 1980s made up the bulk of the Welsh national side, with up to seven players appearing in the starting line-up, including the likes of Leighton James, Brian Flynn and Robbie James.

Then it all went catastrophically wrong. Money problems off the field left the club struggling for survival, and by 1986 the Swans were back in the bottom rung of the league ladder.

Legends? Swansea is awash with them. The greatest of them all never played for the first team. Gentle giant John Charles – the only player Britain has ever produced who was world class at centre half and centre forward – played schoolboy football for Swansea, but was snapped up by Leeds United before going on to become a legend at Juventus.

A statue of Ivor Allchurch can be found at the Liberty Stadium, home to Swansea since leaving the Vetch in 2005. He played 445 times for the Swans in two spells, bagging 164 goals, and played a pivotal part in Wales reaching the quarter-finals of the 1958 World Cup, where they lost 1-0 to eventual winners Brazil – undone by a goal from a young lad called Pele.

It may be some time before Swansea is supplying most of the Welsh team again – the 14 players who played in the side that beat Southend 3-0 last season included five Englishmen, three Spaniards, three Irishmen, two Dutchmen and one from Trinidad & Tobago: not a Welshman among them.

Potential good news for Swansea... is that FIFA boss Michel Platini is said to be unhappy at the rule introduced in 1995 that bars Welsh clubs competing in English leagues from entering the Welsh Cup – the winner of which has a passport to the UEFA Cup.

Swindon Town

"I prepared for this game with four Page Three models and a snort of coke. And I loved every minute of it – the match I mean."

David Thompson made meticulous preparations for his Swindon debut.

These have been tumultuous times for Swindon. The first team to drop from the Premier League to the fourth division, lurching from one financial crisis to the next. Twice in administration, things got so bad in 2000 that boss Jimmy Quinn was ordered not to pick teenage midfielder Robin Hulbert as it would trigger a payment to his former club Everton – the unfortunate youngster was banished to the north-east to train with Newcastle's reserves.

It's all a far cry from the golden period at the end of the sixties when Don Rogers reigned supreme. Swindon were in the third division but the country sat up and took notice of the flying left-winger who was also a prolific goalscorer, netting 90 goals in three seasons. Their greatest ever player, he was the architect of the finest moment in the history of the Robins when they defeated first division Arsenal 3-1 in the 1969 League Cup final at Wembley, scoring twice in extra time.

Wembley figured again in the club's darkest moment, the 1989-90 season when Swindon won the play-offs at the Twin Towers to reach the first division for the very first time. Or so they thought. Just ten days

292

after their triumph the roof fell in. The club admitted 35 charges of making illegal payments and the Football League decided to demote the Robins to division three, though it later relented and allowed the club to remain in the second.

Villain of the piece? Chairman Brian Hillier. In 1992 he was jailed for 12 months for tax evasion, after he diverted hundreds of thousands of pounds from sponsorship, gate receipts, programme sales and supporters' club funds and used it to top up wages. His defence? Everyone else was doing it. The judge didn't buy it.

Nickname The Robins

Kit Red shirt, red shorts, red socks

Ground County Ground – 15,728

Contact County Road, Swindon, Wilts SN1 2ED 0871 4236433

Tickets 0871 2232300

Website www.swindontownfc.co.uk

Don't mention... Leeds chairman Ken Bates. There was tremendous excitement at the start of the 2005-6 season when the new management team of Dennis Wise and Gus Poyet arrived and won the first six matches. Wise barely had time to pick up his Manager of the Month

> "My goalkeeper had trouble kicking with the wind, never mind against it. Yet all his team-mates insisted on passing back to him. It was schoolboy stuff."
>
> Boss Steve McMahon after seeing his side dumped out of the cup by non-league Stevenage.

award before Bates moved in and lured him to Leeds United. It's a familiar story for Swindon fans, who lost manager Glenn Hoddle to Bates and Chelsea back in 1993, just days after Hoddle had steered Swindon to the Premier League for the very first time.

Did you know?... Money raised from the Community Shield – formerly the Charity Shield but rebranded by the FA in 2004 to stop the Charity Commission looking at it too closely – is distributed via hundreds of small grants chosen by clubs. Not so when Swindon made their one and only appearance in 1911. By the time the FA got round to distributing the money, the *Titanic* had sunk and the proceeds from the game (and the following year's) were given to the fund set up for the survivors. The match at Stamford Bridge was the highest scoring in the history of the competition, Swindon going down to Manchester United 8-4.

Tottenham Hotspur

"The great fallacy is that the game is first and last about winning. It's nothing of the kind. The game is about glory. It's about doing things in style, with a flourish, about going out and beating the other lot, not waiting for them to die of boredom."

Danny Blanchflower, Spurs legend

You wouldn't bet your house on Spurs. Actually, someone did. Three-up at half-time against Manchester United at home, a mug internet punter thought he'd impress his girlfriend by putting everything they had or were likely to have on Tottenham to win the match. They lost 5-3.

Don't get me wrong, Tottenham have had some fabulous players over the years and have played some blindingly entertaining football.

Nickname Spurs

Kit White shirt, navy blue shorts, navy blue and white hooped socks

Ground White Hart Lane – 36,214

Contact Bill Nicholson Way, 748 High Rd, London N17 0AP 0844 4995000

Tickets 0844 8440102

Website www.tottenhamhotspur.com

Whenever a crowd-pleaser comes on the market, Tottenham are always head of the queue to sign him up.

Their greatest coup came in 1986 when Argentine World Cup winners Ossie Ardiles and Ricky Villa found themselves on a plane to White Hart Lane. Ardiles was mesmerisingly good – according to Oldham manager Joe Royle, the midfield wizard was the difference when the two clubs met in the 1988 FA Cup: "It was like trying to tackle dust."

Then there was Paul Gascoigne; England manager Bobby Robson famously dubbed him daft as a brush. When George Best declared Gazza's IQ was less than his shirt number, a perplexed Gazza enquired, "What's an IQ?" But when given his chance in the England team he took it, single-handedly transforming a mediocre England side to the point where they were a penalty shoot-out away from making the 1990 World Cup final.

The dominant player

Spurs fans back Venables in his High Court clash with Sir Alan on the pitch almost every time he played and their best player in the last 20 years, he was never the same after a reckless tackle in the 1991 cup final crocked him for a year, although Spurs still succeeded in offloading him to Lazio for what was then a Spurs record of £5.5m.

Last year the club made enquiries about two of the most entertaining footballers in the world, Ronaldinho and Riquelme, and had their noses put out of joint by Real Madrid's Brazilian winger Robinho, who turned them down on the grounds that he didn't consider Spurs to be a big club, though ironically he ended up at Manchester City – no bigger but since August 2008, immeasurably richer.

Just how big are Spurs? Their illustrious history stretches back to 1901 when they became the only non-league side to win the FA Cup

Gazza's reputation preceded him at Lazio

since the Football League was founded. Since then, another seven FA Cup wins, four League Cups and three UEFA Cups as well as two league titles – most recently with the legendary 1961 team, the first to pull off a league and cup double in the 20th century.

Rivals? Arsenal, obviously. When former Gunners boss George Graham took over the reins at White Hart Lane, the fans couldn't quite bring themselves to say his name and the ground resounded to strains of "Man in the raincoat's blue and white army". And when keeper Paul Robinson was warming up for the UEFA Cup clash at Slava Prague and was invited to sing a song by cheeky away fans, he had them in ecstasy seconds later with a belting version of "Stand up if you hate Arsenal".

Legends? Danny Blanchflower and Dave Mackay, the brains and heart of the 1961 double-winning side. Bill Nicholson, manager then and winner of another six major trophies in his 16 years. And Jimmy Greaves, 266 goals in 379 matches.

Bizarre injury... Spurs midfielder Alan Mullery was unavailable for the England tour of South America in 1964 after putting his back out while brushing his teeth.

Glenn Hoddle? When comedian Jasper Carrott heard the midfielder had found God, he exclaimed: "That must have been one hell of a pass." A man who could land a ball on the proverbial sixpence with superb balance and a thunderous shot, to many of the Spurs faithful he will always be God. His talent divided the nation – some thought he was the best midfielder in England. And others... John Lennon, when asked if Ringo Starr really was the best drummer in the world, quipped: "Best drummer in the world? He's not even the best drummer in The Beatles." Hoddle was too rarely the best performer in a Spurs midfield where he was regularly outshone by a fab three of Ardiles, Mickey Hazard and Chris Waddle. His England career was equally frustrating – Bobby Robson picked him 19 times in 22 matches without Hoddle ever truly stamping his class on the team.

Saviour? The often unpopular figure of Sir Alan Sugar. His footballing credentials weren't the best when he bought the club in 1991, confessing that he knew more about smalz herring than he did about football. And he outraged many fans when he sacked popular manager Terry Venables, at one point protesting: "I feel like the guy who shot Bambi, I am not an egotistic loony." His greatest achievement was to save the club from the predatory clutches of Robert Maxwell. It feels wrong to kick a man when he's dead but in this case we can make an exception. Who knows what would have happened to White Hart Lane had that fat megalomaniac bully and serial fraudster managed to get his hands on the ground? He might have put luxury flats on it. Or swallowed it whole.

And now? A club that looked in great shape at the start of 2008 with three top-class forwards ended it with all three sold – Jermain Defoe to Portsmouth, Robbie Keane to Liverpool, and Dimitar Berbatov to Manchester United, after a summer-long sulk during which it became very clear that Spurs would be unable to keep him. The result? 2008-09 saw their worst start to a season since 1912.

Believe it or not… when Spurs played Getafe in the UEFA Cup in October 2007, Martin Jol was the last person at White Hart Lane to know he had been sacked. He only found out after the game when his nephew filled him in on what the crowd already knew. But when was the decision taken? Visitors to the club shop could give us a clue – Jol's name had already been expunged from the latest edition of the Spurs Monopoly game days before he was given the bullet.

Tranmere Rovers

"That boy throws a ball further than I go on holiday."

"Big" Ron Atkinson is awestruck when world-record holder Dave Challinor opens up his arms and shows his class.

Some clubs live in the shadow of a bigger neighbour. Tranmere Rovers exist in the shadow of two, just six miles and a ten-minute drive through the tunnel away from the Merseyside giants at Anfield and Goodison. Which is why Prenton Park is the only ground in the league which regularly hosts football on a Friday night: the club would rather retain – or even share – its supporters than have them seduced for ever by their more glamorous neighbours.

Rovers limbered up for 2008-09 with a pre-season friendly against Liverpool, going down by a single goal but, more importantly, banking a tidy sum from a sell-out crowd and attracting a host of young fans to the ground who had never been before.

Perhaps that's the solution to the 39th game, the Premier League's contemptible scheme to generate hundreds of millions by playing the climax of our season thousands of miles away from the fans in some lucrative if far-flung corner of the globe. Instead, the top club in the Premier League could play an away match against the team at the bottom of the basement league, second plays second bottom, and so on. Last season this would have seen Manchester United at Wrexham, Chelsea at Mansfield, Arsenal at Dagenham, Liverpool at Chester. A bonkers idea? Obviously. But it would guarantee the weakest clubs in the league one full house and one massive TV pay day and reverse ever so slightly the one-way redistribution of wealth that has tainted football since 1992.

Liverpool and Everton have played a big part in Tranmere's history. As well as competing with them for players and supporters, the club's record attendance of just over 61,000 came in a "home" FA Cup tie match against the Reds in 1934 which was switched to Anfield, while the biggest crowd to watch a Tranmere match of just under 62,000 came at a fifth-round tie at Everton in the sixties. Then there was Ron Yeats, the granite-like centre half who took the Reds from the second division to two championships and an FA Cup. He was well into his thirties when he moved to the Wirral and, after becoming player-manager, decided to pack the team with a selection of Liverpool old boys, in some cases, very old. Ian St John, Tommy Lawrence, Bobby Graham and Willie Stevenson all followed their former skipper to Prenton Park and formed the backbone of the team that pulled off one of Tranmere's greatest results, a 1-0 win at Highbury, which knocked Arsenal out of the League Cup in 1973.

It is in cup competitions that Tranmere have really made their mark. Many football supporters who weren't entirely sure where Tranmere was started to sit up and take notice from the mid-nineties as they established themselves as the top cup side from the lower leagues. Between 2000 and 2004 they reached the quarter-finals of the FA Cup no fewer

Nickname The Rovers

Kit White shirt, white shorts, white socks

Ground Prenton Park – 16,587

Contact Prenton Rd West, Birkenhead, Cheshire CH42 9PY

0871 2212001

Website www.tranmererovers.co.uk

than three times, in 1994 they made the League Cup semi-final, and in 2000 got to the final of the same competition, going down 2-1 to Leicester.

Premier League teams beaten over the years included West Ham, Sunderland and Middlesbrough, while the Mighty Whites put five past Coventry. In terms of pure football theatre, the FA Cup run in 2001 was perhaps the most astonishing. Tranmere were drawn away to neighbours Everton in the fourth round and stunned the football world by trouncing them 3-0. The fifth-round tie against Southampton was, if anything, more extraordinary – three down at home at half-time and seemingly dead and buried, Tranmere staged an incredible second-half comeback, with Paul Rideout hitting a hat-trick before Stuart Barlow scored the winner.

The architect of much of this was John Aldridge, another former Liverpool hero who scored 63 goals in just 104 games for the Reds before decamping to Spain and success with Real Sociedad. By the time he arrived at Prenton Park, he was nearly 33, a little late to be carving out a career as a club legend. Yet he served the club for ten years as player, player-manager, then manager, and played an astonishing 294 times for the team, notching up an equally incredible 174 goals. The League Cup final was preceded by a row over whether or not players would be allowed to use towels to wipe the ball at throw-ins – defender Dave Challinor held (and holds) the world record for the longest throw-in (46.57m, since you ask) and was much feared by teams who realised that conceding a throw-in to Tranmere on the halfway line was pretty much like conceding a corner to any other team.

Is it a coincidence that the areas that suffered most during the Thatcher years were the footballing hotbeds of Britain? Mrs Thatcher certainly hated football. In the mid-eighties when the Wirral was in the grip of misery and mass unemployment and the club was hovering at the bottom of the fourth division with crowds of around 1,600, the then chairman famously announced that the club would die in three weeks and that keeping football at Prenton was akin to flogging a dead horse.

A group of supporters saved the club in the short term, although Rovers were the first club in the country to go into administration back in 1987 and have had their fare share of financial worries since. However, in the last decade they've had the benefit of the wisdom of high-flying financial lawyer Lorraine Rogers who arrived in 1999 to sort out a short-term crisis and ended up as one of the few women to become club chairman. Rogers plans to stand down at the end of the 2008-09 season. A staunch supporter, she has said she is disillusioned with the way the game is going and by the growing gap between the richer and the smaller clubs.

Loyal servant?... Look no further than Harold Bell, who holds the all-time English club record for consecutive matches. He played 401 games in an unbroken record stretching from 1946 to 1955 and made a total of 595 league appearances for the club.

Walsall

"I even stopped having sex. Expectations had been raised to such a height, I didn't want to let anyone down."
Manager Ray Graydon counts the cost of his promotion push, 1999.

Everyone remembers their first time. Half-time, in my case, freezing my nuts off at an icy Upton Park and scanning the familiar fare at the food kiosk, craving something warm and filling, pie or pasty, pasty or pie, thermonuclear or lukewarm, didn't mind.

Which is when I first clapped eyes on a tray of chicken balti pies, a concept so alien, at first I couldn't quite take it in. It boggled my mind. Pies, so quintessentially unmistakably traditionally English. Balti chicken, available only in Bangladeshi restaurants. There are restaurants, posh restaurants even, that will serve you bacon and egg ice cream or snail porridge. Neither seemed as mad or as radical a concept as the chicken balti pie.

With hindsight, of course, it's a work of genius, combining as it does the football fans' genetic dependence on pies with the British obsession with curry, now our national dish. Now available at over 70 clubs and counting. this great culinary experiment can be traced back to Walsall, the first club in the country to offer chicken balti pies to its fans. Which is only just and right as the country's first Balti houses sprung up within a few miles of the Bescot Stadium where the Saddlers (the town is the traditional home of the saddle industry) play.

There have been times when they looked likely to lose it. A small club with 120 years of history behind them, including a handful of years in the second division, they've had to fight off the unwanted attentions of their predatory bigger neighbours. Twice in the eighties they came close to being swallowed up – once by Wolves, once by Birmingham – and were saved only by a brilliant rearguard action by their fans. Though on occasion it's been a case of out of the frying pan, into the fire. Back in 1986 they were rescued from oblivion by the intervention of multi-millionaire and massive gambler, Terry Ramsden, who achieved hero status for a short while. But that all went pear-shaped quite quickly, with Ramsden losing his £150m fortune in record time and later being jailed for fraud. But not before the council had named a block of flats after him.

Relations between the club and the council haven't always been cordial. There was a big falling-out around 1990 when the club moved from its old home in Fellows Park to the Bescot. The club needed to buy a small strip of land which it already rented off the council in order to build the new stadium. The council, which could have charged them next to nothing for it, knew it had the club over a barrel and insisted on half a million. There was a long-festering sore when the club, desperate for cash so as not to go bust, tried

Nickname The Saddlers

Kit White shirt, red shorts, white socks

Ground Banks Stadium (affectionately known as the Bescot Stadium) – 11,300

Contact Bescot Crescent, Walsall, Staffs WS1 4SA 0871 2210442

Tickets 0871 6630111

Website www.saddlers.co.uk

in vain for years to open a Sunday market at the ground to raise some money. Because of council opposition, it took years before it was finally opened.

Relations between club and fans have also been strained at times. Former chairman Jeff Bonser was constantly at war with his own supporters' association, starting a High Court action against them over some piddling dispute and threatening to clamp members who dared to park in the club car park. Fans really like the club's new training ground in Essington, so much so that they keep breaking into it to have a kickabout. The police have been kept very busy turfing them out.

Great moments? Arsenal figure heavily in two of them. The Gunners won the title in 1933 but were bundled out of the FA Cup 2-0 in what was then indisputably the greatest ever cup upset. Exactly 50 years later the clubs met again, this time in the League Cup, and Walsall did it again, winning 2-1 at Highbury in a run that saw them come within minutes of getting to Wembley, going down narrowly to Liverpool in the semi-finals. And a sensational five-goal thriller against Reading at the Millennium Stadium in 2001 which saw the Saddlers promoted for the second time in three years. Heroes of the hour were the club's popular keeper, Jimmy Walker, who made more than 470 appearances for the club over 11 years, and Ray Graydon – the no-nonsense manager with a hatred of mobile phones and earrings who was controversially sacked a few months later.

Don't miss... a fabulous 1997 hat-trick, including a great overhead kick, from pint-sized striker Roger Boli for the Saddlers against Southend. Available to view on YouTube, it would ordinarily have made huge headlines the next day. But not on the day that Princess Diana died.

Watford

"I speak to Sir Elton every week. Wherever he is he gets on the phone because he is a massive fan and wants to know what is going on, who am I picking and have I seen this player and that player. He is the world's most famous chief scout."

Aidy Boothroyd

Few managers have enjoyed a longer honeymoon period with the fans than Aidy Boothroyd. Unknown and inexperienced, the 33-year-old was a surprise appointment in March 2004 when Watford were on the brink of relegation to the third division. Fans were sceptical when he vowed to beat the drop, delighted when he pulled it off, incredulous when he suggested his distinctly average team would go up the following season, and ecstatic when they did just that – defeating Palace and Leeds to win the play-offs. It was clear to everyone that the team would never be able to compete in the top flight and no-one blamed Boothroyd when

Nickname The Hornets
Kit Yellow shirt, black shorts, yellow socks
Ground Vicarage Road – 19,920
Contact Watford, Herts WD18 0ER 0845 4421881
Tickets 0870 1111881
Website www.watfordfc.co.uk

the Hornets went straight back down. In 2007-08 it looked for a while like Watford would bounce straight up, winning ten of their first 13 matches to go nine points clear at the top of the second division. But they faded away and lost out to Hull in the play-offs.

Sir Elton is a pivotal figure in the Watford story. As a schoolboy, young Reg Dwight cheered the Hornets from the terraces. His first and best decision as chairman was to appoint Graham Taylor as manager. The club was then languishing in the fourth division, but in just six years he took them to the first where they finished second behind Liverpool in their first season and reached the FA Cup final for the first time the following year, losing out to Everton.

A key figure in the side was Luther Blissett, who played in all four divisions in the team's incredible rise and who holds the record for both appearances and goals during three spells at the club. But when he moved to AC Milan there was widespread suspicion that the Italians had boobed, confusing Blissett with his silky-skilled team-mate John Barnes. Football myth? Probably. Milan were in desperate need of a goalscorer in 1983, Blissett was banging them in at Vicarage Road and had announced himself on the international stage by hitting a hat-trick on his first full start for England. Barnes, always less prolific, had yet to score his wonder goal against Brazil that catapulted him to the world's attention.

It all started to go wrong in 1987 when Taylor was seduced by Aston Villa, and Watford went down the following year. Nine years in the doldrums. Then Taylor returned and did it all over again, leading the club to two promotions and a return to the Premier League. In his final year the Hornets were relegated once more and the club surprised the footballing world with the glamorous appointment of Italian goalscoring hero and former Chelsea boss Gianluca Vialli. It was a gamble – the plan was to spend big and bounce straight back to the Premier League.

It didn't work. When Vialli went, Watford were teetering on the edge of administration. A tenant at Vicarage Road for 80 years, the club finally bought the ground for half a million off the local brewery – only to sell it almost immediately for £6m to stave off bankruptcy. Sir Elton stepped down as chairman, pointing out that football was now big business and needed someone who could give it their full-time attention.

Hero?... Elton came though in the Hornets' hour of crisis, playing a concert at Vicarage Road and donating all the money to the club so it could buy back the ground.

Hornets' legend – Luther Blissett who holds the record for goals and appearances at Watford

West Bromwich Albion

"When Kevin first came to the club he asked to be called 'SuperKev'. To be honest we thought he must be a bit of a knobhead but now we know why."
Baggies skipper Jonathan Greening salutes Kevin Phillips – the veteran striker's 24 goals in just 30 starts fired the Baggies back into the Premier League in 2008.

Longest serving manager in England? No contest – Fred Everiss took charge at the Hawthorns in 1902 and stayed for 46 years. He inherited a side that had already reached five FA Cup finals, winning twice. Under Everiss, the Baggies won the title in 1920, made another three finals and in 1931 pulled off a unique double, the only side to win promotion and the FA Cup in the same season.

Alongside Everiss was club hero Billy Bassett, a tiny winger who won 16 England caps and the first Albion player ever to be sent off. His offence? "Unparliamentary language". The club would have gone bust in 1905 had supporters not rattled tins, and in 1910 Bassett staved off a second crisis by paying players out of his own pocket.

In those days most clubs had a number of Scottish players. Not the Baggies. Eight international matches against Scotland had given Bassett an aversion to all things Scottish. In his 29 years as chairman, Albion didn't sign a single Scottish player.

The pair were not great innovators. By the time Everiss retired in 1948, the directors were still picking the team, and the club cared little about tactics and training. Working on set pieces? Not at the Hawthorns where training was purely about getting fit. They didn't use footballs.

The club was modernised in the fifties and by 1954 Albion were renowned entertainers and almost pulled off the first league and cup double of the 20th century, coming

Nickname The Baggies
Kit Navy blue and white striped shirt, white shorts, white socks
Ground The Hawthorns – 28,003
Contact Halfords Lane, West Bromwich, West Midlands B71 4LF
0871 2711100
Tickets 0871 2719780
Website www.wba.co.uk

second but winning the FA Cup with a 3-2 win over Preston. The press dubbed them "The team of the century", with the *Daily Mirror* suggesting the entire side be selected to represent England at that year's World Cup.

Heroes? Future England captain Bryan Robson played more than 200 games and marshalled the team's top four finishes in 1979 and 1981 before following Ron Atkinson to Manchester United. Big Ron made his name at the Hawthorns and had three black players at a time when there were just a handful in league football. Cyrille Regis, Brendan Batson and Laurie Cunningham were

Tiny Baggies winger Billy Bassett

dubbed "The Three Degrees" after the black girl pop trio best known for being Prince Charles's favourite group, and were immensely popular with Baggies fans.

But Jeff Astle was the King, scoring in every round during the 1968 FA Cup run – including the winner against Everton in the Wembley final – and chalking up 174 goals in his decade at the Hawthorns. When he died of a degenerative brain disease aged just 59, the coroner reckoned it had been caused by heading the heavy leather balls used in the sixties and seventies and recorded a verdict of death by industrial injury, a landmark decision which could lead to compensation claims by former players similarly affected.

Humiliating bid? In 1979 West Brom offered Birmingham City £175,000 for Trevor Francis, but kept it secret. Just as well – four weeks later the striker was sold to Nottingham Forest in a record-breaking £1.1m deal.

A yo-yo team? Three promotions and two relegations to and from the Premier League since 2002 suggest as much, although October 2008 found the Baggies sitting in the top half of the table after an encouraging start to the season.

International betting scandals... a modern phenomenon resulting from easy access to telephone and internet betting? Not always – in 1913 Pascoe Bioletti offered Baggies left-back and England captain Jesse Pennington £55 (£5 a man) to throw a game against Everton. Pennington tipped off the police who arrested Bioletti and discovered that his son owned a football betting business based in Geneva. Bioletti got five months, the Baggies drew one-all.

West Ham United

"Even when they had Moore, Hurst and Peters, West Ham's average finish was about 17th. It just shows how crap the other eight of us were."

Harry Redknapp

A great cup team? Let's start with the World Cup. Bobby Moore was captain, and all four goals in the 1966 final against West Germany came from West Ham players, courtesy of hat-trick hero Geoff Hurst and midfielder Martin Peters.

Closer to home? Five FA Cup finals, three wins and two European Cup Winners' Cup finals, winning once. So far, no league title, their highest finish third in 1986.

The club began life in the late 19th century as Thames Ironworks FC – a pair of crossed iron hammers survives on the club crest as does the terrace cry of "Up the Irons".

Hammers fans talk reverentially about the Old Academy. But what is it, and where? Certainly not at the club's training ground Chadwell Heath, best known as the place where hulking Welsh striker John Hartson landed a blood-curdling boot on the head of team-mate Eyal Berkovic in an ugly spat caught on video and replayed endlessly on YouTube.

The Academy traces its roots back to Cassetari's cafe just across the road from Upton Park. The most important cafe in the history of

Nickname The Hammers

Kit Claret and blue shirt, white socks, white shorts

Ground Boleyn Ground (still known as Upton Park) – 35, 303

Contact Green St, London E13 9AZ 0208 548 2748

Tickets 0870 1122700

Website www.whufc.com

English football, it was there in the late fifties that player-turned-coach Malcolm Allison would talk tactics, formations and coaching with his colleagues. Armed with pepper pots and a clutch of sugar cubes their ambition, no less, was to revolutionise English football.

An ethos that ran through the club first under manager Ted Fenton and later with Ron Greenwood was that they nurtured young talent. The youth team reached the FA Cup final twice in three years, while chairman Reg Pratt urged players to take FA Coaching Badges to qualify them for life after football.

Enormously influential, the foundations of England's World Cup win were laid there, while an astonishing number of Academy graduates went on to make their mark as managers. The roll call includes Dave Sexton, Frank O'Farrell, Noel Cantwell, John Lyall, John Bond, Jimmy Bloomfield, Harry Redknapp, Billy Bonds, Geoff Hurst and Ken Brown, while Allison was the brains behind Manchester City's FA Cup and title wins in the late sixties. Trevor Brooking had only a brief stint as caretaker manager but carved out a distinguished career and gained a knighthood as a sports administrator.

While Moore, Hurst and Peters went on to their greatest achievements wearing the claret and blue, West Ham benefited fleetingly from the latest crop of outstanding talent nurtured by the club. Rio Ferdinand, Joe Cole, Frank Lampard, Glen Johnson, Jermain Defoe and Michael Carrick learned their trade at Upton Park but were all sold in their teens or early twenties.

So – a selling club? Every club that cannot guarantee Champions League football is a selling club these days. The chasm between the so-called Big Four and the rest remains vast because the top four clubs can

Let's hear it for the Hammers. West Ham fans cheer on their team in the FA Cup 1933 with an assortment of offensive weapons

cherry-pick the best players from every other club and have each accumulated hundreds of millions of pounds from earlier Champions League campaigns (and billionaire owners) to pay for them. Meanwhile, almost every talented player good enough to play in the Champions League wants to be at a club where he can. It's a vicious circle and the Hammers, who have produced so much talent, have suffered more than most.

In October 2008, there was yet another hammer blow when Icelandic owner B.J. Osgolfer Gudmundsson became a high profile victim of the credit crunch, forced to resign as chairman of Landsbanki after the bank was nationalised. Fans were left wondering what that would mean for their team.

Their glory days in the sixties came under Ron Greenwood. When the Irons won the FA Cup in 1964 he accompanied the players to a local cinema to watch the match highlights on the big screen. Travelling as they were by public transport, he hid the trophy beneath a cloth on his lap. A curious passenger wondered what he was hiding. Greenwood's reply: "Sweet FA."

More recently, foreigners have been making the headlines at Upton Park. In the summer of 2006 two top Argentines showed up in the shape of Javier Mascherano and Carlos Tévez. The Hammers appeared to have no idea how to best utilise the defensive midfield brilliance of Mascherano, who played just five times before being offloaded to Liverpool, while Tévez masterminded an extraordinary escape from relegation – with nine games left in 2007, the Hammers looked dead and buried, but won seven of their remaining matches to stay up. The club broke Premier League ownership rules when acquiring Tévez, an error that cost them a world record £5.5m fine.

Volatile Italian Paolo Di Canio was a huge favourite with the fans during his four years with the Hammers. At Sheffield Wednesday he'd made headlines around the world when he knocked over referee Paul

Alcock after being sent off against Arsenal. At West Ham he redeemed himself in spectacular fashion, winning the FIFA Fair Play award in 2001. With Everton keeper Paul Gerrard writhing in agony with a twisted knee and the goal unprotected, Di Canio met a cross in the penalty area – and caught it with both hands.

Not all foreigners have been good news. Million-pound-man Marco Boogers played just over 40 minutes of football for the Hammers, long enough to be red-carded for a horrendous lunge on Manchester United's Gary Neville, then disappeared to Holland for two weeks, where he was reportedly holed up in a caravan in a Dutch trailer park.

"I'm Forever Blowing Bubbles" became West Ham's anthem through a series of coincidences. In the twenties, adverts for Pears Soap featured a small boy with a mop of thick curls gazing at a bubble. At the time West Ham had a triallist who looked uncannily like the boy in the ad – Billy J. "Bubbles" Murray. When the song became a music hall hit, manager Charlie Paynter hired a band to play it as pre-match entertainment. It stuck.

Ever watched your team and thought, even I could do better than that?... Diehard Hammers fan Steve Davies did and directed a volley of four-letter filth at striker Lee Chapman throughout the first half of a pre-season friendly at Oxford City. When Chapman was taken off with an injury, coach Harry Redknapp challenged the tattooed skinhead to do better – then astonished the 27-year-old fan by bringing him on as a second-half sub.

Wigan Athletic

"The only feedback I've had off the chairman is him asking me: 'Do you want a pie?'"

Manager Steve Bruce spills the beans on his relationship with owner Dave Whelan.

Football took a long time to bed down in Wigan. No fewer than five clubs bearing the town name – Rovers, County, Borough, Town, United – bit the dust before Athletic finally took root in the thirties. Gaining league status was even tougher.

The club applied on 34 separate occasions and was knocked back every time. In the early seventies there was even a sensational but abortive bid to join the Scottish Second Division. There is a precedent for this – Berwick Rangers is an English team playing in the Scottish league.

Berwick-Upon-Tweed, however, is not far from Scotland, whereas Wigan is a 440-mile round trip from B-Upon-T, and as for Elgin… That didn't work either, although the club did have a stroke of luck in 1978, the year they finally gained league status. Despite finishing below Boston United in the Northern Premier League, Wigan were put forward for election because Boston's ground wasn't up to it.

The Latics' current Premier League status can be traced back to a leg-breaking tackle in the 1960 FA Cup final. It effectively finished the top-flight career of Blackburn's Dave Whelan but was, as it turned out, a lucky break. He used the compensation cash – just under £500 – to set up two market stalls and is now a multimillionaire who has had his fingers in lots of pies – a grocery business, sportswear retailing, and Poole's Pies.

Nickname The Latics

Kit Royal blue and white striped shirt, blue shorts, white socks

Ground JJB Stadium – 25,023

Contact Robin Park, Newtown, Wigan WN5 0UZ 01942 774000

Tickets 0871 6633552

Website www.wiganlatics.co.uk

When Whelan bought the club in 1995 the Latics were dithering in the fourth division and as few as 1,000 fans were passing through the turnstiles at Springfield Park. There was much hilarity when the new owner promised Premier League football. Fast-forward ten years and Wigan welcomed champions Chelsea as their first opponents in the top flight.

How did he pull it off? It needed a miracle, so he turned to Jesus. Striker Jesus Seba, late of Real Zaragoza, was one of a trio of Spaniards imported by manager Graham Barrow. A man who had spent his formative footballing years in Chorley, Southport and Altrincham was surprised to find himself despatched on a scouting mission to Barcelona. The so-called Three Amigos were an instant hit and the Latics began their steady climb through the divisions.

Central to their success was former striker Paul Jewell, who returned as manager in 2001. In his first three years he guided Wigan through two promotions to the Premier League, as well as an unsuccessful League Cup final appearance against Manchester United.

Believe it or not… there is little love lost between the Latics and Wigan's famous rugby league team, despite the fact that they share a town, a stadium, and until recently, an owner. Fans of the Latics chant "Wigan's turning blue" and sing the praises of Warriors' rivals St Helens while the Warriors faithful respond with "There's only one team in Wigan". There has been the odd high-profile spat between the clubs over the years, most notably in 1989 before they shared a ground when then cash-strapped Athletic were compelled to play the home leg of a League Cup tie against Liverpool away at Anfield because their own ground was too small and the board of the rugby league club refused to lend them their ground, which was three times bigger. The Latics lost a lot of money. But hostility between the two codes goes back a lot further than that. They just don't get on.

Did you know?... Striker Emile Heskey has always divided opinion, with fans forever frustrated that a man with his size, strength and skill doesn't score double the goals he bags each season. But Wigan fans eventually warmed to him, which is why, to the tune of "Winter Wonderland", they sing: "He used to be shite, but now he's alright, walking in a Heskey wonderland."

Wolverhampton Wanderers

"If I could get rid of every player who has ever been through my hands we'd never lose a game, because they all seem to come back and score."

Mick McCarthy, 2008

The best team in the world? Back in the fifties everyone, or at any rate everyone in England, reckoned the honour belonged to Wolverhampton Wanderers. English football had been in the doldrums. For decades we'd assumed we were the world's top footballing nation. Defeats such as the 1-0 loss to the United States in the 1950 World Cup could be dismissed as one-offs, flukes. Deep down we knew we were the best. Until 1953 when the Hungarians came to Wembley and famously took England apart 6-3. The following year, utter humiliation as England was torn to shreds 7-1.

Wolves gave us our pride back. With floodlights still a novelty, a series of floodlit games against some of the top sides in the world was staged at

Nickname Wolves

Kit Orange shirt, black shorts, black socks

Ground Molineux – 28,500

Contact Waterloo Road, Wolverhampton, Staffs WV1 4QR 0871 2222220

Tickets 0871 2221877

Website www.wolves.co.uk

Molineux, with opposition including Spartak Moscow, Moscow Dynamo, and top Argentine team Racing Club. But the big one in November 1954 was against Honvèd, the club side containing six of the Hungarian team that had caned England. The friendly was televised live on the BBC, Wolves came back from two down to win 3-2 and woke up to headlines the next morning proclaiming them champions of the world.

This got up the noses of the French who'd been pushing for a new competition under floodlights featuring Europe's top teams. Which is how the European Cup – now Champions League – was born.

The Wolves side of the fifties was very good indeed. Winners of the FA Cup in 1949, the next decade saw them win the title three times, come second three times and win the cup a second time in 1960.

Architect of all this was Stan Cullis, a man rarely mentioned when the names of all-time great managers come up, but whose achievements speak for themselves. He more or less invented the long-ball game – the theory being that the more time the ball spent in the opposition penalty area, the more likely his team were to score. Pivotal to the side was Billy Wright, who went on to make 105 appearances for England, 90 as captain, and one of the smallest men to distinguish himself at centre-half – he was just 5ft 8in.

After the fifties it never really got that good again for a club that was a founding member of the Football League. There was some success in the seventies in the days when the attack was spearheaded by outspoken Northern Ireland international Derek "The Doog" Dougan – a fourth-place finish in 1971 saw the club qualify for the UEFA Cup, where they made it to the final before losing to Spurs. There was also a League Cup triumph over Manchester City in 1974.

Don't mention… the eighties. The decade promised so much when Wolves defeated reigning European champions Nottingham Forest to win the League Cup in 1980. But by 1986 three successive relegations put the club in the fourth division for the first time – and a nadir was reached when the team was walloped 3-0 in the FA Cup by Northern Premier League outfit Chorley.

Club hero? Has to be Steve Bull. Signed for just £65,000 in 1986 when the club was in the fourth division, he went on to break every one of their goalscoring records, thumping home 306 goals in his 13 years, including 18 hat-tricks. When Wolves were in the third division he made the first of his 13 appearances for England.

More recently… the club's fortunes picked up in 1990 when lifelong fan Sir Jack Hayward bought them for £2m and set about rebuilding the dilapidated Molineux and ploughing tens of millions into the team. Wolves were often there or thereabout in the promotions stakes but only made it to the Premier League once in 2004 – and were relegated in their first season.

Yours for a tenner?… In 2007 Sir Jack sold the club to fanatical Liverpool supporter Steve Morgan for just £10, on condition the businessman invested another £30m in the club.

> **"Our team was the worst in the first division and I'm sure it'll be the worst in the Premier League."**
>
> Did Wolves chairman Sir Jack Hayward really slag off his own team at the moment of their glorious promotion to the Premier League in 2004? Er, no… The following day the Guardian newspaper issued a hasty apology: "Sir Jack had just declined the offer of a hot drink. What he actually said was: 'Our tea was the worst in the first division and I'm sure it will be the worst in the Premier League."

Wycombe Wanderers

"I'm trying to take this light-heartedly, but I'll just finish this interview then go and hang myself."
Martin O'Neill, after Wycombe narrowly missed out on automatic promotion, 1994.

Friendly place, Wycombe. The deeds to Loakes Park, their home for 95 years, were gifted to the club by former captain Frank Adams. Until very recently the club was run as a members' club – the only one in the country – its affairs ultimately controlled by 500 season ticket holders paying the princely sum of a pound a person for the privilege. And when the board decided it needed outside investors and more money to go forward, there were none of the usual bitter battles with the fans that have torn clubs apart. Supporters don't have one representative on the board. They have two.

The Chairboys were founded back in 1884 by a group of young carpenters. Things didn't really start to happen for them until 1931 when they won the FA Amateur Cup, and for most of the century they were in the Isthmian League – a league so resolutely amateur, it didn't hand out trophies to the winners as it believed the honour of winning was its own reward – a shame for Wycombe who won it no fewer than eight times. Another, famous amateur cup final appearance came in 1947 when they lost to amateur giants Bishop Auckland at Wembley in front of an astonishing 90,000. Only in 1990 did things really start to motor.

Two things happened. Wycombe flogged Loakes Park to the health authority and moved to Adams Park, a delightful new home a little way out of town, surrounded by hills and trees, and the sort of place which would grace the Football League. And Martin O'Neill breezed into a debt-free club with ambition to match his own.

At the end of his first full season they won the FA Trophy. The next year they

Nickname The Chairboys
Kit Light blue and dark blue quartered shirt, light blue shorts, light blue socks
Ground Adams Park – 10,000
Contact Hillbottom Road, High Wycombe, Bucks HP12 4HJ
01494 472100
Tickets 01494 441118
Website www.wycombewanderers.co.uk

failed to clamber out of the conference by the narrowest of margins, squeezed into second place on goal difference. But the following year they did the double, winning the trophy again and romping away with the conference title, then followed it up with a back-to-back promotion the following season. O'Neill's loyalty throughout this period was admirable. It took him five years after hanging up his boots to find even a conference team willing to take a gamble on him as manager – his managerial CV included a spell with Shepshed Charterhouse – and he repaid Wycombe's faith by spending five years in Buckinghamshire, despite having a number of much bigger clubs sniffing around.

There have been two glorious highlights since he left. An epic giant-killing FA Cup run in 2000-01 that saw Wolves, Leicester and Wimbledon put to the sword. Manager Lawrie Sanchez scored the winner for Wimbledon in the 1988 cup final against Liverpool, but his Wanderers could not pull it out of the bag in the semis, going down 2-1 to the Reds at Villa Park. And there was a magnificent League Cup run in 2007 in which Wycombe drew all-conquering Chelsea in the semi-finals and held them 1-1 at home before going out. In 2008 the club reached the second division play-off, going out to Stockport, with manager Paul Lambert stepping down days afterwards to be replaced by Peter Taylor.

Fans of the Chairboys immediately began a sweepstake on how long it would be before Junior Taylor joined the club – Peter Taylor has previously signed the veteran midfielder when managing Dover, Gillingham, Leicester, Brighton, Hull and Stevenage Borough.

Believe it or not... club hero Roy Essandoh who scored the winner in the 2001 FA Cup quarter-final against Leicester was signed thanks to... Teletext. Manager Sanchez placed an ad begging for strikers on the TV text service when he was hard up for forwards. Essandoh was the only applicant.

Yeovil Town

"Dickie Dyke was the reserve keeper; he'd never played for the first team. He worked in a solicitor's office down Church Street and I walked down there to tell him, 'Dickie, you're in on Saturday.' 'Righty-ho,' he said. Not a flicker, just got on with his work. He played beautifully, man of the match."

Alec Stock was player-manager on Yeovil's greatest day. Top team talk tip?
"Don't swear – the ref's a vicar."

The dullest afternoon of my life came when an English girl domiciled in Germany who had acquired a thick comedy accent – think Tony Woodcock, 1979-ish following his transfer from Forest to Cologne, or Steve McClaren's fabulous Dutch accent since he moved to Holland – stupefied my family with a slide show consisting of 300 more or less identical pictures of four unidentifiable young women in matching woolly hats, sunglasses and skis posing on a snowy Swiss mountainside. Her commentary on each slide never varied: "Zis is me and also my friends. Again in zis picture, vee are on ze slope."

For 70 years, Yeovil and the slope were inseparable. Somerset has hills – the Mendips, the Quantocks – but none as terrifying as the legendary slope at the Huish. Step forward Alec Stock, Yeovil's delightful if wily player-manager. When the non-league club drew high-flying Sunderland in the FA Cup fourth round in 1949, Everest had yet to be conquered. The way Stock spoke made the Huish seem similarly

Nickname Glovers

Kit Green and white hooped shirt, green shorts, white socks

Ground Huish Park – 9,665 (5,212 seated)

Contact Lufton Way, Yeovil, Somerset BA22 8YF 01935 423662

Tickets 01935 847888

Website www.ytfc.net

insurmountable. He talked up the impossibility of playing on the pitch, and when Sunderland arrived in the West Country, he refused to let them practise on it.

The rest is the stuff of legend. Yeovil played with effectively ten men for 80 minutes after left-winger Jack Hargreaves pulled a muscle early in the match – there were no subs in those days and reserve keeper Dickie Dyke was a solicitor's clerk making his debut – but in a ground where 17,000 struggled to see through thick fog, Yeovil ran out 2-1 winners, with the decisive goals banged in by Stock and Eric Bryant, part-time centre forward, part-time corn chandler's assistant.

Yeovil are the indisputable giants of giant-killing. No fewer than 20 league scalps over the years, including Blackpool, Bournemouth Brentford, Brighton and Bury. Buried too is the sloping pitch, concreted over to make way for a Tesco's car park when the club moved to Huish Park in 1990. In truth, it never sloped that much – ten feet from corner to corner, no better or worse than a lot of non-league grounds.

But then Yeovil are no longer a non-league club. Founded in 1890, they applied for league membership on no fewer than 28 occasions and were turned down every time, a disgrace even by the Football League's then transparently corrupt practices and particularly so given Yeovil's strong football traditions and relative isolation – Exeter City, the nearest league club, is almost 50 miles away.

Hero of the hour was Gary Johnson, a man who until recently was pulling off footballing miracles without anyone noticing. He was assistant manager at Cambridge United in the early nineties when they came within a whisker of achieving three successive promotions. He was manager of Latvia and groomed the side that unexpectedly qualified for Euro 2004. More recently he has been working miracles at Bristol City. In his first full season at Yeovil he guided them to the FA Trophy; in his second he catapulted them into the Football League for the first time in 113 years, breaking all sorts of records along the way, and won yet another promotion two years later.

Controversy? Sacking the manager in 2001 shortly after the side had achieved their highest ever placing seemed mad at the time, though given the success of his successor, it wasn't. Graham Roberts, former Spurs hardman, was at the helm in the nineties and divided opinion right up to the point when he faxed Newcastle United before a cup tie with Stevenage to wish them luck, adding – perhaps unwisely: "We aren't all arseholes in the conference." At which point opinion was united and he was on his bike.

Club hero? Captain Terry Skiverton. Rejected by Chelsea as a youngster, the central defender bounced back to lead the Glovers to two promotions and was the inspiration behind their greatest victory. Three down at Doncaster in the 2002 FA Trophy, the Glovers staged a remarkable comeback to level things at four-all, inspired by Skiverton who hammered in a 25-yard screamer in the last minute to seal victory. After that nothing could stop Yeovil Town and they went on to lift the trophy at Villa Park later that year, overcoming Stevenage in the final and gaining the self-belief to run away with the conference the following year.

The Glovers? Yeovil used to be the centre of the glove-making industry in the 19th century, knocking out three million pairs a year.

Did you know?... Yeovil are arguably the only club in Britain whose most famous ex-player didn't actually play much football. Somerset and England cricketing giant Ian Botham played for the club for a couple of months in 1985.

Acknowledgements

Thanks go to Ken Hayes, Kiki Madden, Aurea Carpenter, Sam Velody and Jackie Ambrosini for their help in getting this book together. Apologies to Jackie, Sam, Freddie, Isabella and Sasha for chaining myself to the laptop all year and being a rubbish partner/dad. If I missed anyone's birthday, I'm sorry.